Ireland's

Ireland's Histories examines aspects of the politics, society and ideology of Ireland from a radical perspective. It addresses key historiographical issues, as well as key moments and aspects of the two states in Ireland. Among the many issues addressed are the history of Irish women in Ireland and abroad, and the politics and ideology of the Protestant working class, including its relationship to the Northern Ireland state. It brings together writing from a number of different and competing perspectives on the formation and development of Irish politics, ideologies and society. Together, these add up to a questioning contribution to contemporary debates on modern Irish history.

The book is intended for academics and Irish Studies students, as well as those with a general interest in Irish issues.

The editors

Seán Hutton taught history at Bridlington School, North Humberside, before taking up his present post as Executive Director of the British Association for Irish Studies. He has written three books of Irish poetry, for one of which he was awarded the Seán ó Ríordáin Prize.

Paul Stewart, Senior Lecturer in Sociology at Sunderland Polytechnic and Director of the Local Studies Unit, has written on the Protestant working class and the nature of the Northern Ireland State. Co-author of *The Nissan Enigma: flexibility at work in the local economy*, he has written widely on the nature of work and flexibility in the automobile industry.

History Workshop Series

General Editor: Raphael Samuel
Ruskin College, Oxford

The Myths We Live By
Raphael Samuel and Paul Thompson (eds)

Metropolis: London
Histories and Representations since 1800
David Feldman and Gareth Stedman Jones (eds)

Patriotism: The Making and Unmaking of British National Identity
Volume 1: History and Politics
Volume 2: Minorities and Outsiders
Volume 3: National Fictions
Raphael Samuel

New Views of Co-operation
Stephen Yeo (ed.)

The Radical Soldier's Tale
John Pearman 1819–1908
Carolyn Steedman

Slavery
And Other Forms of Unfree Labour
Leonie Archer (ed.)

Socialism and the Intelligentsia 1880–1914
Carl Levy (ed.)

Disciplines of Faith
Studies in Religion, Politics and Patriarchy
Jim Obelkevich et al. (eds)

The Enemy Within
Pit Villages and the Miners' Strike of 1984–5
Raphael Samuel et al. (eds)

Voices of the People
The Politics and Life of 'La Sociale' at the End of the Second Empire
Adrian Rifkin and Roger Thomas

Language, Gender and Childhood
Valerie Walkerdene et al. (eds)

The Progress of Romance
The Politics of Popular Fiction
Jean Radford (ed.)

Theatres of the Left 1880–1935
Workers' Theatre Movements in Britain and America
Raphael Samuel et al.

The Worst Street in North London
Campbell Bunk, Islington, between the Wars
Jerry White

For Anarchism
History, Theory, and Practice
David Goodway (ed.)

Ireland's Histories

Aspects of state, society and ideology

Edited by
Seán Hutton and Paul Stewart

London and New York

First published 1991
by Routledge
11 New Fetter Lane, London EC4P 4EE

Simultaneously published in the USA and Canada
by Routledge
a division of Routledge, Chapman and Hall, Inc.
29 West 35th Street, New York, NY 10001

© 1991 collection Routledge; individual chapters, the contributors
Typeset in 10/12pt Times by Selectmove
Printed in Great Britain by
Clays Ltd. St. Ives plc

British Library Cataloguing in Publication Data
Ireland's histories: aspects of state, society and ideology – (History
workshop series).
  1. Ireland. History
  I. Hutton, Seán II. Stewart, Paul
941.5

Library of Congress Cataloging in Publication Data
Ireland's histories / edited by Seán Hutton and Paul Stewart.
  p. cm. – (History workshop series)
  Includes bibliographical references and index.
  1. Ireland–History. 2. Ireland–Social conditions. I. Hutton,
  Seán, 1940– . II. Stewart, Paul. III. Series.
  DA913.I65   1991
  941.5–dc20   91–10365

ISBN 0–415–05334–X.
    0-415-05335-8 (pbk)

To our fathers, who come from differing cultural and political traditions in the island of Ireland, and who have sought to separate themselves from the sectarianism which besets those traditions; and in memory of our mothers, who strove likewise.

The Editors

Contents

Notes on contributors

Donald Graham senior local government official and lead advisor to the Association of London Authorities and the Association of Metropolitan Authorities.

Seán Hutton is Executive Director of the British Association for Irish Studies.

David Johnson is Senior Lecturer in Economic and Social History at Queen's University, Belfast.

Liam Kennedy is a lecturer in Economic and Social History at Queen's University, Belfast.

Joseph Lee is Professor of Modern History at University College, Cork.

Jim McAuley is a lecturer in the Department of Sociology at St Mary's College, Twickenham.

P. J. McCormack is a lecturer in the Department of Social Anthropology and Sociology at the University of Ulster, Coleraine.

Jonathan Moore is a lecturer, writer and broadcaster on Irish Studies.

D. R. O'Connor Lysaght is an historian and a member of the People's Democracy, Irish Section of the Fourth International.

Patrick O'Sullivan is an Honorary Research Fellow of the University of Bradford and editor of the series *The Irish Word Wide*.

Bob Purdie is a Politics Tutor at Ruskin College, Oxford.

Ann Rossiter is Irish Studies Tutor at Kilburn College and Birkbeck College.

Jim Smyth is a lecturer in the Department of Social Studies at Queen's University, Belfast.

Paul Stewart is a Senior Lecturer in Sociology at Sunderland Polytechnic.

Margaret Ward is the author of *Unmanagable Revolutionaries: Women and Irish Nationalism* and *Maud Gonne: Ireland's Joan of Arc*.

Preface

The present volume of essays has been quite long in gestation. This has been due to the vicissitudes both of the publishing world and of the careers of the editors; as well as to the delay and the suspense involved in the obtaining of the promised chapters.[1] The collection's origins lie in a series of conferences which were held under the auspices of the Dublin (later Irish) History Workshop from 1978 onwards, and also from the Irish strands which the editors organized within History Workshop's annual national conferences at Leeds, Newcastle and Brighton between 1986 and 1988. The contents are structured around a number of themes of relevance to the social, economic and political development of Ireland. It has not been the editors' intention to impose a uniform point of view; rather, they have sought to represent a variety of the viewpoints which exist among a group of historians and social scientists who have contributed to those history workshops.

The editors would like to take this opportunity to thank the organizers of the various workshops. They provided an open, undogmatic forum where differing and competing interpretations could be presented. Thanks are also due to the academics, activists and unattached scholars who presented papers to those workshops (or, in the English case, to the Irish strands), as well as to those who attended and who took part in the discussions. All of these contributed to the development of that open and supportive environment. This volume represents merely a further stage in the ongoing debate which arises out of a common concern with the future of Ireland. Our thanks are also due to Claire L'Enfant and her coworkers at Routledge for their continuing interest in this book, and for their patience during the period when it was taking shape.

Seán Hutton
Paul Stewart

NOTE

1 The story is told that, as a train bearing Asa Briggs was pulling out of the station of a northern city, E.P. Thompson rushed up the platform and pressed the promised manuscript of 'Homage to Tom Maguire' into the hands of the editor of *Essays in Labour History*. In an operation requiring somewhat more coordination to make sure that both parties were in the right place at the right time, Ann Rossiter's contribution was delivered to one of the editors when a Heathrow-bound train on the Piccadilly line halted momentarily at Northfields Underground Station.

1 Introduction
Perspectives on Irish history and social studies

Seán Hutton and Paul Stewart

Irish history has been, and continues to be, an area of debate and contestation. This is the case, partly, because of the abiding manner in which populist nationalist, and Unionist/loyalist, versions of Irish history continue to be used to legitimize current political positions and because of the suspicion and hostility with which academic historians regard populist versions of the past. K. T. Hoppen describes the situation thus, in a passage which implies an interesting distinction between academic historians and those 'with an axe to grind'

> Since at least the seventeenth century almost every group with an axe to grind has thought it imperative to control the past in order to provide support for contemporary arguments and ideologies. . . . By the beginning of the present century both nationalists and unionists had each constructed a self-contained theatre of the past in which to play out current aspirations against backdrops painted to represent the triumph of former times . . . though popular political attitudes have often been expressed in a manner which seems to be 'historical', this is so only in the superficial sense that references to past events are involved. For many people it is, indeed, the approach adopted by the writers of the early nineteenth century which still holds sway and, by virtue of having done so for almost two hundred years, gives continued energy to sectarian attitudes of unyielding resonance and power.[1]

Roy Foster has recently referred to 'the uncomfortable fact of the legitimization, and even sanctification, of violence in Irish history';[2] and Marianne Elliott's definition of 'revisionism' in its Irish context acknowledges the field of Irish history as an abiding area of contestation a term normally applied to scholars using scientific standards of research to re-interpret the myths and long-held truths of the past, now used more frequently as a term of abuse to describe those who attack romantic nationalist historiography.[3]

All of this might form a mere footnote to Irish historiography, were not history (for which read also pseudo-history) still seen as a crucial legitimizer. In the case of Ireland, this situation points to the limited nature of the success of the historiographical 'revolution' set in train in the 1930s.[4] This gave to Irish historians the structure which would enable them to professionalize their calling, generalizing a set of standards and practices which came to dominate historical production in the universities.[5] At one level, this historiography was concerned with a methodology for the handling of historical evidence.[6] At another, it was concerned to replace populist nationalist readings of history with another, which had greater validity in the eyes of the reformers and which appeared to have, also, the added benefit of objectivity.[7] As Brendan Bradshaw has perceptively written,

> the modern tradition actually developed in self-conscious reaction against an earlier nationalist tradition of historical interpretation and aspired to produce 'value-free' history . . . a moulding influence on the tradition . . . is the aspiration towards the study of the past 'for its own sake' based on a scientific examination of the documentary sources.[8]

Both Peter Gibbon and Bradshaw have made valid criticisms of this dominant form of Irish academic historiography. Gibbon has pointed out that this particular historiography '[relies] upon exactly the same methodological devices with which the straightforwardly ideological contributions engage in their special pleading'; and he has pointed to the procedural problems inherent in the way in which conclusions are drawn from documentary sources.[9] Bradshaw quite rightly points to the epistemological problem thrown up by the centrality of the category of 'objectivity' to Irish academic history.[10] He identifies such history as history which, in its 'negative bias', is equally open to distortion as populist nationalist history. 'What have changed are the forms in which distortion has manifested itself.'[11] Most interestingly, Bradshaw, acknowledging his debt to Herbert Butterfield, argues convincingly 'the inability of practitioners of value-free history to cope with the catastrophic dimensions of the Irish past'.[12]

If the 'new' historiography has been conservative, with a heavy political emphasis, Irish academic historians have been willing, even eager, to communicate with a wider audience by such means as the Thomas Davis [radio] lectures, initiated in 1953 – where economic, cultural and social history also featured – and through the production of general histories (J. C. Beckett's *The Making of Modern Ireland* (London, 1966) and F. S. L. Lyons's *Ireland Since the Famine* (London, 1971), for example) accessible to non-academic readers.[13] It has been a feature of such histories, with their conscious striving for neutrality and balance, that they have smoothed some of the rougher surfaces of Irish history.

In Ireland, history has tended to dominate in the field of the social sciences up to comparatively recent times. Economic and social history were late to develop fully as separate disciplines; and other branches of the social sciences lagged even further behind.[14] Alongside the developments which have taken place in the social sciences since the 1960s, however, there has been development, as well, in areas which would once have been regarded as the fringes of history. An Irish Labour History Society was set up in 1973, and its journal *Saothar* began publication in 1975;[15] and the somewhat later revival in the writing of women's history has been manifest in general surveys, specific studies, and biographies.[16] The publication of Maria Luddy and Cliona Murphy's *Women Surviving: Studies in Irish Women's History in the 19th and 20th Centuries*, indicates the maturity achieved in this field. The editors stress that the history of Irish women 'is not just the history of the oppressed "other"',

> living in a separate dimension as one might have supposed from either reading the traditional textbooks in Irish history or the books which are relegated to the discreet corners of bookshops under the label of 'Feminist Studies'. Their lives are firmly connected to, and dictated by, the political, social, demographic and economic happenings of the time. They are a part of history, not on the fringes of it.[17]

David S. Johnson and Liam Kennedy open the volume with an essay which, in its consideration of George O'Brien's writings as an economic historian, in itself illustrates the degree to which economic history has developed since the beginning of the century. The weight which they attach to economic, as opposed to political, factors indicates the line of revisionist development in this area. At the same time, the residual importance which they attach to political factors marks them off from the most rigorous of revisionists. Their essay forms a contrast to a later chapter, by Jim Smyth, which demonstrates the continuing importance of political economy in radical and Marxist readings. Seán Hutton's overview of the politics of labour in the independent Irish state is based on the premise that the history of labour cannot be considered as part of a discrete 'labour history', ignoring the general pattern of social relationships within the state. He deals with structural and ideological factors affecting the development of the institutions of labour, as well as the more personal factors which, at certain points in time, have affected outcomes. He reflects on the success of bourgeois parties in establishing a cross-class basis of power, enjoying the support of the majority of the working class, in each of the two Irish states originating after 1920; examining, in particular, the circumstances leading to this development in the southern state.

Two contributions in the present volume bear specifically on the subject of women's history. Ann Rossiter, in an overview on the subject of Irish women's experience of emigration, deals with the economic and ideological factors in Ireland which lay behind the emigration of women. She describes the social and economic categories into which Irish women fitted in Britain and the USA on emigration; and the way in which they put down roots in their adopted countries. With regard to the more recent past, she deals with the impact of women's/political struggles both in the Republic of Ireland and Northern Ireland on the women's movement in Britain. Margaret Ward traces the history of the women's movement in Northern Ireland in the last twenty years, making constant reference to the contemporary developments in the Republic of Ireland. She deals with a range of issues, including women's control of human reproduction, which are obviously of key importance; but she also deals at some length with the way in which political struggles in Northern Ireland have affected the lives of women as well as women's politics in the northern state.

The absence of a strong socialist or Marxist movement in Ireland, with its own intellectual strata, has meant that an Irish Marxist-socialist critique – most notably developed by James Connolly in the early twentieth century in *Labour in Irish History* (Dublin, 1910) and *The Reconquest of Ireland* (Dublin, 1915) – had been carried little further by the 1960s. Connolly identified the causes of nationalism and socialism in Ireland and used history as part of a revolutionary project which had for its object the driving of a wedge between the nationalist and Unionist bourgeoisie and their working-class supporters. British communist historians like T. A. Jackson and

C. Desmond Greaves produced a version of history under the influence of a particular view of anti-imperialist struggle which restricted their ability to deal with the problematic of nationalism. Trotskyist historians like D. R. O'Connor Lysaght and Michael Farrell have worked in relative isolation in a Connollyist tradition, producing histories which constitute radical critiques of bourgeois nationalism and political Unionism, and of the two states set up in Ireland in the 1920s. In Lysaght's work, in particular, a wide empirical knowledge is strongly informed by his understanding of Marxism; but it is a Marxism which is relatively unaffected by the enriching aspects of intra-communist theoretical debate which has raised questions around the unidirectional, economistic base–superstructure model. He contributes an essay to the present volume which examines British state strategy and the balance of political forces within Ireland, and outside it, which led to the setting up of the Irish Free State in 1922. He concludes his narrative-analysis with an examination of the development of the Irish Free State into the era of Fianna Fáil dominance in the 1930s. J. J. Lee is a revisionist of revisionism, as *The Modernisation of Irish Society 1848–1918* (Dublin, 1973) and *Ireland 1912–1985: Politics and Society* (Cambridge, 1989) have shown; as well as an eclectic, non-Marxist, radical commentator on modern Irish society. Despite the fact that he kept us on tenterhooks up to the very last moment, we are flattered that we appear to have been preferred before a number of other claimants on his time and industry. Lee points out, in his survey of the De Valera Constitution of 1937, the degree to which it was a consensus document in its day, and how it possesses an inbuilt element of flexibility through revision by the Supreme Court and the possibility of amendment by referendum. While he reflects on ambiguities surrounding the concept of the 'nation' embodied in the document, he questions some of the criticisms which have been made of the Constitution, indicating that the issues are more complex than such criticism would allow.

It was the British and Irish Communist Organization (B & ICO) which opened a currently ongoing debate on nationalism, in a series of historically based pamphlets dealing with some of the more reactionary aspects of Irish nationalism, as well as its sectarian character in certain forms.[18] It also sought to rescue for history forms of progressive Irish thought which were anti-clerical or anti-nationalist.[19] The reactive nature of the exercise has rendered certain aspects of this project problematic. It is only in the work of Bew, Gibbon and Patterson, however, that the theoretical basis for a Marxist critique of Irish nationalism has been systematically explored. While Peter Gibbon had stressed the importance of an analysis based on modes of production in his *The Origins of Ulster Unionism* (Manchester, 1975), it was largely as part of a critique of history produced in the Connolly tradition that a wider project was embarked upon by the trio in the introduction to *The State in Northern Ireland* (Manchester, 1979). Here, the Trotskyist/Republican concept of imperialism was challenged by reference to Leninist texts; and texts of Marx and Lenin were used to demonstrate that both these revolutionary thinkers regarded national struggle as progressive only under certain specific conditions. A feature of the collective and individual work of the trio, dealing with Northern Ireland, has been an emphasis upon the relatively autonomous nature of popular Ulster Unionism and the compatibility of this with a labourist consciousness. Paul Stewart recognizes the innovative nature of their work in the area of the social analysis of the origins and formation of the Northern Ireland state. The major problem regarding their work, he argues, lies neither in their insistence that Protestant working-class politics and culture are relatively autonomous of the bourgeois state nor that, at decisive moments, a break from bourgeois Protestant sectarianism was witnessed. What can be questioned, he believes, is the assumption that moments of relative independence for the Protestant working class signalled a political moment of potentially positive significance. While agreeing that such developments did not negate the possibility of a shift to a labourist politics of sorts, he argues that what was precluded was a break on anything like a radical democratic, not to speak of a socialist, agenda. This was because the actions of the state and the Protestant working class were compromised by their inscription in the very fabric of a society founded on a peculiarly capitalist regime of Catholic subordination; and he argues that it is only by ignoring the effect of this culture of exclusion that Bew, Gibbon and Patterson could come to the conclusions they do. In an important argument that seeks to continue the debate opened up by Bew, Gibbon and Patterson, J. W. McAuley and Joe McCormack address the extent to which a progressive, socialist agenda can be articulated within the context of popular working-class politics in Belfast. Despite the negative role of sectarianism, McAuley and McCormack insist that Protestant working-class identities are contradictory and consistently produce radical, democratic imperatives that many socialists have failed to identify. They argue that failure derives from a misplaced and vulgar attempt to apply inappropriate, or often wrong, Marxist categories. For Bob Purdie, the importance of Bew, Gibbon and

Patterson has to be registered in the way they have broken down what he perceives as cherished, but fatally flawed Marxist dogma. That the trio are committed to a resurgence in the use of Marxist categories, which Purdie himself feels are no longer of any historical or political utility, is of secondary importance. For Purdie, they are leading an assault on icons of ignorance.

A challenge to assumptions taken for granted about the relationship of the Irish economy to the new global order is paramount in Jim Smyth's contribution. In contrast to Lee,[20] who regards the performance of the Irish economy as a mark of the failure of the national role of the Irish bourgeoisie, an underlying assumption of Smyth's contribution is that there is no necessary correlation between the class interest of the Irish bourgeoisie and Lee's perceived national interest. He argues that the regeneration of the Irish economy is unsustainable by a bourgeoisie which has always sold its soul to the highest bidder. This is quite apart from the economy's subordination within the new post-Fordist international division of labour. All of this he would see as constituting a double bind for the Irish working class.

Emigration is an integral factor in the history of Ireland from the nineteenth century onwards. As Gearóid ó Tuathaigh and Lee have suggested, emigration was the way in which Ireland solved a number of its structural problems, both before and after the creation of an independent Irish state. They have also indicated the differential impact of emigration in terms of both class and gender.[21] Two essays in this volume address the issue of emigration. Patrick O'Sullivan's appraisal of the formation and practice of Patrick MacGill's writing represents an important departure from the usual assessment of this untypical Irish navvy emigrant. His methodology locates MacGill's work within the context of the writer as cultural producer and of the consequences for that product (his fictions) as MacGill's own life is transformed from that of a worker by hand to a worker by brain. O'Sullivan argues that MacGill's reception as a migrant Irish worker was articulated in two distinct but related moments: on the one hand, there were the middle classes for whom the lives of the 'poor' were revealed; on the other were the navvies who could find resonance of their own lives in MacGill's writing. Increasingly, his discourse obscured the character of the Irish migrant, for his Irishness was distinct from those more recent emigrants whose skills and biographies he could not really assume. Increasingly also, his writing was drawn into a culture that represented it as Irish writing, in Britain – although it was not Irish writing and it was not about Ireland. Ann

Rossiter's article, mentioned above, deals with a hitherto somewhat neglected aspect – the impact of emigration on women.

Viewing sectarianism simply as the voluntarist outcome of strategies of the various Unionist regimes fails to recognize the ways in which the structural links between the state and Northern Ireland civil society could continue to reproduce sectarian structures of domination. As one of the main bulwarks of sectarian discrimination in Northern Ireland since its foundation, housing was a critical site of conflict during the movement for civil rights in the late 1960s and early 1970s. Donald Graham's incisive critique of the sectarian nature of employment practices and housing strategy within the Northern Ireland Housing Executive (NIHE) sets out to test the claims of politicians of many hues in Ireland and Britain concerning progress in the elimination of sectarianism during the past twenty years. According to Graham, sectarianism has been inscribed in and impacts upon housing strategies in four interrelated ways: recruitment and the operation of the internal labour market within the NIHE itself; sectarian pressure in the area of planning and building; links between members of the executive and loyalist councils; pressure from loyalist councils in the implementation of executive policies. Added to these, he argues, has been another pressure against democratic housing – intervention by the British army, under the auspices of the Belfast Development Office, in the overall planning of estate layout. It is within this context, Graham argues, that the NIHE continues to reproduce sectarian housing strategies.

Jonathan Moore, in the last essay in the volume, looks at the Irish–British relationship at the level of political leadership, from the point of view of the British Labour Party's attitude to Ireland. He places this in the context of the 'new politics' introduced by Labour into parliament, a politics influenced by British imperial strategy and ideology, just as was the earlier 'new' liberalism. He indicates a constant theme of taking Ireland out of British politics, and of keeping it out. He shows the way in which it was easier after partition and the setting up of the two states in Ireland for would-be Labour reformers to argue, as did the Campaign for Democracy in Ulster (CDU), for the extension of the rights of British citizens to the Catholic/nationalist population of Northern Ireland. But he also argues that this strategy ignored the pressures which would be inevitably unleashed as liberal solutions were proposed to the problems arising from the situation which had been sustained by Unionism in Northern Ireland since the foundation of the state.

Notes

1 K. T. Hoppen, *Ireland Since 1800: Conflict and Conformity* (London, 1989) pp. 1, 2–3.
2 R. F. Foster, ed., *The Oxford Illustrated History of Ireland* (Oxford, 1989) p. vii.
3 Marianne Elliott, *Wolfe Tone* (London, 1989) p. 418.
4 On this see F. S. L. Lyons, 'TWM,' in F. S. L. Lyons and R. A. J. Hawkins, eds, *Ireland Under the Union – Varieties of Tension: Essays in Honour of T. W. Moody* (Oxford, 1980).
5 Lyons, op. cit., pp. 321–2.
6 ibid., p. 10.
7 ibid., pp. 11, 321.
8 Brendan Bradshaw, 'Nationalism and historical scholarship in modern Ireland', *Irish Historical Studies* 104 (November, 1989) p. 329.
9 Peter Gibbon, *The Origins of Ulster Unionism* (Manchester, 1975) pp. 5, 7.
10 Bradshaw, op. cit., p. 337.
11 ibid., p. 343.
12 ibid., pp. 340, 337–42.
13 There has recently been a spate of new single-volume general histories, among them the works of Hoppen, op. cit., Foster, ed., op. cit., R. F. Foster, *Modern Ireland 1600–1972* (London, 1988) and J. J. Lee, *Ireland 1912–1985: Politics and Society* (Cambridge, 1989); as well as general interpretative studies which place Ireland in a broader context, such as Hugh Kearney, *The British Isles: A History of Four Nations* (Cambridge, 1989) and Oliver MacDonagh, *States of Mind: A Study of Anglo-Irish Conflict 1780–1980* (London, 1983).
14 L. A. Clarkson, 'Introduction: K. H. Connell and economic and social history at Queen's University, Belfast', in J. M. Goldstrom and L. A. Clarkson, eds, *Irish Population, Economy, and Society: Essays in Honour of the Late K. H. Connell* (Oxford, 1981) pp. 1–7; Lee, op. cit., pp. 584–6.
15 Paul Cullen, 'Irish Labour History Society: 1982–83', *Saothar* 9 (1983) pp. 6–7; Francis Devine and Emmet O'Connor, 'Editorial: Labour and Irish history', *Saothar* 10 (1984) pp. 3–8.
16 For example, Margaret Mac Curtain and Donncha ó Corráin, eds, *Women in Irish Society: The Historical Dimension* (Dublin, 1978); Margaret Ward, *Unmanageable Revolutionaries: Women and Irish Nationalism* (London, 1983); Rosemary Cullen Owens, *Smashing Times: A History of the Irish Women's Suffrage Movement* (Dublin, 1984).
17 Maria Luddy and Cliona Murphy, eds, *Women Surviving: Studies in Irish Women's History in the 19th and 20th Centuries* (Dublin, 1990) pp. 7–8.
18 For example, *The Economics of Partition* ([Belfast], 1969); *The Home Rule Crisis 1912–14* (Belfast, 1971); *Aspects of Nationalism* (Belfast, 1972).
19 For example, *A Belligerent Liberal (M. J. F. McCarthy)* (Belfast, 1979); *Reprints from the Cork Free Press 1910–1916: An Account of Ireland's Only Democratic Anti-Partition Movement* (Belfast, 1984).
20 In *Ireland 1912–1985: Politics and Society*.

21 M. A. G. ó Tuathaigh, 'The land question, politics and Irish society, 1922–1960', in P. J. Drudy, ed., *Irish Studies 2 – Ireland: Land, Politics and People* (Cambridge, 1982) pp. 178–81; J. J. Lee, 'Irish agriculture', *Agricultural History Review* XVII, part i (1969) p. 65; Lee, *Politics and Society*, pp. 374–5, 376.

2 Nationalist historiography and the decline of the Irish economy

George O'Brien revisited

David S. Johnson and Liam Kennedy

INTRODUCTION

The historical works of George O'Brien represent the *locus classicus* of the nationalist interpretation of Irish underdevelopment. His trilogy of economic histories, researched and written at breathtaking speed between 1918 and 1921, quickly established itself as the definitive account of England's wrongs and Ireland's economic woes.[1] In industry, for example, 'Centuries of penal laws and restrictive legislation had resulted in the immaturity of some Irish manufactures and the decay of others.'[2] In agriculture, by the early nineteenth century 'a long course of the most oppressive behaviour on the part of the landlords, connived at, if not actually abetted, by the government, had plunged the mass of the people into a state of unexampled misery'.[3]

This historiographical essay largely confines itself to a discussion of O'Brien's views on the decline of the Irish economy after 1800. His case consists of a number of high level generalizations regarding the interrelationship between economics and politics, the limitations of the doctrine of *laissez faire*, and the necessity of different industrial policies for different stages of economic development. We return to these wider issues in the concluding section. But the essence of O'Brien's case is the historically specific claim that the absence of political autonomy condemned Ireland to economic backwardness in the eighteenth and nineteenth centuries. This conclusion rests on four main arguments.

First, there were the economic benefits conferred on Ireland during the brief interlude of legislative autonomy between 1782 and 1800. This experiment, popularly known as Grattan's Parliament, afforded a positive demonstration of the economic advantages of self-government. Second, there were the malign effects of the Act of Union which made clear the disadvantages of self-government. Third, the apparently deviant case of Ulster, where there was industrial growth rather than decline in the nineteenth century, far from contradicting the overall argument, actually reinforced it. Finally, the system of land tenure was a long-standing source of economic weakness, though again the potential for a prosperous society was demonstrated by the peculiar agrarian conditions of Ulster. We will examine the four pillars of O'Brien's explanatory structure in detail, but first it is helpful to know a little more about the man who was the architect of the nationalist economic historiography of Ireland.

GEORGE O'BRIEN

George O'Brien was born in 1892, the son of a Catholic Unionist. In 1904 he was sent to a Catholic public school in Weybridge, England. He returned in 1908 intending to enrol at Trinity College, Dublin. However, his Unionist father was by now dead and the political climate seemed to be moving towards Home Rule. It was likely that once this was enacted Trinity College, the bastion of Unionist ascendancy, would fall from favour. It was decided, therefore, that he should opt instead for University College, Dublin (effectively the Catholic counterpart to Trinity) having first enrolled for two years at Belvedere College. The choice of 'UCD' was to have an important influence on O'Brien's subsequent career and writings. In later life he felt that, had he attended Trinity, he might 'have developed an anti-Irish and perhaps even an anti-Catholic bias'.[4] Instead he became acquainted with fellow students who were later to become important figures in Irish nationalist politics, such as Patrick McGilligan, Kevin O'Higgins and Patrick Hogan.

At UCD O'Brien absorbed, in its essentials, the version of the economic history of Ireland that was later to find expression in his writings: namely that Ireland's economy had languished under the Penal Laws; that it had flourished under Grattan's Parliament; and that this prosperity had been destroyed by the Act of Union. Indeed, in the stronger version of this thesis, as expounded by Arthur Griffith, for example, the Union had been expressly designed by England to impoverish Ireland.[5] These ideas could in fact be traced back to Daniel O'Connell and the Repeal movement.[6]

The background to the writing of the economic histories is, however, curious. Although attending courses in economics at UCD, O'Brien specialized in law and went on to train for the Bar where he practised for three years. Then in 1916, as a result of botching a case, he suffered a type of nervous breakdown. He spent most of 1917 in Glasgow undergoing treatment. Early in the following year he decided to give up his legal practice, with his career in ruins. He then made a conscious decision to try to make a second career for himself in university life. Within a year he had written *The Economic History of Ireland in the Eighteenth Century*, which was published in 1918. *The Economic History of Ireland in the Seventeenth Century* followed the next year. The third volume of the trilogy, *The Economic History of Ireland from the Union to the Famine*, was not published until 1921, although in 1920 O'Brien found time to write *An Essay on Medieval Economic Teaching*. This was an extraordinary performance. In later life O'Brien openly admitted his motives for writing the books: namely, to secure an academic post at UCD. He wrote little on Irish economic history during the rest of his long life. In his own words the books 'served the purpose for which they were designed'.[7] He could not even bring himself to reread them for fear of finding them unsatisfactory.

In one sense it is surprising that books written in such haste by a man with little training in the subject, and indeed little interest, until his legal career collapsed, should have so greatly influenced the perception of Irish economic history for almost half a century. Yet in another sense it is easily explained. With few exceptions, the writing of Irish history after 1920 was dominated by the nationalist view which O'Brien had expressed so well, but which he had by no means originated. His books were simply an elegant and lengthy expression of the conventional wisdom. Although it would be grossly unfair to accuse O'Brien of simply pandering to popular prejudices, it is most unlikely that he would have been appointed to an academic post in UCD if, for instance, his books had denigrated Grattan's Parliament and extolled the benefits of the Union. But it is extraordinary how quickly many of his views changed. In 1923 as a member of the Fiscal Inquiry Committee – an appointment brought about as a result of the influence of his old university friends, who were now in government – the great advocate of the potential virtues of protectionism after 1800 came down firmly in favour of free trade for the newly independent Irish Free State.[8] In 1928, as a member of the Select Committee on Wheat Growing, the opponent of the extension of pasture in the nineteenth century became its advocate for the twentieth.[9] Perhaps times had changed; if so, they had changed within a remarkably short space of time.

In fairness it should be remembered that O'Brien was not alone in performing intellectual somersaults. Ministers prominent in the new Free State government, such as Hogan and O'Higgins, who had come to power apparently adhering to Sinn Féin views on protectionism, became noted free traders once in office.[10] Timing and political context, as well as opportunism, are no doubt important in explaining these gyrations. The period 1918–21, in which O'Brien's trilogy was written, were years of heady nationalism. The solution to Irish problems seemed straightforward. Once the British were banished, the millennium would dawn. The civil war and the realities of self-government led many into a painful reappraisal of cherished notions.

GRATTAN'S PARLIAMENT

That there was striking economic progress under Grattan's Parliament was virtually an article of faith among nationalist writers of the early twentieth century. This belief had strong political resonance, since it dovetailed neatly with contemporary economic arguments for Home Rule. Prevailing ideas on the subject were seriously questioned for the first time by the Scottish-born socialist, James Connolly, in the course of a blistering attack on 'Parliamentarian historians'. In his highly original *Labour in Irish History*, published in 1910, he exclaimed

> The prosperity of Ireland under Grattan's Parliament was almost as little due to that Parliament as the dust caused by the revolution of the coach-wheel was due to the presence of the fly who, sitting on the coach, viewed the dust, and fancied himself the author thereof.[11]

Connolly was sceptical of any gains in living standards among the poor and, while admitting that there may have been significant increases in aggregate output during this period, concluded that these should be attributed to the impact of the Industrial Revolution on Ireland. Not surprisingly, George O'Brien took issue with Connolly's attempt to revise nationalist orthodoxy. O'Brien selected a number of indicators which he construed as showing clear advances in prosperity during the tenure of the quasi-independent Irish parliament. Chief among these were a rise in rents, increased population, an expansion of tillage, higher *per capita* consumption of 'articles of common use among the poor' and a larger volume of industrial output.[12] Two problems are immediately apparent. First, all of the indicators, with the possible exception of the last, are ambiguous. Indeed, if applied consistently to subsequent time periods as measures of economic progress, O'Brien's argument becomes internally contradictory. Rents and population both maintained an upward trend between the Union and the Famine

– a period which most writers (including O'Brien) see as one of declining economic prospects. Tillage also expanded after 1800, and did not go into serious retreat until after the Famine. The articles of allegedly common consumption turn out to be tea, tobacco, sugar and coal. It is clear, however, from the household accounts and information on diets presented to the Poor Inquiry of 1836 that these were not items of common purchase among the poor, and it is extremely unlikely that expenditure patterns were very different a generation earlier. Recent research on tea and tobacco duty in the 1830s and 1840s suggests rising levels of consumption for these semi-luxury items, but few would now take this as indicating improving living standards among the poor in the lead up to the Great Famine.

The second range of problems is that the temporal connection between parliamentary independence and economic expansion in the later eighteenth century may be accidental rather than causal. This is strongly suggested by the fact that upward trends in rents, population and tillage were well established before the 'charmed' interval of 1782–1800. In industry, linen manufacture grew, with periodic interruptions, throughout the eighteenth century. Its vigour derived from preferential access to British and empire markets and the progressive absorption of improved techniques of production and organization. The case of the woollen industry is more complex. This ancient industry had declined in the last quarter of the eighteenth century, rallied in the late 1790s, and did not finally succumb to British competition until after 1825.[13] Its partial resilience seems to have been due mainly to the adoption of larger units of production. The fledgling cotton industry, initiated on a factory basis in the 1780s, was a product of private, rather than state, initiative. The tariff on cotton of 1793 was, it appears, a purely *ad hoc* measure, designed to tide the industry over a trade depression, and not an application of protectionist thinking.[14] Nevertheless, the measure almost certainly helped, though the success of the industry depended ultimately on the use of modern forms of capitalist organization.

To move from textiles to agro-industry; both the brewing and distilling sectors advanced in the late eighteenth century. The growth in brewing, it is argued, was due to a lowering of excise duties during the tenure of Grattan's Parliament and a simplification of the laws governing the brewing trade. At best, though, this is only a partial explanation.[15]

The spectacular increase in pork and butter production, as reflected in buoyant export figures, dates back at least to the 1760s and the same decade saw the beginnings of reorganization in corn milling with the emergence of larger, power driven flour mills.[16] The salted beef and tanning trades declined in the late eighteenth century in response to changing market conditions. Even in the case of Foster's Corn Law of 1784, credited with producing a great increase in tillage and frequently regarded as the most concrete example of effective state policy, the impact seems to have been slight. That Ireland had emerged as a net exporter of cereals in the decade before 1784 was, as in the case of pork and butter, essentially a response to market opportunities.[17] Finally, and most ironically in view of the significance with which the Irish parliament had been invested with economic significance by earlier writers, Grattan's Parliament was not, even in principle, protectionist. Indeed, according to Black, free trade notions seem to have enjoyed a wider currency in Ireland than in England during the later eighteenth century.[18]

The heroic theory of Grattan's Parliament is rooted more firmly in fantastic political expectations surrounding the Home Rule movement than in economic or historical analysis. Expansion in agriculture and industry in the period 1750–1800 owed little to Irish parliamentary action. The dynamic of growth was supplied by market, organizational and technological changes associated with the rise of urban, industrial capitalism in Britain. Warfare, and its demands on the economy, and the development of imperial markets were related stimuli. Consistent with this interpretation is Cullen's observation that economic growth in the late eighteenth century is best viewed as part of a long wave of expansion extending back to mid-century and forward to the end of the Napoleonic wars; or as Lee puts it, 'Grattan's Parliament has been extravagantly praised for having the good fortune to exist concurrently with a phenomenon for which it was not responsible.'[19]

These conclusions should not, however, be taken to suggest that political institutions, Anglo-Irish economic relationships and tariff policies were an irrelevance. The two main industries, linen textiles and agriculture, benefited greatly from access to British markets. Furthermore, there were the benefits to Ireland of British tariff barriers against European competitors.[20] This was important for linens in particular. In the cotton industry, where Ireland did not possess a clear comparative advantage, Irish tariffs introduced in the 1790s may well have been significant for the survival and expansion of the industry. Also, current orthodoxy notwithstanding, the prohibition on Irish woollen exports can hardly have been other than damaging. It is interesting to note in this regard that a critical element in the rise of the Yorkshire woollen trade, predating the introduction of the factory system, was its involvement in foreign markets.[21] Commercial contacts abroad and aggressive marketing laid the basis for sustained development. The stimulus of export trade was not an option open to the Irish industry over much of the eighteenth century. Woollen exports were prohibited between 1698 and 1779, and between the latter date and 1800 differential tariffs discouraged Irish exports to Britain. It is at least conceivable that the inability to build up commercial networks abroad, and the limited involvement with the British market (where the major technical, organizational and product changes were occurring) deprived the Irish industry of dynamism and powers of adaptation.

Ideally, Ireland would have benefited most from a combination of free trade and selective tariffs, in a world where economic retaliation was absent. But the eighteenth century was not, alas, constructed around the exclusive interests of Ireland. Ireland could not have been simultaneously an integral part of the British economy, enjoying all the associated advantages, and an independent political entity, pursuing wholly self-interested economic and trading policies. Greater scope for autonomy lay in the next century, as we shall argue later.

THE UNION AND ITS CONSEQUENCES

The second component of O'Brien's general case, and in many respects the most interesting, is his discussion of the economic consequences of the Act of Union. But the Union cannot be considered in isolation from the conditions that gave rise to it, namely the political failure of Grattan's Parliament. As ó Tuathaigh has noted, even after 1782 the Irish parliament remained 'unrepresentative and corrupt'.[22] Although Roman Catholics were given the vote in 1793, they remained excluded from parliament. During the 1790s the United Irishmen increased in strength as did the activities of the rural secret societies. The combination of these two forces, with French assistance, led in 1798 to a massive insurrection against the Irish government, which was suppressed only with British help. In essence, the rebellion challenged a key premise on which conceptions of Irish political and social development had come to be based. 'For nearly thirty years', according to McDowell, 'it had been assumed that Ireland was a nation . . . in which old antagonisms were vanishing.' The risings revealed the deep divisions in Irish society and 'made it difficult to view the future with optimism'.[23] In these circumstances the British government determined upon a bold initiative, the Act of Union. The economic outcome, O'Brien argues, was calamitous. Ireland was adversely affected in three main areas: public finance; agriculture; and industry. We will now explore the impact of the Union on each of these in turn.

Public finance

There is some substance to the view that the fiscal arrangements established in 1801, and amended in 1817, were a burden to the Irish economy. Under the Act of Union it was envisaged that Ireland would keep its own exchequer but contribute 2/17 of the total revenue raised to cover British expenditure. Although this was probably reasonable at the time – certainly there was no malice on Castlereagh's part in fixing the proportion – increases in government expenditure of over 70 per cent between 1801 and 1814 meant that Ireland found it difficult to keep up its contributions without heavy borrowing.[24] The result was that by 1816 the Irish exchequer was virtually bankrupt. In 1817 the crisis was overcome by the merger of the British and Irish exchequers.

But there were continuing complications. It was not so much that Ireland was in an absolute sense overtaxed, though this allegation was sometimes made. In 1819, in *per capita* terms, the country paid only 21 per cent as much in taxation as Britain, rising to 30 per cent in 1849.[25] The 'problem' was twofold. First, after 1816, taxation in Britain fell much more rapidly than in Ireland: by 31.1 per cent as against 3.4 per cent. Although O'Brien makes much of this, it was largely a result of the abolition in Britain of income tax, which had never been levied in Ireland. Furthermore on several items, the most notable of which was whiskey, Ireland continued to enjoy lower rates of duty than Britain. The more substantial problem, however, was the possible drain of funds out of the country that the unification of the exchequers involved. Taken at face value this would appear to have been considerable:[26]

1819	1829	1839	1849	1859	1879
£3.7M	£4.2M	£3.6M	£2.6M	£5.4M	£3.2M

To put these figures in perspective, Mokyr has estimated Irish national income in 1841 as being between £75 and £85 million.[27] In other words, again taken at face value, the tax drain represented roughly 4.5 per cent of national income in that year.

O'Brien ends his analysis in 1849, though his argument would have been strengthened if he had examined what happened on taxation account in the 1850s and 1860s, when the gap between revenue and expenditure in Ireland widened markedly. This was a result of

Gladstone's decision to equalize British and Irish taxes. His measures included the imposition of income tax for the first time in Ireland in 1853 (income tax had been reintroduced in Britain in 1842) and the raising of the duty on whiskey to British levels. As a result, in 1859 the Irish paid in taxes £5.4 million more than the British government apparently spent in Ireland. Although there was a reduction in the deficit thereafter, it was still as high as a £3.2 million in 1879.[28]

But the situation is not as simple as these figures suggest. The deficit is exaggerated because the sums for 'expenditure in Ireland' do not take into consideration all the monies disbursed on 'imperial' account in the country. Thus interest payments on the national debt to Irish bondholders are excluded. These totalled £1.7 million in 1819, £1.3 million in 1829, £1.2 million in 1839, £1.4 million in 1849 and £1.5 million in 1859.[29] Additionally there was the expenditure on the army. Although Irish nationalist opinion might well argue that this was unwanted, it nevertheless marked a real transfer of resources to the country. The precise amounts of money paid to the army and ordnance service are difficult to determine. A parliamentary return for 1847 indicates figures of £1.51 million for 1819, £0.99 million for 1829 and £1.11 million for 1839.[30] True, not all the money issued on army account in Ireland would necessarily have been spent there: the British regiments in the country, for example, may have sent some of their money home, though this is likely to have been offset by remittances from Irish soldiers serving in Britain and abroad.

But at all events the true drain of funds out of Ireland on taxation account was considerably less than the raw data indicate. We would suggest a real deficit of approximately £0.5 million for 1819, £2.0 million for 1829 and £1.3 million for 1839.[31] This would represent for the last year roughly 1.6 per cent of national income. In the following decades the amount of excess taxation paid by Ireland seems to have diminished; by the early twentieth century there was a substantial net flow of public funds from Britain to Ireland. In conclusion, therefore, O'Brien's basic contention that there was a drain on taxation account out of Ireland is correct, though exaggerated.

Agricultural trade and the Union

The incorporation of Ireland into the United Kingdom after 1800 transformed the economic status of the island from one of a national economy to that of a mere region of a multi-regional state. However, being simply a region of the United Kingdom had two positive effects for Irish agriculture: it ensured continuing and secure access to the expanding British market and it conferred on Ireland the benefits of UK agricultural protectionism. These benefits cannot be taken for granted. They were conditional on membership of the UK. The seriousness of the issues can best be appreciated by reference to later experience. One recalls the crisis of agriculture in the Irish Free State during the 1930s, when the British state took punitive measures against food imports from Ireland. In the post-war period, one is aware of the severe marketing problems, and consequent low prices, which faced Irish farmers before they gained access to the highly-protected markets of the European Economic Community.

But would Britain, like other European countries, have erected tariffs against Irish agricultural exports during the first half of the nineteenth century? This seems likely after 1813. Even before the end of the Napoleonic wars, fearing an outbreak of peace, landlords and farmers were mobilizing in county agricultural associations to protect the 'farming interest' against foreign imports.[32] Agriculture, it should be remembered, was still the largest industry and also the largest employer, and its interests were unlikely to be neglected in a landlord dominated parliament. The Corn Law of 1815, enacted in response to post-war depression, entailed an absolute prohibition on the sale of imported grains unless grain prices rose above what were virtually famine price levels (80 shillings per quarter in the case of wheat, for example). Appropriately enough, the pressure for higher protection came initially from a select committee chaired by Sir Henry Parnell, 'an Irish landlord who had the interests of his homeland very much at heart'.[33] There were further modifications to the apparatus of protection in the succeeding decades, as agricultural interests contended with free trade advocates, before the final Repeal of the Corn Laws in 1846. In the early nineteenth century Ireland was a useful but relatively minor source of grain for the British market.[34] She was certainly not indispensable. Even in wartime there were alternative suppliers in the Baltic countries and North America. In the depressed agricultural conditions following 1813, it is difficult to see why an independent Ireland would have been excluded automatically from the operations of the Corn Laws. British livestock farmers fared somewhat better than arable farmers after 1813, but again there can be no ready assumption of privileged treatment for outside suppliers. Livestock imports from outside the United Kingdom were in fact prohibited until 1842.[35]

The issue of limited access to or exclusion from the British market raises complex possibilities regarding the welfare of different social classes. The landed ascendancy and commercial farmers would have experienced major losses. Rents and farm revenue would have declined and, inevitably, also the demand for labour. The wage income of cottiers and labourers would, as a result, have been lowered. In addition, lower farm rents might have altered the pattern of land use, favouring livestock production with its lower labour requirement at the expense of labour intensive tillage. A preference for pastoral products in British tariff policy, which would have been quite conceivable given that the major problems in post-war British agriculture were in the arable sector, would have accentuated this unfavourable impact on labour. On the other hand, the reduction in rents, which would also have been reflected in conacre rents, would have redounded to the benefit of the rural poor. Thus, the conflict centring on land use between (export) commodity production and subsistence food production would have slackened. It is even conceivable that cottiers and labourers would have gained access to more land, and hence reduced dependence on the vulnerable potato crop. The net outcome of these contradictory tendencies is difficult to assess, but clearly there was no long-term future in Ireland for a rural proletariat experiencing rapid population growth, in the context of falling agricultural income and declining rural industry.

Before leaving agriculture, it is important to consider also the implications of economic union for the closely related food processing trades. By 1800 the provisions trade had become heavily focused on Britain and, to a declining extent, on the transatlantic colonies. The Union had the positive effect of ensuring continued access to these markets. Butter exports increased substantially in the first half of the century.[36] The barrelled beef and pork trades were given an artificial stimulus by the French wars, but after 1815 beef exports declined as the trade was reoriented towards the live export of cattle. Live pig exports to Britain gained similarly at the expense of pork exports, though less rapidly. This shift away from processing livestock implies a loss of jobs and incomes in the provisions industry and a related decline in coopering and tanning. These changes, however, had little to do with legislative change; they were in response to market demands and improved transport facilities (the introduction of the steamship and, later, rail transport being particularly significant).

Industry and the Union

Linen textiles represented the leading industrial sector in terms of employment, output and exports in 1800. The British market was of particular significance, though by mid-century the United States was taking some 40 per cent of Ireland's exports.[37] Reinforcing the importance of the British market in the early nineteenth century was the fact that the home market was being lost increasingly to cheaper cotton substitutes. Free trade in linen goods within the United Kingdom was clearly beneficial to Ireland, given the competitiveness of the Irish industry. Conversely, tariff barriers separating the two economies would have handed a competitive advantage to the major competing centres in Scotland and the north of England, with potentially grave consequences. Furthermore, the outer protective shell of UK tariffs handicapped Silesian, Belgian and French producers in competition with the Irish. Aided by these advantages, the Irish (essentially Ulster) linen industry achieved a position of pre-eminence in world markets. By 1914 its factory labour force numbered some 75,000 workers, while most of its output was exported to diverse parts of the globe.[38] O'Brien's comment on the survival and success of linen manufacturing is worth noting, both because it identifies key elements in the story and also because of the subversive implications of the argument for his own preoccupation with policy, as opposed to market processes. Capitalist relations of production, technological change and factory production were

> the principal changes which the industrial revolution wrought in the linen manufacture; and, *as in the case of every other manufacture*, where they were adopted the industry not alone survived but increased, whereas, where they were not adopted, it waned and ultimately disappeared.[39] [emphasis added]

Given this admission, one need only add that modern large-scale production – one of the conditions of survival in the textile industry – was in turn dependent on continuing access to extensive markets, such as those of the United Kingdom.

To assess the impact of the Union on woollen textiles it is helpful to review developments in the English as well as the Irish industry. The final quarter of the eighteenth century was a period of fundamental change, both organizational and technological, in English woollen manufacture. In Yorkshire, which was destined to dominate the British industry, the first phase of the new mill-system of production was concentrated in the period 1790–1800. (This was in the woollen branch of manufacture; in worsteds the surge in mill building came in the following decade.) Earlier technical developments in the 1770s and 1780s involved the widespread adoption of the flying shuttle and the spinning jenny, both of which were compatible with the domestic mode of production. Carding machinery and multiple spindles driven by water or steam power formed the technical basis of the new factory system. Still, the pace of change should not be exaggerated. There were only twenty-two mills in the worsted branch of the industry in Yorkshire in 1800 (less than 10 per cent of the 1835 total), while the effective mechanization of weaving had to wait in the case of worsteds until the late 1830s, and in the case of woollens until the 1850s.[40]

The Irish industry, largely the woollen branch, was losing ground to English imports on the home market in the 1770s.[41] Its problems intensified in the next two decades. The timing is significant, relating as it does to a period before the adoption of the factory innovation. A number of hypotheses, none of which have been adequately tested, have been put forward to explain the industry's lack of competitiveness: high wages and problems of labour management associated with its traditionally urban as opposed to countryside location; a less elaborate division of labour as compared to England, and hence lower labour productivity; poor quality yarn; too many products; and an inelastic response to changing market demands. Additionally, where the industry was based in the countryside, it tended to take the rudimentary form of merely catering for household and local needs. This offered limited possibilities for capital accumulation and transition to modern forms of organization and production.

But alongside this picture of decline, the worsted trade managed to hold its position in the home market, though admittedly it found little success in export markets after 1779. If the Union and repeal of tariff duties were critical for the wool textile industry, then it is curious that Irish worsteds held off the challenge of English imports for the first quarter of the nineteenth century. There was, after all, virtually free trade in wool textiles from 1801. Alice Murray rightly describes the 10 per cent protective duty as a 'trifling advantage' for home producers.[42] When the end came, it came very quickly; not following the repeal of this duty in 1823, but with the depression of the whole of the British Isles in 1825–6. There was extensive off-loading of cheap goods onto the Irish market during the crisis, and by the mid-1830s the Irish wool textile industry was in a state of terminal decay.

In the larger context of locational change in the UK economy this was of course unremarkable. The English woollen industry was increasingly centred on the West Riding of Yorkshire in the early nineteenth century. Ancient seats of the industry in East Anglia and the West Country declined. Even in Yorkshire the worsted trades of Ripon, Selby and York, for example, lost out to expanding centres such as Bradford.[43] The weaknesses of the Irish industry had little to do with the Union. Taking a longer view, the legislative restrictions of the eighteenth century may, however, have sapped some of its vitality.

While linen and, to a lesser extent, woollen textiles were sheltered from massive technological change in the eighteenth century, cotton manufacture was exposed to the immediate impact of modern industrial methods. The Irish industry developed in the image of its powerful cross-channel neighbours in Lancashire and the west of Scotland. Power-driven spinning mills produced yarn which was distributed under the 'putting-out' system to thousands of handloom weavers. The organization of the industry was thus on a large scale from the outset. It was also highly regionally concentrated, focusing on Belfast and its environs. Production was geared to the home market. Because cotton manufacture was in its infancy in 1800 it secured favourable treatment under the Union. Existing duties on cotton cloth were maintained until 1808 after which they were progressively reduced to a level of 10 per cent by 1816.[44] They were finally abolished in 1824. However, the duties on spun yarn were abolished much earlier, in 1816.[45] This is an important and frequently neglected point, particularly as it is clear that the modern factory-based cotton industry in Ireland was located in the spinning sector. The abolition of the duties and exposure to competition had no immediately discernible effect on the industry's fortunes.

Decline set in during the late 1820s and early 1830s with the conversion of some cotton-spinning mills to linen manufacture. Until recently the conventional interpretation, shared by modern revisionist scholars and nationalist historians, was that the Irish cotton industry was driven out of existence by its cross-channel rivals. However, Geary has suggested that the switch from cotton to linen in east Ulster may have been voluntary, being largely in response to higher profits in the latter.[46] If this is true, then tariff structures were irrelevant to the issue of decline. The fact that the Irish spinning industry had already survived more than a decade without protection lends some support to this view. Still, a reimposition of the duty on yarn might well have prolonged the industry's existence. But this hypothetical pathway opens up further possibilities, illustrating again some of the complexities of counterfactual history. Increasing the profitability of cotton spinning might have delayed the movement towards rapid adoption of the wet-spinning process in the linen industry. It was relatively easy to convert cotton factories to linen manufacture; no massive new investment was required. If the transition had been postponed, then it could have allowed linen spinners in Leeds, or more particularly Scotland where the new technology had been invented, to steal a march on their Irish competitors.[47] This highlights the more general point that tariff policy which favours one industrial subsector may have adverse implications for another, sometimes in quite unexpected ways.

While the absence of fiscal autonomy may have created problems for the spinning section of the cotton industry, the same was not true of the weaving sector. Muslin weaving in particular benefited in the 1820s and 1830s from economic integration. Scottish merchants put out work to Ulster handloom weavers, thus integrating them into a larger pattern of regional specialization. Similarly, the sewn muslin trade, also controlled by Scottish firms, was facilitated by liberal trading conditions. This developed strongly from the end of the 1820s and may have employed over 100,000 workers when it peaked about 1857.[48]

With respect to the smaller industries examined by O'Brien there is little evidence that they were damaged by the Union. They were, in any case, of minor economic significance. By his own admission pottery-making was unaffected simply because it barely existed in eighteenth-century Ireland, owing to the absence of coal.[49] Again, using O'Brien's own figures, the output of shipbuilding increased, though the industry remained insignificant. As regards paper and printing, O'Brien's treatment is both cursory and ambiguous. With no evidence, he suggests that paper-making declined in Ireland between 1814 and 1823. Yet in the same paragraph he notes an increase in the number of mills from forty-two in 1822 to fifty-seven in 1835. Furthermore, as shown by a parliamentary return for 1842, which O'Brien ignored, there was a considerable increase in paper manufacture during the 1830s, from 2.5 million lb in 1833 to 4.0 million lb in 1841.[50] O'Brien's explanation of the decline of the printing industry – again assumed without proof – is quite singular; namely that Irish printers after 1800 were subject to copyright laws, so they could no longer reprint British books with impunity. In fact the Irish printing industry saw an expansion in the years before the Famine due to the spread of newspapers. The numbers of stamps issued for newspapers in Ireland rose from 2.5 million in 1817 to 6.0 million in 1840.[51]

The final industry mentioned by O'Brien is glass. Here again his treatment is marred by a failure to use the available evidence. Between 1825 and 1827 the British excise duties were extended to Ireland. This, O'Brien assumes, must have harmed the manufacture of glass in Ireland. His only hard evidence for this – polemical tracts emanating from O'Connell's Repeal Association can be given only limited credence – is a table from Thom's directory which shows a decline in the number of glass bottles and the amount of flint glass produced in the early 1840s.[52] However, information from the parliamentary returns shows that there was no marked decline in domestic glass production following the legislation of the 1820s. The output of bottle glass averaged 493 tons between 1822 and 1826 and 520 tons between 1836 and 1840. With respect to flint glass, where no figures are available before 1826, output rose marginally from an average of 337 tons between 1826 and 1830 to 362 tons between 1836 and 1840. Although there was a perceptible decline in glass production in the 1840s this was not because of the injurious effects of the excise duties. It was rather a result of Belgian competition, which was causing similar problems for British glass-making at the time.[53]

With respect to Ireland's evident lack of natural resources, O'Brien dismissed the absence of coal reserves as a contributory factor in Ireland's failure to industrialize. Following Kane, he argued that the higher price of the fuel added little to the total final cost of important products like textiles. This view has recently been endorsed by Mokyr, who also points out that the experiences of Switzerland and Japan show 'that coal and iron were not indispensable in the Industrial Revolution'.[54] This is true, although it needs to be mentioned that the proportion of the population involved in industry in Japan remained lower than that in Ireland until the 1930s.[55] But Japan and Switzerland are the exceptions rather than the rule. Those countries that industrialized earliest, and in which the process went furthest – Britain, Belgium, Germany and the United States, for example – possessed abundant mineral resources. For coal and iron are not simply inputs into other industries; they are outputs in their own right. Coal and iron ore are the gifts of a bountiful nature, providing employment, incomes and exports. It cannot be seriously maintained that if Ireland had possessed the mineral resources of the Ruhr it would not have been a more industrialized country. Abundant resources of coal and iron may not have been a necessary condition of industrialization in nineteenth-century Europe, but they were usually sufficient.

While O'Brien's analysis of industrial change in the period 1800–45 is generally unsatisfactory, his conclusion of widespread deindustrialization may still be valid. Modern scholars are divided on the issue and reliable evidence is scarce. According to census data on occupations, the proportion of the labour force employed in trades, manufacturing and handicrafts fell from 41 per cent in 1821 to 33 per cent in 1841. However, some doubt surrounds the classification of occupations in 1821, thus the downward trend could be more apparent than real. Against this, the 1841 census recorded 516,000 female spinners, representing 45 per cent of the total industrial labour force. We know from other sources that the rapid diffusion of the wet-spinning process in linen manufacture during the 1830s either destroyed the livelihood of most spinners, or reduced their incomes to a pittance. If we exclude female spinners, then the proportion of the labour force in industry shrinks to a mere 18 per cent. Unless the 1821 level is grossly overstated, it seems clear that there was indeed a major contraction in industrial occupations in pre-Famine Ireland. In an employment sense, therefore, O'Brien seems correct in saying that Ireland deindustrialized. But focusing on employment alone is to miss the real point. The army of hand spinners, necessary under conditions of handicraft technology, was being displaced by machine production. According to Green, one mill girl was able to produce as much linen yarn as some 300 hand spinners.[56] Thus, it was the very success of the transition to modern industry that caused a steep decline in the demand for textile labour. The more general paradox, therefore, is that the process of industrialization within Ireland was in considerable part responsible for the fall in the industrial population.

O'Brien ends his analysis of Ireland's industrial decline with the Famine. This choice of a terminal date weakens his case, particularly with reference to protection. From 1846 onwards Britain was firmly committed to free trade. Thus the danger of retaliation against Irish tariff policy was removed. During the second half of the nineteenth century a whole host of Irish industries, particularly those in rural areas, decayed: candles, boots and shoes, the clothing trade, furniture making are prime examples. The coming of the railways and cheaper transport meant that local production was replaced by goods made in Dublin or, to a greater extent, in Britain. By 1907, for example, Ireland imported boots and shoes to the value of £1.73 million, compared to domestic production of £219,000. The output of the Irish clothing trades was £4.57 million compared to imports of £6.5 million.[57] There is little doubt that quite moderate rates of protection could have increased the domestic production of these sorts of industries. Indeed, they were amongst the first to be protected in independent Ireland. Nevertheless, protection could not have prevented the decline of industry in small Irish towns. It would have meant instead that goods produced in Dublin, Cork or

Belfast supplanted goods produced in Britain. Furthermore, if this process had taken place without significant export success, it would have led inevitably to a net loss of jobs as factory production replaced handicraft methods. There would also, by definition, have been a rise in prices to the agricultural community. Nevertheless, it seems reasonable to suggest that, after mid-century, an independent Irish government, imposing selective tariffs and pursuing complementary industrial policies, would have saved some jobs and created others, though hardly on a scale necessary to prevent emigration. Economic conditions for the exercise of autonomy in the first half of the nineteenth century were far less favourable. Being a region of the UK economy was then, perhaps, the optimal arrangement for Ireland.

ULSTER AND LAND TENURE

East Ulster industrialized in the nineteenth century. Over most of the rest of the island there was reversion to a more purely agrarian economy. This uneven development is not particularly remarkable. Industrialization everywhere in Europe was limited to particular regions.[58] Nonetheless, within Ireland the conspicuous deviation of Ulster from the general experience excited much contemporary prejudice. Unionists tended to attribute the province's successful industrialization to its Protestant heritage and to its inhabitants' Scottish and English ancestry. These had given Ulster its special 'character'.[59] Naturally, nationalists scorned this explanation. 'The only way in which the special character of the Ulster people influenced the industrial development of the province', scoffed O'Brien, 'was by hastening on the introduction of the factory system on account of their dishonesty in dealing with the yarn in their own homes.'[60] Whatever about the dishonest Ulsterman, how does the case of Ulster serve the cause of O'Brien and nationalist Ireland?

As the argument was essentially one about land tenure, it is convenient to locate the question of Ulster in a broader discussion of tenurial systems. While the withdrawal of protection from Irish industry under the Union was held to have aggravated the country's problems, 'the ultimate cause of the failure of Ireland to achieve industrial success in the first half of the nineteenth century was the impossibility of accumulating capital under the existing land system'.[61] If anything, these problems intensified in the decades after the Union but the exception of Ulster is said to prove the rule. Here was a region which allegedly enjoyed freedom from the worst burdens of the land system. The Penal Laws were less severe in the province because of its Protestant population; tenure was more secure and the level of rents lower. Hence it was easier to accumulate capital in Ulster than elsewhere in Ireland, which in turn led to industrialization.[62]

The scope and severity of the Penal Laws have been questioned by a number of writers.[63] Recent scholarship has also cast severe doubt on the insecurity hypothesis.[64] Rents, however, increased during the period of the French wars, pushed up by buoyant agricultural prices, and probably maintained an upward trend (in real terms) in the period 1815–45. Although O'Brien has no evidence on the issue, this is consistent with his assertion of an increasingly oppressive land system. But the real point is about differential rents, and the test case for the inhibiting effect of rents on capital accumulation is Ulster. We should expect, therefore, to find a lower rent level in Ulster as compared to other regions. Comparative data on rents (per acre) for the mid-1830s are presented in Table 1.1.

Table 1.1 Head rents and conacre rents in Ireland, c.1835

Province	Head rent(£)	Number of cases	Conacre rent(£)	Number of cases
Connacht	1.28	93	4.88	132
Leinster	1.60	253	5.62	306
Munster	1.74	199	5.01	281
Ulster	1.60	152	6.52	171

Source: Calculated from the *Poor Inquiry (Ireland)*: *Appendix D* (*British Parliamentary Papers*, XXXI, *1836*)

The estimates are crude but there is no suggestion that Ulster was lightly rented relative to other Irish provinces, despite its poorer natural resource endowment as compared to Leinster, for example. The modern view is that Ulster Custom has been greatly exaggerated as an explanatory factor in the separate development of the north-east.[65] Absenteeism, as a recent study suggests, may have been more, rather than less, pronounced in Ulster in the 1830s.[66] More generally, if the system of land tenure was the crucial barrier to growth, then the expansion of the Irish economy in the second half of the eighteenth century, in the face of such restraints, becomes exceedingly difficult to explain.

Perhaps the real problem goes back further in time. The imposition, through confiscation and terror, of an alien landlord class in the seventeenth century may have unleashed a diffuse set of historical forces that constrained Ireland to a pathway of underdevelopment. Mokyr, for instance, in a neo-O'Brienite interpretation has argued that Ireland suffered from massive entrepreneurial failure, particularly on the part of the landed elite.[67] While this possibility cannot be dismissed, it must be recognized that counterfactual history extending across several centuries has such an open-ended character as to tend towards metaphysical inquiry.[68]

CONCLUSION

Three of the four components of O'Brien's explanatory structure are deeply flawed. Grattan's Parliament did not regenerate the Irish economy; the Act of Union did not have the uniformly malign consequences claimed (in fact the economic implications seem to have been strikingly favourable); and the unique development of east Ulster did not rest on privileged opportunities for capital accumulation in the agrarian sector. The final element – the system of land tenure – cannot be held to explain satisfactorily the problems of the Irish economy, if understood in terms of rackrenting, absenteeism and tenant insecurity. But if the issue is understood more broadly as the seventeenth-century confiscations and the imposition of an alien ruling class, with all the associated political and cultural consequences, then O'Brien's interpretation cannot be dismissed so easily. This is partly because the argument exists simply at the level of assertion but also because an assessment of the hypothesis involves counterfactual speculation on a grand scale.

Examined from the standpoint of historical method, O'Brien's trilogy must be heavily faulted. A narrow range of sources, generally the most readily available books, pamphlets and parliamentary reports, are exploited. The use of these sources is often uncritical, as if materials were selected simply to buttress pre-determined conclusions. Prize essays for O'Connell's Repeal Association, and other contemporary polemical writings are not necessarily founts of historical truth. The use of statistical data is rudimentary and sometimes misleading, being symptomatic of a generally weak empirical underpinning to many of the arguments. There are extensive borrowings from other secondary sources. In particular, generous helpings from Alice Murray's *Commercial Relations* are less than adequately acknowledged. Finally, the world-view embodied in O'Brien's writings is not only conventionally nationalist but also narrowly bourgeois. Social classes and conflict between social groups figure only in so far as they conform to middle-class nationalist categories of thought.

More positively, one can say that O'Brien's works are well organized, well written and contain a wealth of historical detail. But there are more important reasons for revisiting O'Brien and the earlier tradition of nationalist historiography. These writings still pose, even though they fail to resolve, some of the major questions of Irish economic history. O'Brien was right to emphasize the possible interaction between political independence and economic development. Issues of political economy, and Anglo-Irish relations in particular, deserve further investigation by historians. But O'Brien oversimplified a complex problem. Following Arthur Griffith, he assumed that legislative autonomy ensured economic growth. The Irish experience after 1922, however, lends no support to this article of economic faith. Moreover, political autonomy has costs as well as benefits. O'Brien minimized the constraints on an Irish state in terms of its freedom to adopt unilateral trading policies, while at the same time exaggerating the potential of protection as a means for promoting growth.

One must agree also with O'Brien's claims regarding the limitations of *laissez-faire* policies, especially in the context of the rural economy. This doctrine achieved its cruellest expression during the Great Famine under Lord John Russell's whig administration. One wonders, though, if an independent Irish parliament, probably dominated by landlords and commercial farmers, would have responded very differently. As noted, O'Brien had little to say about class relations or the political representation of class interests in a self-governing Ireland. As with *laissez faire* and its deficiencies, O'Brien's related generalization – that different economic policies are appropriate to different stages of economic development – is surely correct. Both were commonplace notions by 1920, but it is still worth emphasizing that diffusionist notions of the automatic spread of economic growth through market mechanisms are weakly founded.[69] The historical experience of backward economies from Russia and Japan in the nineteenth century to the newly industrializing countries of the contemporary Third World suggests the necessity of nurturing and channelling market forces at the national level. Finally, in the context of the revisionist revolution in Irish historiography since the 1960s, one may conclude that the political economy of George O'Brien and the nationalist school has been not so much refuted as neglected.

Notes

1 George O'Brien, *The Economic History of Ireland in the Seventeenth Century* (Dublin and London: Maunsel, 1919); *The Economic History of Ireland in the Eighteenth Century* (Dublin and London: Maunsel, 1918); *The Economic History of Ireland from the Union to the Famine* (London: Longmans, 1921). An unrelated work, *An Essay on Medieval Economic Teaching* (London: Longman, Green & Co., 1920) was also published in this period.
2 O'Brien, *Union to the Famine*, p. 589.
3 ibid., p. 588.
4 James Meenan, *George O'Brien: A Biographical Memoir* (Dublin: Gill & Macmillan, 1980) p. 24.
5 Arthur Griffith, *The Resurrection of Hungary: A Parallel for Ireland* (3rd edn, Dublin: Duffy, 1918) pp. 118, 138.
6 See in particular R. F. B. O'Ferrall, *The Growth of Political Consciousness in Ireland, 1823–1847: A Study of O'Connellite Politics and Political Education* (Ph D thesis, Trinity College, Dublin, 1978) and, by the same author, *Daniel O'Connell* (Dublin: Gill & Macmillan, 1981).
7 Meenan, *O'Brien*, pp. 187, 212.
8 *Report of the Fiscal Inquiry Committee* (Dublin: Stationery Office, 1924).
9 *First and Second Interim Reports on Wheat-growing and the Question of a Tariff on Flour* (Dublin: Stationery Office, 1928).
10 T. K. Daniel, 'Griffith on his noble head: the determinants of Cumann na nGaedheal economic policy 1922–32', *Irish Economic and Social History* 3 (1976) pp. 55–65.
11 James Connolly, *Labour in Ireland* (Dublin: Three Candles, 1951) p. 42.
12 O'Brien, *Ireland in the Eighteenth Century*, p. 406.
13 L. M. Cullen, *An Economic History of Ireland* (London: Batsford, 1972) p. 105; L. A. Clarkson, 'The Carrick-on-Suir woollen industry in the eighteenth century', *Irish Economic and Social History* 16 (1989) pp. 23–41.
14 R. D. C. Black, *Economic Thought and the Irish Question, 1817–1870* (Cambridge: Cambridge University Press, 1960) p. 320.
15 Compare O'Brien, *Ireland in the Eighteenth Century*, pp. 279–84 and Patrick Lynch and John Vaizey, *Guinness's Brewery in the Irish Economy, 1759–1876* (London: Cambridge University Press, 1960) pp. 2–3.
16 L. M. Cullen, 'Eighteenth-century flour milling in Ireland', *Irish Economic and Social History* 4 (1977) pp. 5–25.
17 R. D. Crotty, *Irish Agricultural Production: Its Volume and Structure* (Cork: Cork University Press, 1966) pp. 22–3.
18 Black, *Economic Thought*, p. 320.
19 Cullen, *Economic History*, p. 100; J. Lee, 'Grattan's Parliament', in Brian Farrell, ed., *The Irish Parliamentary Tradition* (Dublin: Gill & Macmillan, 1973) pp. 151–2.
20 *Customs Tariffs of the United Kingdom from 1800 to 1897 with some notes upon the history of the more important branches of receipts from the year 1660 (British Parliamentary Papers (BPP)*, LXXXV, 1898).
21 D. T. Jenkins and K. G. Ponting, *The British Wool Textile Industry, 1770–1914* (London: Heinemann, 1982) pp. 57–76.

22 Gearóid ó Tuathaigh, *Ireland before the Famine, 1798–1848* (Dublin: Gill & Macmillan, 1972) p. 9.
23 R. B. McDowell, 'The age of the United Irishmen: Revolution and the Union, 1794–1800', in T. W. Moody and W. E. Vaughan, eds, *A New History of Ireland, IV. Eighteenth-Century Ireland, 1691–1800* (Oxford: Clarendon Press, 1986) p. 362.
24 *Final Report by Her Majesty's Commissioners appointed to inquire into the Financial Relations between Great Britain and Ireland* (*BPP*, XXXIII, 1896).
25 ibid., p. 9.
26 ibid., p. 499.
27 Joel Mokyr, *Why Ireland Starved: A Quantitative and Analytical History of the Irish Economy, 1800–1850* (London: Allen & Unwin, 1985) p. 11.
28 *Commission on Financial Relations*, p. 499.
29 *Finance Accounts of the United Kingdom* (*BPP*, X, 1820) pp. 312–13; (*BPP*, XVII, 1830) pp. 150–3; (*BPP*, XXIX, 1840) pp. 76–7; (*BPP*, XXXIII, 1850) pp. 193–4.
30 *Account of the Public Income and Expenditure of Ireland; Charges; and Excess or Deficiency of Income, 1817–1846* (*BPP*, LIV, 1847) p. 208. However, another return suggests a slightly lower expenditure for 1839 of £0.9 million, while manuscript evidence from the Exchequer and Audit Department indicates £1.01 million. Still, these various estimates are sufficiently close to each other to suggest the broad accuracy of the data contained in the 1847 return. See *Naval Force, Army Force, and Ordnance Department (Ireland)* (*BPP*, XXXIII, 1844) p. 351; Public Record Office, London, A.03.
31 *Commission on Financial Relations*, p. 499; *Finance Accounts for the United Kingdom, for the Year ended Thirty-First March 1860* (*BPP*, XXXIX, 1860) pp. 74–5.
32 J. D. Chambers and G. E. Mingay, *The Agricultural Revolution, 1750–1880* (London: Batsford, 1965) pp. 123–6; G. Hueckel, 'Agriculture during industrialisation', in Roderick Floud and Donald McCloskey, eds, *The Economic History of Britain since 1700* (Cambridge: Cambridge University Press, 1981) vol. 1, pp. 192–3.
33 Chambers and Mingay, *Agricultural Revolution*, p. 124.
34 During the five-year period 1803–7, for instance, the annual average level of wheat exports was only 13,500 tons, while that of oats was 31,000 tons. The great surge in grain exports came in the next decade. See Raymond Crotty, *Irish Agricultural Production: Its Volume and Structure* (Cork: Cork University Press, 1966) p. 276. By 1845, on the eve of the Great Famine, Ireland was exporting the equivalent of half a million tons of grain (P. M. A. Bourke, 'The Irish grain trade, 1839–48', *Irish Historical Studies*, XX, 1976–7, p. 168).
35 *Customs Tariffs of the United Kingdom*, p. 39.
36 This section is based largely on Cullen, *Economic History*, pp. 53–9; Crotty, *Agricultural Production*, p. 277; and J. O'Donovan, *The Economic History of Live Stock in Ireland* (Cork: Cork University Press, 1940).
37 Philip Ollerenshaw, 'Industry, 1820–1914', in Liam Kennedy and

Philip Ollerenshaw, eds, *An Economic History of Ulster, 1820–1939* (Manchester: Manchester University Press, 1985) p. 74.

38 D. A. Armstrong, 'Social and economic conditions in the Belfast linen industry, 1850–1900', *Irish Historical Studies* 7 (1951) p. 240.

39 O'Brien, *Union to the Famine*, p. 326.

40 Jenkins and Ponting, *Wool Textile Industry*, pp. 29–56.

41 Cullen, *Economic History*, p. 65.

42 Alice Murray, *A History of the Commercial and Financial Relations between England and Ireland from the period of the Restoration* (London: P. S. King, 1903) p. 347.

43 Jenkins and Ponting, *Wool Textile Industry*, p. 78.

44 *Customs Tariffs of the United Kingdom*, p. 33.

45 E. R. R. Green, 'Industrial decline in the nineteenth century', in L. M Cullen, ed., *The Formation of the Irish Economy* (Cork: Mercier Press, 1969) p. 92.

46 Frank Geary, 'The rise and fall of the Belfast cotton industry: some problems', *Irish Economic and Social History* 8 (1981) pp. 30–9.

47 For a similar argument, but in the context of the nineteenth-century Indian cotton textile industry, see James Foreman-Peck, *A History of the World Economy* (Brighton: Harvester Press, 1983) p. 10.

48 Ollerenshaw, 'Industry', pp. 68–9.

49 For O'Brien's discussion of the minor industries see *Union to the Famine*, pp. 360–7.

50 *Account relating to the Duties on Papers in the United Kingdom, from 1833 to 1841 inclusive* (*BPP*, XXVI, 1846) pp. 620–1.

51 O'Brien, *Union to the Famine*, pp. 368–9; *Stamps issued for Newspapers, Ireland, 1817–26* (*BPP*, XVII, 1826–7) p. 47; *A Return of the Aggregate Number of Stamps issued for Newspapers in Great Britain and Ireland each year, from 1 Jan. 1827 to 1 Jan. 1842* (*BPP*, XXVI, 1842) p. 599.

52 O'Brien, *Union to the Famine*, p. 364. But see *Returns relating to Glass Retained for Home Use, and Quantities Exported, Duty Charged, and Drawback paid on each Description, in the United Kingdom, from 1814 to 1841, both inclusive* (*BPP*, XXVI, 1841) p. 160.

53 T. C. Barker, *The Glassmakers: Pilkington – the Rise of an International Company, 1826–1976* (London: Weidenfeld & Nicolson, 1977) pp. 117–28.

54 O'Brien, *Union to the Famine*, p. 412; Mokyr, *Why Ireland Starved*, p. 153.

55 On Japan see W. W. Lockwood, *The Economic Development of Japan: Growth and Structural Change* (Princeton NJ: Princeton University Press, 1968) pp. 109–32.

56 E. R. R. Green, *The Lagan Valley, 1800–50* (London: Faber & Faber, 1949) p. 117.

57 *Final Report on the First Census of Production of the United Kingdom (1907)* (*BPP*, CIX, 1912–13) pp. 240–1, 254–9.

58 Sidney Pollard, *Peaceful Conquest* (Oxford: Oxford University Press, 1981); John Langton and R. J. Morris, eds, *Atlas of Industrialising Britain, 1780–1914* (London: Methuen, 1986).

59 For the flavour of some of these sentiments see Patrick Buckland, ed.,

Irish Unionism 1885–1923: A Documentary History (Belfast: Public Record Office, Northern Ireland, 1973) especially pp. 15–17.
60 George O'Brien, 'Foreword' to E. J. Riordan, *Modern Irish Trade and Industry* (London: Methuen, 1920).
61 O'Brien, *Union to the Famine*, p. 447.
62 'the true secret of the industrial success of Ulster was the prevalence of the Ulster custom of land tenure': O'Brien, *Union to the Famine*, p. 442.
63 J. L. McCracken, 'The ecclesiastical structure' in Moody and Vaughan, eds, *A New History of Ireland*, vol. IV, pp. 91–9.
64 Mokyr, *Why Ireland Starved*, pp. 101–3.
65 Liam Kennedy, 'The rural economy, 1820–1914', in Kennedy and Ollerenshaw, eds, *Ulster*, pp. 40–1.
66 Mokyr, *Why Ireland Starved*, p. 201.
67 *ibid.*, pp. 199–200, 278–86.
68 Liam Kennedy, 'Why one million starved: an open verdict', *Irish Economic and Social History*, 11 (1984) pp. 91–7.
69 For a critique of diffusionist views see Ian Roxborough, *Theories of Underdevelopment* (London: Macmillan, 1979) and Eoin O'Malley, 'The problem of late industrialisation and the experience of the republic of Ireland', *Cambridge Journal of Economics* 9 (1985) pp. 141–54.

3 A Saorstát is born

How the Irish Free State came into being

D. R. O'Connor Lysaght

On 6 December 1921, plenipotentiaries representing the cabinets of the Irish Republic and the United Kingdom signed Articles of Agreement for a Treaty between the two countries. These superseded the previous direct colonial relationship between Britain and Ireland (the parliamentary Union) and replaced it with the relationship, part colonial and part semi- or neo-colonial, that exists, despite vicissitudes, to this day.

The basis of the settlement was that it allowed most of nationalist Ireland a dominion status that could and would eventually become political independence, while Britain kept control of certain spheres in which it had decisive economic and defence interests. Economically, it conceded the new twenty-six county regime full tariff powers, but this meant less than it might have done a century earlier. By 1921, Britain controlled Irish trade and finance through a network of links that had been strengthened by its own superior economic development in the previous century. This was not an imperial relationship in Lenin's sense of it being based on the export of the dominant partner's capital to exploit its raw materials for extra-large profits. Britain had not exported its capital to Ireland, rather it had imported Irish capital, attracted by the superior profit potential in Britain and other British colonies. (An exception to this was the Irish railway system, of which half the major companies were subsidiaries of British lines.) The largest capitalist interests in Ireland were integrated into British concerns. Above all, Britain still controlled the Irish export market, both in the volume of business it did and in the fact that most Irish foreign trade was carried by Britain's Merchant Navy (and continued to be until the Second World War). None of these problems could be overcome by protective tariffs alone.

A twenty-six county government might have made a serious attempt to extend its economic freedom; it could have tried to do this by allying with the new power of Soviet Russia, or as seemed more likely, with aid from capitalist America. For this reason, as well as for the long-standing one (going back to its original invasion of 1171) of military security, Britain retained two strongpoints in Ireland itself. The first consisted of its naval bases in the twenty-six counties: the so-called Treaty Ports. The second has proved more lasting. The capitalists of north-east Ulster had been able to maintain and build their industries at the cost of increasing sectarian division among their workers. Protestant capitalism, encouraged and headed by leaders with political and economic links to the hardest British imperialists, and opposed to the Catholicism of the Irish majority, gave Britain a stronger foothold than any group of isolated ports. Already, before the Treaty, the province of Northern Ireland was an accomplished fact and it was recognized as such in Articles 11 to 16 of the Treaty.

These were the realities behind the new order in Ireland. It must be understood, however, that their significance was immediately very much masked by other clauses that caused Irish Republicans much more heart-searching, since they denied the formal reality of the Republic. In particular, many who had taken the Republican oath found it impossible to accept the article providing for an oath to the King of England, against whom the Republic had been in arms. This oath would remain for more than ten years the major political issue dividing the defenders of the new Irish Free State or Saorstát Eireann, from the state's opponents. In the end, it was abolished quite easily, without breaching the balance of forces behind the Treaty. More serious were the financial agreements made later to clarify Anglo-Irish business left outstanding in the Treaty. These agreements would leave the Saorstát accepting responsibility for settling the land question that had been the best known cause for dispute between Britain and Ireland. This acceptance gave the question new life in the 1920s and 1930s. Nevertheless although it provoked an economic war in the later decade, it would be resolved at the end of the period, again with the Treaty settlement shaken but not stirred.

That the Irish Republic's plenipotentiaries should have signed an agreement that gave them so much less than they claimed, needs some explanation. On the British side, matters were comparatively straightforward. The previous settlement, the parliamentary Union of 1801, was obsolete. It had been established to serve the current needs of British military security and of the landlord class on the two islands. The latter's importance diminished during the nineteenth century, particularly after trans-oceanic agricultural supplies from America and even Australia and New Zealand had caused local food prices to fall. From the Land Purchase Acts of 1885, and particularly 1904, Irish landlords were tending to cut and run from their estates, with the United Kingdom exchequer paying half the purchase price of their estates and their ex-tenants paying the remainder in the face of the increased international competition.

The departure of the landlords came, in fact, too late to save the Union. Most of the Irish people had reasons to object to it from its beginnings. It had been understood that Britain would accompany its passing with an extension of voting rights to the disenfranchised Catholics, whose religion was that of the Irish majority; the British-dominated United Kingdom parliament refused to honour this for nearly thirty years. Meanwhile, the Union created more lasting grievances. It stimulated a major increase in Irish capital exports and, outside the north-east, a collapse of Irish industry: a development that was probably inevitable given Irish lack of coal and iron, but which did emphasize the difference in fortune between Irish and British. This contrast was emphasized and encapsulated most decisively in the Great Famine of 1845–7.

The Famine created the condition for a continuous movement for a revolutionary split between Britain and Ireland. The Irish plebians learned from the failure of the pre-Famine movement for constitutional parliamentary separation, as well as from the industrial stagnation that had begun before the Famine and the fall in population that the Famine escalated. The change caused by the disaster in the balance of interests within the remainder of the Irish population dictated the form of the revolutionary movement. In the countryside, the chief losses had been suffered by the agricultural labourers; from 1850, the farm population outside a few counties in the east and south was dominated by tenant farmers holding tenancies that differed widely in size and value. They could and would be united against the landlords and the colonial government that upheld their interests; as the landlords retreated, the farmers' militancy on the national issue varied according to their interests *vis-à-vis* the state (whose land laws would give it the role of land divider and capital investor in the west), each other (small against large farmer) and their remaining landless labourers. Revolutionary nationalism, the programme of an Irish Republic, was maintained in the cities both in Ireland and among Irish emigrants to the USA. The more prosperous of the Irish national bourgeoisie, those who owned their portion of real estate, saw their future as centred on the control of the colonial administration. Those with less security sought full legislative freedom to rebuild their country's ravaged economy. This aim was supported by the skilled section of the working class. In a manufacturing economy unable (outside Ulster) to grow beyond the norm of the small workshop, its members were unable to present a more advanced programme; this would become a permanent factor as a result of the organization of the unskilled workers after 1900. Nevertheless, backed by increasingly influential forces in the USA, the Irish Republican classes proved to be the most serious revolutionaries in the United Kingdom in the second half of the nineteenth century. Land tenancy might have been reformed successfully by the colonial regime but the demands of the Republicans could not be satisfied within the 1801 settlement.

The reaction of British capital to this problem was divided. It was fortunate at this time in having the Liberal Gladstone, the only politician in eight centuries to try seriously and scientifically to place on firm foundations Britain's interests on the neighbouring island. He sought to do there what had been done in Britain: to win over the more prosperous of the country's middle class and use it to discipline the rest. This meant changing British policy to strengthen the Irish tenant against the landlord. It meant, too, reducing the power of the unpopular state Protestant church. The constitutional nationalists would be further conciliated by Irish university reform to give them educational equality with the British and the Protestants who dominated the professions and the civil service. Here, however, Gladstone's ideas clashed with those of the Irish bishops of the Catholic hierarchy. Many of these gave support to the new constitutional demand of Home Rule, a call for an Irish parliament vague enough to unite Republican veterans of defeated insurrections in the 1860s with those who saw some sort of Irish parliament, however subordinate to that of Britain, a necessity for keeping disorder in check. This latter, the principled Home Rule bourgeoisie, was encouraged to commit itself further after 1882. For three years the Home Rule movement had provided leadership for a major land agitation that won a measure of tenant relief. Then, when the movement split between those who accepted the reform and those who wanted more, it allied with the right wing of that agitation to consolidate itself. Its success in this convinced Gladstone that, to achieve his aim, a measure of limited Home Rule for Ireland was necessary.

This was quite out of the question for the largest British business interests. When a Home Rule Bill was introduced in 1886, the richest Liberals broke with Gladstone and joined his Conservative opponents. The new alliance to defend the parliamentary Union (it became a single Unionist party only in 1912) accepted that

Ireland was a colony, but, unlike the Home Rule Liberals, it was prepared to run it as a colony, even without the Union's franchise rights if it did not conform. British Unionism was supported by the remaining Irish groups in favour of the Union: the diminishing numbers of landlords, the colonial bureaucracy and, most substantially in the long run, the community of Irish, and particularly Ulster, Protestants, of which the vanguard was the Orange Order. Yet its priority was British; it defied its Irish base to argue that local government reform and land laws, passed by Unionist, even more enthusiastically than by Liberal, governments, would create a strong Irish middle class that would support the Union. This perspective was right-wing utopianism, but it had money and influence behind it. Its chief constitutional support lay in the House of Lords, and the limiting of that body's veto in 1911 was a major blow to it. Yet it won extra-constitutional support in Britain (and Ulster) to neutralize its new constitutional weakness and stop the enacted measure of Home Rule being brought into operation in 1914.

By then, Home Rule was in danger of being superseded. Its likelihood had won support from members of the Republican movement and isolated its less compromising leaders. From 1905, Arthur Griffith's Sinn Féin had made explicit the Republican economic and social programme, with some success, but it overstretched its resources (among other initiatives, it tried to produce a daily paper) and after 1910 could do little more than make propaganda. However, below and even partly within the traditional Republican class alliance, an alternative to all the major Irish political movements was developing. In 1907, James Larkin began the lasting organization of Irish unskilled workers, founding the Irish Transport and General Workers' Union (ITGWU). This was not just an extension of trade or industrial unionism, but a centre for socialist ideas; the unskilled could have no illusions that their talents could give them prosperity in a capitalist republic. Griffith accused Larkin of being a British saboteur of the remaining Irish businesses and thereby lost his party's left wing. A distinct, independent, working-class interest was established. In 1913, its vanguard in Dublin survived the worst that the largest employers – Unionist and nationalist alike – could throw at it, over a five-month lockout.

Labour's more lasting problems were political. Its new mass movement, led by socialists, was bound to suffer from its share of infantile disorders, the more so because it was isolated from what was in any case still a politically underdeveloped Socialist (Second)

International. It embraced the central idea of syndicalism, of the organization of the working class through an industrial union, or unions, that would create an alternative state to those of the bourgeoisie without too much political action. This was attractive to newly organized workers and was attacked accordingly not only by capital, but also by the Catholic clergy and, in Unionist Ulster, by the Orange Order. Syndicalism made it appear that the achievement of socialism would be spontaneous and inevitable. Such hopes seemed to be justified by James Connolly when he returned in 1910 from the United States, with his pamphlet *Socialism Made Easy*. Connolly took pains to oppose the total hostility to political (i.e. non-industrial) action that he had found among American syndicalists. He fought elections, supporting women's right to the vote and Ireland's right to independence. The trouble was that syndicalism emphasized the union as both the force creating the Workers' Republic (that was bound to come) and its prospective state form. This perspective reduced politics to one more aspect of union work. Additional and necessary political action was left to propaganda groups and, in practice, to a few individuals like Connolly and Frederick Ryan in the Independent Labour Party of Ireland. Unlike its British namesake, this party had no formal relationship to any mass party. Such a party was founded in 1912 as an extra function of the Irish Trade Union Congress, now, literally, the Irish Trade Union Congress and Labour party.

The dual role of a combined congress and party magnified its problems in winning members to its affiliates at a time when Home Rule was about to be passed against massive Orange opposition, and when the Irish workers were as divided on the issue as any other class. The Congress-Party leaders responded by avoiding the issue. Even Connolly accepted this line, because he believed Home Rule to be inevitable. Only in 1914, when the Home Rulers began to negotiate with the Unionists to allow Orangeism its own territory separate from the rest of Ireland, did Congress move. Its annual meeting that year denounced partition, but without stating whether it supported any sort of distinct Irish parliament. This position could have been accepted by the Unionists as much as by nationalists.

From August 1914, syndicalism did allow the Congress-Party to stay united under an executive that opposed the First World War, while Home Rule and Unionist politicians supported the British. On the other hand, it could not move on the issue beyond demanding that Ireland not be despoiled of its foodstocks to make up for Britain's curtailed imports. Connolly accepted this. His plan of action centred on Larkin's Irish Transport and General Workers' Union, the most militant in the United Kingdom, of which he was now acting general secretary. In common with other socialist revolutionary defeatists he sought to turn the imperialist war into class war; in Ireland, this had to begin with national revolution. At first Connolly tried to create subversive propaganda to provoke the colonial regime to attack his union and confront the rest of the Irish workers. But as the war continued, economic conditions worsened and the workers revived the militancy that had been suppressed after 1913. From November 1915 Dublin docks were closed by a strike. Connolly began to consider more offensive action. He allied with a group of Republicans in the leadership of the nationalist militia, the Irish Volunteers, with the aim of rebelling the following Easter. By then, his hopes had been reduced, and many of his own union members doubted his perspective. The dock strike that would have given its militants a first-hand opportunity to experience British imperialism in action was ended by scabbery from the British National Seamen and Firemen's Union. Finally, Connolly's Republican allies were unable to obtain a rising in most areas outside Dublin. Even so, Connolly's own force, the Irish Citizen Army, was the junior partner to the Volunteers in the actual rebellion, giving it the impression of a piece of 'propaganda by the deed'. He was executed afterwards by the British, leaving no political successor outside his family.

Yet the Easter Rising was successful even in its defeat. The Home Rule party had presented its support for the British war effort to its supporters as being payment in return for the Home Rule Act. More dangerously, they portrayed the measure as giving Ireland the free status of a dominion within the empire, and as being actually in operation. But this was untrue. The act conferred only provincial status and had in any case been suspended for the duration of the war. Now, after the rebellion, Britain suspended its civilian control of the country and appointed a military governor with powers of life and death, which he exercised. This exposed the Home Rule party, the self-styled ruling party of Ireland, as impotent to decide on the basic questions of life, death and national sovereignty. It could not win: either Britain had the right to appoint a military governor, in which case the party had been lying, or it had no right, in which case 'poor little Catholic Ireland' was being treated as badly as 'poor little Catholic Belgium' on whose behalf the party was recruiting Irish soldiers to the army of Ireland's oppressor. All the party could do was press for immediate self-government, which no United Kingdom war ministry could allow, and hope more than ever that the war would soon end.

Instead, the war lasted a further two and a half years. For most of this time the revolutionaries kept the initiative, particularly during the first half, as the imprisoned Volunteers and their allies were released. The question was: what would be the nature of their revived and expanded movement? The Volunteers were reconstituted in November 1916, but would their political functions be organized separately and, if so, would they be organized by a broad movement or by a party; if a party, which class would it represent? These questions had been answered by October 1917. A conference that month confirmed that the political wing of Irish Republicanism was a party of revolutionary nationalists with a social and economic programme, as well as with a name taken from Griffith's Sinn Féin.

Peadar O'Donnell would remark later: 'Connolly's chair was left vacant.' Subsequent myth has placed the blame for this on the new party's President, Eamon de Valera, for ordering Irish Labour to 'wait' until the achievement of full independence, and on Labour's own leaders for accepting this order out of pure nationalism. In fact, de Valera never did try to order Labour to wait, though he may have agreed that it should. For its part, Labour could have allied with Sinn Féin with its socialist aspirations intact and codified, as long as it upheld as a principle the 'virtual establishment' of the Irish Republic and refused, accordingly, to take any United Kingdom parliamentary seats it might win. This would have handicapped the strategy of the Trade Union Congress and Labour party. Its plan was to build its own industrial republic through the organization of all Irish workers, of whatever political opinions, including those on the vexed national issue. As far as that was concerned, there was no distinct socialist group to intervene; Connolly's attempt to use his union had succeeded only in justifying British attacks on its officials and headquarters. So the Congress-Party leaders counterposed building their organization with participating in the national struggle. Connolly's friend, William O'Brien discovered this for himself. In April 1917, while the revolutionary national movement had still to take its final shape, O'Brien joined the committee that headed the front later to become the nucleus for the new Sinn Féin. In doing so, he was considered to have breached his mandate from the Dublin Trades Council, although he made it clear that he was acting as an individual. Even his closest comrades there were hostile and in May he had to resign from the committee. This was taken over the more easily, as a result, by Griffith and his allies, who were the most experienced and effective people remaining in the Republican movement. They expanded it still further. By the general election at the end of 1918, the new Sinn Féin was able to dictate terms by which the Congress-Party might contest seats without its opposition. Rather than agree to principled abstention from the United Kingdom parliament, or oppose Sinn Féin in a series of doomed fights, Labour withdrew its candidates except in non-nationalist Belfast. Sinn Féin won 47 per cent of the Irish vote and 73 of the country's 105 seats, 26 without contests.

This meant that the Irish national democratic revolution had come to be led by a national revolutionary party with a general social analysis centred on the alleged qualitative division between the owners of real estate and the rest. Its ultimate social vision was that of a society like that believed vaguely to have existed in Ireland before the Normans introduced feudalism. Its minimum aim was class conciliation. It was able to maintain this contradictory position because the wartime boom continued from 1918 to 1920. Sinn Féin was able to allow Labour to make the running on the industrial scene, although it took the precaution of founding a series of Republican arbitration tribunals. It did clash more determinedly with local branches of the Irish Transport and General Workers' Union in the west, when the latter organized a land agitation in the spring of 1920. The leaders of the union did not protest at its members' initiative being smashed by forces of the new Irish Republic.

The Republic was one of the two contenders for full state power, the other being the colonial administration. This condition of dual power had been formalized by the establishing of Dáil Eireann in January 1919. Irish Labour did not remain altogether outside this contest. In each year from 1918 to 1920, it organized nationwide general strikes which asserted its own aspiring industrial Republic, producing what could be termed a 'triple power situation' that was too unstable to survive for more than a few days at a time.

Even before the Treaty compromise, the Republican strategy had revealed its flaws. It is an open question whether direct participation by Labour in the national struggle would have helped reconcile the Ulster Protestant workers to an Irish Republic. What is sure is that there was no way that the Republic could win over Protestant workers from communal politics that at least gave them a junior share in Protestant hegemony over Catholics, to the role of victim of exploitation equal to that of Catholic workers, and subject to Catholic as well as Protestant employers. As the Anglo-Irish war proceeded, the Orange leaders kept their community loyal to Britain by harping on the threat to Protestant rights. (Contrary to the views of some modern apologists, these rights were not held then by their advocates to include divorce and contraception, let alone abortion.) In 1921, this loyalty was rewarded by their being given their own provincial Home Rule over the largest area they could control separately from the rest of Ireland: the province of Northern Ireland. Meanwhile, in July 1920, Ulster Labour had paid the price of its national leaders' political evasions. Orange workers drove Catholics (and also Protestants who were socialists) from their places of employment. In the elections for the new Northern Irish Parliament in May 1921, all forty Unionist candidates won seats compared to the twelve won by nationalists (six each for Sinn Féin and for old Home Rule), and none by Labour.

The Ulster 'pogroms' were only the most acute form of Irish Labour's difficulties in 1920. As the Anglo-Irish war increased in intensity, the occupying forces began to ignore the unions' formal neutrality in the military struggle and to treat their branches as fair game. Moreover, from May, the Party-Congress (it had switched its title around in 1918) found itself locked in a struggle that nearly destroyed it. It gave its support to a strike of railwaymen against the carriage of munitions on the railways, which was done openly only by the occupying forces. Unlike the previous occasions of Labour action against them, the British refused to accept a compromise. Instead, the colonial regime closed or curtailed services on most lines outside Ulster, giving Labour the choice of either surrendering or ruining itself. In the end, Britain's own escalation of the military struggle created the disorder that gave Irish Labour the excuse to end the strike for reasons beyond its control. Nevertheless, for the last months of the war in 1921, its national executive could do no more than make propaganda.

With Labour weakened, the Dáil had to approach economic and social issues under conditions of recession, and with its institutions being destroyed by the British. To this was added the strain put by the war on the Irish Volunteers. Their struggle had varied in militancy according to local conditions. While the politicians came mainly from the upper groups of the Republican classes in the towns, though often with a background in the countryside, the Volunteer leaders sprang directly from the rural environment, and fought according to the different conditions in each area. So the cockpit of the war was south-east Tipperary, where the contrast between large and small farmers was more extreme than anywhere outside the western areas. In County Clare, the larger farmers played an active militant role that was related to the fact that comparatively few had bought their lands.

Strong organization by Connolly's union seems to have affected areas like County Meath, where the farmers had little cause for revolutionary nationalism, but where a conscious and strong working class existed to replace them. As the war entered its third year, there was a general tendency for local Volunteer commands to become declassed. With Labour paralysed, many activists concentrated on the military struggle. Such fighters held more radical social and economic views than their general headquarters approved; Peadar O'Donnell and Sean O'Dwyer had both organized workplace occupations under the Red Flag. In County Tipperary, a veteran fighter was expelled for declaring publicly that the Republic would make Lord Dunally snag turnips. Militarily, too, the train of command from headquarters was becoming less dependable. Local units had to stand on their own feet or go under. When they succeeded, they were less inclined to accept the GHQ line.

For a time, these internal problems were ended when a truce was agreed with Britain in July 1921, but the social problems got worse. With prices falling, the employers sought to cut wages. Against them were the workers, who were organizationally weaker, but undefeated outside Ulster. In the new struggles, the Volunteers were used or threatened against strikers and occupiers. Constance Markievicz, Dáil Minister for Labour and former officer in Connolly's Citizen Army, was as interested as her colleagues in maintaining national unity at any cost, rather than supporting the workers' claims. Griffith, an advocate of Irish tariffs since before he had founded Sinn Féin, was willing, as head of the Dáil peace delegation, to drop his old economic demand in order to gain peace in which to deal with the strike wave, but he was overruled by his colleagues.

Once the Articles of Agreement were signed, it was not these class divisions but the apparently less important embryo organizational divisions in the Volunteers that proved important. Many in the still surviving Citizen Army, and their friends like Peadar O'Donnell, had expected that Sinn Féin would betray the Republic. Their hopes were that William O'Brien would lead Labour to save it and turn it, in the process, into a Workers' Republic. O'Brien did not oblige. Once the Dáil had ratified the Treaty, he and his colleagues declared the end of the national struggle and the 'beginning' of industrial struggle. What they thought had been taking place during the truce is not clear.

Indeed, this formulation should have given cause for thought to many in sympathy with the idea behind it. It did not mean mobilizing the full membership of the Party-Congress affiliates (an estimated half of the employed work force) to break the shell of Republic, Saorstát and colony alike and proclaim the Industrial Republic, although the social upsurges in the first half of 1922 showed great potential support for this line of action. The basic difficulty with it was that O'Brien and his colleagues had been too cautious too long. In particular, the growth of the Irish Transport and General Workers' Union, from 5,000 in April 1916 to 100,000–120,000 in 1920 had given it financial reserves as well as members. It seemed safer to trust to the apparently inevitable growth of union membership than to risk what they had in a possibly ill-judged intervention. This caution had been shown already when Labour had stood idly by while its comrades were victimized in the Orange 'pogroms'. Compared to that provocation, the Treaty split over what appeared an academic choice of words seemed an issue on which a *putsch* or even an agitation seemed the depth of stupidity. So the proclamation of the industrial struggle meant, in practice, a decision by a narrow majority at a special meeting of the Party-Congress that it would contest the General Election to be held in the twenty-six counties on the Treaty. Those who wanted more direct action on industrial issues were disciplined. Some, like the new Communist party of Ireland and, later, the left wing of the Citizen Army turned to the anti-Treaty vanguard, calling on it to rise immediately.

The strength of this vanguard surrounded the Volunteers. Most Sinn Féin activists would probably have opposed the Treaty, but the probability was not tested. The party conference (Ard Fheis) on the issue was postponed by agreement, never to meet again. What is certain is that two-thirds of the fighting men (unlike the Citizen Army, the Volunteers excluded women) and the majority of their women's auxiliary, Cumann na mBan, declared against the Treaty. This was done for various reasons: Cumann na mBan was particularly dubious about the continuing of partition. However, the overall critique was reduced to a lowest common denominator on lines summarized by the Tipperary Dáil (parliamentary) deputy and Volunteer commandant, Seamus Robinson; the Republic had been won before the plenipotentiaries had betrayed it in London. This classical formulation made it seem unnecessary to go any further. It united all who opposed the Treaty for whatever reason. At the same time, it could not appeal to those who knew that the betrayed Republic had given them little more than they had taken for themselves. It had nothing to say to those who were just happy with the prospect of peace. Nor did it give any incentive to prepare arguments outside the divided ranks of those who had led the national struggle. The

Communist party of Ireland and the anti-Treaty Volunteers made no appeal to labour. Labour made no gesture to them. The CPI and the Citizen Army limited their appeal to the anti-Treatyites, urging them to attack immediately.

Against this divided opposition, the Irish bourgeoisie united behind the Treaty. Their non-Socialist opponents in the anti-Treaty movement were, with the exception of Cathal Brugha the candle-maker, all people from the traditional Republican class alliance; petty bourgeois and skilled workers who did not own land or dwellings, backed by those whom socialists would regard as more definitively propertyless. Unionists, Home Rulers and old Sinn Féin capitalists united behind Treaty, Saorstát and, of course, 'peace'. This unity had a parallel in the Catholic hierarchy. During the Anglo-Irish war it had not been able to unite except, as Labour had mobilized, in opposition to specific British excesses. Its old Home Rule majority could not recognize the Republic. Now all the bishops moved to support the new settlement.

That this position involved big evasions of reality was shown in April. On the 24th, the Party-Congress organized a successful general strike (the last in the twenty-six counties for nearly fifty years) against 'militarism' and for the supremacy of civil government. As the Treatyites themselves were administering the only civil government in the twenty-six counties, the main target of the stoppage was the anti-Treaty Volunteer garrison in the Dublin Four Courts. At the same time, Labour's bias was implicit rather than otherwise and the strike organizers did find enough evidence of abuses by the new Saorstát army to provoke that army's command to protest. What was more, the strike encouraged the workers in the twenty-six counties to their highest level of militancy. The Munster creamery occupations, revived land agitations and the occupations in 'red' Tipperary were all encouraged, if not caused directly by the new revelation of Labour's power.

Another after-effect of the strike went against this upsurge and was more lasting. On 27 April, the united Catholic hierarchy in Ireland issued a political statement on behalf of all its members. This repeated the Irish Labour leaders' appeal for peace, but concentrated responsibility for its breach entirely on the opponents of the Treaty. For nearly ten years after this the Catholic bishops acted as committed chaplains for the Treatyite party.

The anti-Treatyites did not try to counter such attacks by any serious social initiatives. They organized land agitations in Counties Leitrim and Mayo and at Ballinacourtie, County Tipperary, but these were linked to plans for resettling refugees from the northern 'pogroms' rather than to land-hungry local farmers and labourers. In June, more than one-third of the anti-Treaty candidates were defeated at the general election and more would have failed had they not made a pact with the Treatyites to try to fudge the issue. The latter interpreted their relative success as a mandate to dictate the political agenda. They took police action against the more militant anti-Treaty Volunteers, united all anti-Treatyites against them and started a twenty-six county civil war. Despite that, the Treaty regime continued to be portrayed by its allies as peace-loving (against the 'militarists') and democratic (upholding its electoral victory). They were able to do this credibly because, apart from the imprisoned anti-Treaty leader, Liam Mellows, their opponents continued as non-politically as they had begun. Meanwhile, the Labour party and TUC accepted the role of loyal opposition in the Saorstát Dáil. By 6 December, when the new state was officially established, the anti-Treaty struggle was relegated to the status of a guerilla annoyance rather than constituting a challenge for state power.

The story does not quite end there. Politically and socially, the new Saorstát proved to be a retreat from the standards asserted under the Republic. It did win the civil war, with the aid of those who had stayed in the British Army through the previous conflict but politically it failed to achieve Irish unity. Its government was more directly responsible for lumbering its population with the secret financial agreements that surrendered vast sums of money to the British. The institutions of the Republic were scrapped in favour of refurbished forms of those of their colonial opponents. Socially and economically, all traces of socialism, even 'Celtic socialism', were banished, in what would now be called an ultra-monetarist policy. Pensions and wages were cut. The Saorstát army was used to help smash the Irish Transport and General Workers' Union organization of the rural labourers. These policies did no more than intensify trends that had started in the Republic before the Treaty. They were probably inevitable for any contemporary capitalist government. They were notable, too, for being far less thorough than those imposed on both workers and Catholics by the Northern Ireland government: it was opposed to the democratic revolution as a whole, while the Saorstát's counter-revolution was a holding operation in the interests of some who had benefited from the revolutionary change in state power. For all that, the Treatyites intensified social counter-revolution and backed it by suspending local councils and gerrymandering the Dublin municipal franchise.

The party that benefited from the reaction to all this was not Labour but the political organization of the opponents of the Treaty. Their political incompetence had lost them the civil war, but they had fought it while Labour had worked within the new order. Those who opposed that order bypassed the Party-Congress to join the Saorstát's political enemies. In 1927, the largest Republican party, Fianna Fáil, recognized the Saorstát Dáil. Five years later, it took office, in the greatest political change in twenty-six-county history.

Labour's electoral supersession was more than paralleled by the fall in membership of its affiliated unions. By 1927, their numbers were exceeded by Labour's twenty-six-county electors, even though Labour's numbers were also falling. Faith in the inevitability of syndicalism waned. Non-unionized voters had to be organized. In 1930, Party and Congress divided without making any balance sheet of the syndicalist experience. Only such an audit could have allowed the party to escape its political past. It has remained a bad third (at best) to this day in the twenty-six counties.

This result was helped by the comparative success of Fianna Fáil. After 1932, it ended the financial agreements, revised the Treaty to get rid of the oath to the king and produced a constitution that might be called Republican, though the word was never used. It also reformed the social welfare system.

But this was as far as it wanted to go. To prevent the movement that had elected it from getting out of control, it turned to the Catholic hierarchy that it had defeated to help put the country to sleep again. It did more than compensate the bishops for its impiety: contraception was made illegal, and the ban on divorce maintained as a convention by the previous government was written into the new Constitution. Catholic power in Ireland had reached its present position in the state. By then, of course, Saorstát Eireann was constitutionally dead but the settlement it represented was very much alive.

It is interesting but unprofitable to speculate upon what might have happened had Labour been prepared to occupy the place left for it by Connolly in the leadership of the Irish national revolution. What is certain is that the Irish Republic of 1919 could only be maintained by struggle and could be secured only by going beyond its terms of reference, probably geographical, certainly social. By remaining within these borders, it produced an abortion: instead of a Republic, a Saorstát was born.

Bibliography

Most of the above text is based on primary sources: daily newspapers, working-class journals, Minutes of Dáil Eireann and of the Annual Meetings of the Irish Trade Union Congress and Labour party, as well as on the Thomas Johnson and William O'Brien papers in the National Library of Ireland and the Richard Mulcahy papers in the Archives of University College, Dublin. There are a number of books published that give extra information and insights:

Andrews, C. S. (1979) *Dublin Made Me*, Dublin and Cork.

Connolly, James (1987) *Collected Works I*, Dublin.

——(1988) *Collected Works II*, Dublin.

——(1971) *Socialism Made Easy*, Dublin.

Dáil Eireann (1921) *Constructive Work of Dáil Eireann*, Dublin.

Fitzpatrick, David (1977) *Politics and Irish Life, 1913–1921*, Dublin.

Greaves, C. Desmond (1961) *The Life and Times of James Connolly*, London.

London and Cambridge Economic Service (1972) *The British Economy, Key Statistics 1900–1970*, London.

Lyons, F. S. L. (1973) *Ireland Since the Famine*, London.

Lysaght, D. R. O'Connor (1985) 'Class and national struggle in Co. Tipperary, 1916–1924', in William Nolan and Thomas McGrath, eds, *Tipperary, History and Society*, Dublin.

——(1970) *The Republic of Ireland*, Cork.

Marx, K. and Engels, F. (1971) *Ireland and the Irish Question*, ed. R. Dixon, London.

Mellows, Liam (1965) *Notes from Mountjoy Jail*, London.

Mitchell, Arthur (1974) *Labour in Irish Politics, 1890–1930*, Dublin.

O'Brien, William and MacLysaght, Edward (1969) *Forth the Banners Go*, Dublin.

O'Connor, Emmett (1988) *Syndicalism in Ireland, 1917–1923*, Cork.

O'Donnell, Peadar (1963) *There Will Be Another Day*, Dublin.

Pakenham, Frank (1972) *Peace by Ordeal*, London.

4 Labour in the post-independence Irish state

An overview

Seán Hutton

Populist nationalist historiography and much left-wing historiography have tended to view the historical process in the light of its predicated end. In the one case the united march of a people towards self-realization in a nation state forms a unifying theme; in the other there has been an elision of the factors of class and nationalism – factors never found in their idealized, free-standing forms but more problematic in their relationship than much of that historiography would allow. The actual tensions between the ideologies of class and nation, which form an identifiable strand within the history of Irish labour, as well as the widespread and profound hostility within sections of Irish society to socialist ideas and policies, tend to be underplayed. This is equally true of the influence of Catholic social thought, which, with nationalism, has functioned as a predominantly conservative force within the independent Irish state; though a section of the left in Ireland – and in Britain – has, at various times, seen the completion of Ireland's national struggle as the key to the destabilization and overthrow of the bourgeois parties north and south, and even in the two islands.

Anti-metropolitan nationalism has certainly been a driving force in modern Irish history. The historic relationship of Ireland and Great Britain, resulting in the permeation of large sections of the Irish society by a modern ideology of anti-metropolitan nationalism in the course of the nineteenth century, is obviously a factor of great importance in the context of Irish labour. Of equal significance, likewise, has been the allegiance of a section of the Irish population (including a substantial working-class segment) – largely Protestant and sufficiently concentrated in areas of Ulster to be politically significant – to the ideology of political Unionism. These political developments contributed to the setting up of two states in Ireland in the early 1920s, the virtually independent Irish Free State and the dependent state of Northern Ireland. In the context of Irish labour, the impact of partition on the economy and social structures of the two states was marked. In the mid-1920s, for example, 35 per cent of the working population was engaged in industry in Northern Ireland, while in the Free State only 14 per cent was so employed. The respective percentages for employment in agriculture were 26 per cent and 51 per cent.[1] In the southern state, moreover, of the sections within the working class on whom the Labour party might rely, the agricultural labourers were declining in numbers and the skilled and semi-skilled working class constituted relatively small segments of the political nation. Radical hopes centred on an alliance of the urban and town workers with another declining sector, the small farmers.[2]

The purpose of this essay is to examine the way in which the working class in what became the Irish Free State related to the new Irish state and its political parties, and to give an account of the institutions of the left and labour. The outcome will show a certain similarity with the situation in Northern Ireland: to the extent that Fianna Fáil, like the Unionist Party, succeeded, early in the history of the state, in constituting a durable cross-class alliance. Nationalism and Catholicism, as integrationist ideologies, performed a similar function in the southern state to those of loyalism and Protestantism in Northern Ireland. However, there the similarity ends, for loyalism and Protestantism also divided Northern Ireland, while the independent Irish state was sufficiently homogeneous for nationalism and Catholicism to perform an integrating function – as far as the vast majority of the inhabitants of the state were concerned. Further, while the Unionist party held a monopoly of power up to 1972, the government of Northern Ireland was destabilized and removed as a result of the ongoing crisis provoked by the civil rights campaign of 1968–9. The southern state, on the other hand, has enjoyed remarkable stability, with long runs of Fianna Fáil government, interspersed with Fine-Gael-led coalitions, between 1932 and 1989. In both areas the Labour movement was weakened by the process which brought the states into existence, as well as, subsequently, by the pressure of those integrationist ideologies. In Northern Ireland the labour movement has also been affected by the polarization of politics around nationalism and political Unionism.

The first task of the Irish Free State was to ensure its own survival. This it did successfully by using draconian measures. Around the cause of the Republic were gathered a hotchpotch of intellectually 'pure' Republicans and those who refused to abandon the diffuse hopes built up during the 'four glorious years', as well as a handful of social Republicans, in what Peadar O'Donnell described as a 'Fenian' tradition,[3] and the revolutionary socialists of the small Irish Citizen Army and the Irish Communist party.[4]

Labour was represented by the Irish Labour Party and Trade Union Congress, a trade union party. For a mixture of strategic and ideological reasons, the leaders of Labour had adopted an attitude which regarded the revolutionary nationalist struggle of 1918–21 as a form of shadow boxing. This led it to stand aside in the General Election of 1918, while adopting a form of 'benevolent neutrality' towards Sinn Féin down to 1922. Those who believed the leaders of Irish Labour would now initiate the industrial struggle for the Workers' Republic, in line with previous syndicalist rhetoric, were mistaken. In the absence of the republicans from the Free State Dáil [parliament], the Labour party constituted the parliamentary opposition to the government between 1922 and 1927. Under the leadership successively of the English-born Thomas Johnson – a key figure in the labourist reorientation of Labour after 1923[5] – and T. J. O'Connell of the Irish National Teachers' Organization (INTO), the Labour party unsuccessfully opposed the regressive policies of the Free State government, whose strategy for economic development was closely linked to the interests of the more substantial farmers.[6]

The Labour movement suffered two major setbacks in the 1920s. First, the slump which began in 1920 narrowed the room for accommodation between employers and labour. The desire of the nationalist revolutionaries to establish the 'national' credentials of the movement could, and did on occasion, result in conflict with the interests of workers during the period of the Anglo-Irish war. However, the coalition of conservative interests around the Free State brought about a situation which was far more clear-cut. The advance of the Free State Army in the civil war was associated with the restoration of the 'rights' of employers and property holders; and the deployment of the army and the new police force was an important factor affecting the outcome of the wave of strikes organized against wage cuts in 1923.[7] Trade unionism among rural labourers, for example, was smashed and would not revive again until the 1940s. Trade union membership in general declined radically. The Irish Transport and General Workers' Union (ITGWU), which had 100,000 members in 1921, had a membership of 15,453 in 1929.[8]

However, the fall in membership of the ITGWU was also due to the second factor affecting the Labour movement: the struggle for power between James Larkin and William O'Brien, which split the ITGWU, leading to the formation of the Workers' Union of Ireland (WUI) in 1924, when the majority of the Dublin membership followed Larkin out of the union he had founded. Substantial issues of tactics were lost sight of in the reaction provoked by Larkin's difficult character and lack of constructive abilities.[9] The conflict between the two men continued into the 1940s, with serious consequences for the unity of the already weakened Labour movement in the southern Irish state. For Larkin's stature among large sections of the Dublin working class was unrivalled, as demonstrated by the outcome of the split in the ITGWU. His ramshackle Irish Workers' League (IWL) was able to bring 6,000 people on to the streets to mourn Lenin's death in 1924, and the three IWL candidates standing for Dublin constituencies in 1927 polled a higher total than the combined Labour party vote in Dublin. In 1923 and 1927, Larkin ran IWL candidates against the Labour party; bringing about the defeat of Thomas Johnson, the then leader of the party, in the second General Election of 1927, at a time when Larkin was working closely with Fianna Fáil.[10] At the same time, Larkin's relationship with the minuscule Irish communist movement was problematic. His IWL was run as a 'one-man-band'; and the backing which the Comintern gave Larkin was understandable in terms of his popularity in Dublin, but frustrating for other Irish communists (who were, anyway, divided on class and national issues). Comintern representatives were unable to compensate for Larkin's lack of interest in organizational matters.[11] In short, Larkin's influence was helpful neither to the Irish Labour party nor to the Irish communist movement. That influence could, depending on how it was used, have allowed one or the other to build a base in Dublin, the one major city of the state. Instead, Fianna Fáil was to accomplish this task in the 1920s and early 1930s, with the compliance, to varying degrees, of the political institutions of the Labour movement and their leaders.

In the late 1920s and early 1930s, however, it still seemed that a left alliance might be constructed with Republican participation. A section of the IRA (Irish Republican Army) leadership began to move to the left, participating in the formation of Comintern sponsored organizations. It also set up the short lived Saor Eire as a left-orientated political movement (in the face of the 'red scare', provoked by the government, Saor Eire redefined its aim as the construction of 'a new Christian civilization').[12] In 1935 the Republican Congress, 'probably the most representative gathering of working class and republican militants ever seen in Ireland',[13] met in Rathmines Town Hall. It split on the issue of whether to become a party seeking the establishment of a Workers' Republic – which seemed to its proposers to offer the best hope of uniting the Irish working classes north and south – or a popular front seeking the establishment of an Irish Republic. The latter was supported by the Communist party, which was now following the line developed by Seán Murray at the refounding conference in 1933: that the fight for communism in Ireland would grow out of the national struggle. Following the failure of the Republican Congress experiment, a more traditionally nationalist leadership asserted itself within the IRA.[14]

It was the success of Fianna Fáil in establishing its own cross-class alliance that constituted the major factor closing off the openings available to other left-wing and radical groupings in Ireland. This success was largely due to the skill of the party leaders in seizing the opportunities which presented themselves in a formative period of Irish politics. But the position of Fianna Fáil was not unchallenged or unchallengeable; and that its victory was handed to it, by Labour and by the residual Republican movement, was also, to an extent, true. The swing to the right in Irish Labour after 1923, and the decline into clientist opportunism which followed,[15] as well as the lack of unity in the movement, was important – not only in the late 1920s and early 1930s, but also in the period from the late 1930s into the 1950s, when disillusion with Fianna Fáil, among elements of its own constituency, opened the real possibility of a left coalition of parties to challenge its power. The dissipation of social Republicanism – internally divided over tactics and marginalized by both the strategy of the Republican right and the success of Fianna Fáil – was equally significant. When a 'socially radical and unequivocally republican'[16] grouping emerged in the 1940s, in the form of Clann na Poblachta, it did so under an essentially right-wing Republican leadership. The lack of a left base and, in fact, the narrowing of the political space for left-wing strategies in the twenties and the thirties would be of considerable significance subsequently.

The social base of Irish politics, of which one characteristic was a strong *petit bourgeois* configuration,[17] was not conducive to the development of a strong Labour movement. In addition, Catholic social ethics as enunciated in the papal documents *Rerum Novarum* and *Quadragessimo Anno*, had, like populist nationalist ideology, considerable currency. Varieties of vocationalist thinking expressed themselves in the search for order and stability in the new Irish state in the 1930s and 1940s. The Roman Catholic Church had immense authority over a wide field, and an informal alliance between Church and state was sustained by both conviction and mutual convenience.[18]

Fianna Fáil was seen as dangerous enough in the late 1920s to be denounced as being tainted with communism by the Cumann na nGaedheal party.[19] It was not, however, until the early 1930s that a full blooded 'red scare' was raised. In 1931, worried by the spread of left-wing activity, and by the threat from Fianna Fáil and the republicans, the government drew up a dossier on subversive activity, which it passed to the bishops. The pastoral letter issued by the Catholic bishops referred to 'the growing evidence of a campaign of Revolution and Communism'.[20] This was the signal for the unleashing of a campaign of political, clerical and mob pressure which reached its height in 1933, when Jim Gralton, the leader of a Revolutionary Workers' Group in County Leitrim, and a naturalized American citizen, was deported from Ireland; in Dublin the headquarters of the Revolutionary Workers' Groups was destroyed, and the Workers' College, the headquarters of the Larkinite WUI and the Kevin Barry Hall, a Republican meeting place, were attacked by Dublin mobs. The bishops, in their pastorals, continued their attacks on socialism and radical Republicanism through the decade and the mob violence continued.[21] A Catholic newspaper, the *Standard*, dedicated to 'the creation of a united public opinion in the cause of Catholic reconstruction',[22] played an active part in the campaign against communism up to the 1950s. Perhaps its most scurrilous contribution in this sphere occurred in 1953 when it published photos of members of the Irish Workers' League, with their names, addresses and details of their employment.[23]

During the 'red scare' of 1933, provoked by the announcement that the relaunching of an Irish Communist party was imminent, many rural Labour party branches organized meetings to protest their abhorrence of communism, and in 1934 the party resolved to oppose any attempt to 'introduce anti-Christian Communistic doctrines into the Movement'.[24] Events in Spain gave further encouragement to anti-communist feeling in Catholic Ireland, resulting in the formation of an Irish Christian Front. The outbreak of the 'cold war' in the post-war period reinforced a feeling, by now widespread in the southern state, in which national destiny, Roman Catholicism and anti-communism were combined. On May Day 1949, trades unions were strongly represented in a demonstration in O'Connell Street, Dublin, of some 150,000 people to protest against the evils of communism in

Eastern Europe.[25] Against this background, the 'red scare' became an obvious tactic to be resorted to, used by sections of the Labour movement itself as well as by its opponents, including Fianna Fáil – once, itself, the butt of such attacks.

Comfortable folk, viewing the new state through a complacent ideological haze, could regard Ireland as 'the best country in the world to be poor and unfortunate in'.[26] In fact, it was a society where petty snobbery, subservience and clientism thrived, enabling those who wielded various forms of economic and political power to act as little caesars.[27] 'They can come to my back door and ask for it, if they need it,' said a priest, in the course of a sermon denouncing a proposal to provide children with a free school meal as communism.[28] Emigration was an integral part of the structure of this society: affecting the poorer classes of the population disproportionately, and women more than men. It was emigration which gave some hundreds of thousands of the sons and daughters of small farmers, as well as labourers, unskilled and semi-skilled workers and their offspring, the freedom that went with the ability to earn a steady income.[29] Emigration was the price paid to maintain the stability of the state and the standards of living of those who remained at home.[30]

That emigration was 'to an extent unusual in Europe, female emigration'[31] was not perhaps surprising. Up to the 1960s, in what was to become the twenty-six-county state, opportunities for women's work, outside the home and outside a series of low-paid and poorly-regarded occupations, were severely limited.[32] In the 1920s and 1930s there were attempts to restrict further the opportunities of women to work outside the home. In 1926, legislation was passed which allowed the government to restrict the entry of women into certain areas of the civil service. The position of women teachers offers an interesting example here. In 1933 a rule was introduced by the Fianna Fáil government which required that women should retire from teaching on marriage. The need to alleviate the current unemployment situation, as well as various reasons which were held to render married women unsatisfactory members of the teaching force, were advanced in support of the bill. While the INTO opposed the bar and campaigned for its repeal, pay and conditions of service other than this were seen as of greater importance to teachers; and its removal, in 1958, was due to the need to make up a shortage of teachers, rather than to any fundamental change of heart on this issue. Another example in this field was the Conditions of Employment Bill, introduced by Seán Lemass in 1935, sections of which had the effect of restricting women's entry into industrial employment. It was the Irish Women Workers' Union and a group of women senators, rather than the Labour party or the trade union movement in general, which was responsible for the ultimately unsuccessful opposition to this aspect of the bill.[33]

In the course of the Senate debate on the Conditions of Employment Bill, Senator Kathleen Clarke argued eloquently for equal pay for women, basing her demand on the recognition of equal rights for men and women enunciated in the 1916 proclamation, of which her executed husband had been a signatory.[34] However, general thinking on the social position of women, and the pressures of an economy with a high rate of unemployment and only limited room for expansion, meant that such views carried little weight either within the Labour and trade union movement, or outside it.

The expectation that women who worked would cease to do so on marriage was a general one.[35] Legislation concerning the social role of women, divorce and the regulation of sexual reproduction, which tended to bring the law of the state and Catholic social teaching into line with each other, met with little resistance. Demands tended to be for that degree of support which would enable a woman to fulfil her role as wife and/or mother in society.[36] Although the emphasis placed on women's domestic role in the Constitution of 1937 was denounced as reactionary by some of its opponents, the predominant view, and one which became part of the internalized world view of most women, was that this was, in fact, the case.[37]

William Norton could say with truth in 1929 'not one of the thirteen Labour Deputies held his seat by trade union votes'[38] (i.e. by trade union votes alone). The contraction of trade unionism and the decline of the Labour party into clientism in rural areas, as Teachtaí Dála (members of parliament: TDs) sought to build up local bases of support, and made those calculations inherent in a system of voting involving the single transferable vote, led to adjustments. Local party branches had been set up in 1925 and the Labour Party and Trade Union Congress had separated in 1930 in an attempt to broaden the party's base of support.[39]

Once Fianna Fáil decided to take the parliamentary road after 1927, the Labour party, despite continuing denunciation of all forms of bourgeois politics, could not avoid limited cooperation with the new party on a range of issues. It proved unsuccessful in preventing the initiative passing to what was then a radical nationalist party, with a policy which many found difficult to distinguish from its own.[40] Fianna Fáil, when it came to power in 1932 with the support of the Labour party, had radical agrarian and protectionist industrial policies which appeared to offer a solution to the problems of unemployment and emigration, as well as offering immediate advantages to workers, small farmers and agricultural labourers.[41] Fianna Fáil's popularity was also due to such policies as the abolition of the Oath of Allegiance and the enactment of the Constitution of 1937, steps towards the achievement of a republican concept of independence. Then, having stood up to the right-wing Blueshirts, whose chief base of support lay among the strong farmers, and to Britain in the 'economic war' – disarming criticism from the left – the government was able to sign a series of agreements with Britain which reconciled sections of moderate conservative opinion to the party.

However, key aspects of the government's strategy were not succeeding. There was growing dissatisfaction at the speed of land division, and unemployment among rural and urban workers continued. Further, while the industrial workforce increased from a narrow base by some 50 per cent from 1931 to 1938 as a result of Fianna Fáil's protectionist policies, unemployment remained high and, when opportunities for employment in Britain improved in the later 1930s, the volume of emigration increased once more.[42] '[T]he nascent industrial base remained weak and vulnerable',[43] and Fianna Fáil failed to resolve the economic problems which its programme appeared to address. However, one of the undoubted successes of Fianna Fáil in this decade lay in establishing a broad base of support for the party.[44]

William Norton, who led the Labour party between 1932 and 1960, shared the dominant Republican ethos of the time and found no difficulty in moving with the tide. While the party had rejected 'anti-Christian Communist doctrines' in 1935, it had incorporated the object of establishing a workers' republic in its constitution in 1936; and it opposed the 1937 Constitution because it did not contain a specific declaration of a republic. Labour did well in the municipal elections of 1936 and gained seats in the general election of 1937. Social Republicans like Michael Price, Roderick Connolly and Nora Connolly-O'Brien were joining the party.[45] James Larkin was admitted in 1941, along with his son, 'Young' Jim, who quickly established his influence within the Dublin executive committee of the party. In 1941 also the Communist party dissolved its one remaining branch in Éire and urged its members to enter the Labour party.[46] At the same time, the dissatisfaction caused among its erstwhile supporters by the rightwards movement of Fianna Fáil, the apparent continuing decline of Fine Gael, the gains of the Labour party from the late 1930s onwards, and the emergence of two new parties, Clann na Talmhan (founded in 1938) and Clann na Poblachta (founded in 1946) – both aimed at sections of Fianna Fáil's constituency – suggested the possibility of realignments in Irish politics from the later 1930s onwards.[47]

Evidence of the anxieties caused in the trade union movement by the apparent leftward movement of the Labour party was provided when the Irish National Teachers' Organization took ecclesiastical advice on the party's commitment to a Worker's Republic. Word came down the line that this commitment was incompatible with Catholic moral law, and the commitment was withdrawn in 1940.[48] However, in the general election of 1943 Labour won seventeen seats, the number it had won in 1922 and which it had only ever exceeded in the first General Election of 1927.[49] But the labour movement was, in fact, about to enter a renewed period of crisis. This was partly due to the outbreak of a further instalment of that personal struggle between William O'Brien and the man he described as 'the arch-wrecker James Larkin',[50] provoked by the fact that Larkin appeared to be staging a comeback. In 1934, when Larkin's WUI had been admitted to the Dublin Council of Trade Unions, the ITGWU had withdrawn in protest. Larkin had been able to use the trades council as a base to gain access to the ITUC, from which his own union was excluded. In 1936 he was elected to Dublin Corporation and in 1937 as an independent Labour TD for Dublin North-East. In 1941 he played a leading part in the Council of Action established by the Dublin Council of Trade Unions to fight both the government's Trade Union Bill and the proposed wages standstill orders.[51] In 1942, however, his critics sought to disable him politically. A rule change resulted in Larkin's exclusion from Congress. Then, in 1943 the ITGWU members on the administrative council of the Labour party succeeded in blocking Larkin's nomination as a candidate in the general election. The Dublin executive committee of the party supported his nomination, and Larkin stood and was elected. The ITGWU members now proposed that the chair and secretary of the Dublin executive committee be expelled from the party; and when the administrative council refused, the ITGWU disaffiliated from the Labour party and five ITGWU-sponsored deputies seceded from the Parliamentary Labour party to form a National Labour party.[52] An aspect of this conflict was the 'red scare' tactics adopted by the ITGWU.

It was the Communists in the Labour Party who sponsored the campaign to have Larkin adopted as an official Labour Party candidate in the last election. It was before them and their threats that Mr Norton quailed. It was in deference to the intimidation of the self-appointed Dublin Executive, the hub of the Communist organisation inside the Party, that the Party Constitution was violated.[53]

The Catholic *Standard* joined in, as did that master of invective, Seán MacEntee. Expulsions of left-wing members of the party followed, disabling the left. In the general election of 1944, Fianna Fáil regained its overall majority while Labour lost 70,000 votes and nine seats.[54]

The two issues in terms of which the second crisis, which was to split the ITUC, was argued through were (1) the role of the British based, amalgamated unions in an independent Irish state and (2) the problems arising from the multiplicity of unions and the consequent need for an agreed system of rationalization. In fact, underlying both issues was, once again, the desire of the ITGWU to carve out the leading role to which it felt entitled within the Labour movement of the independent state. Following the failure of William O'Brien and the ITGWU delegates to carry the strategy which O'Brien had outlined for the Congress commission on trade union rationalization at the special conference of 1939, an advisory Council of Irish Unions was established by the ITGWU and a number of other Irish unions. In 1945 annual Congress adopted a motion regretting the failure of the executive to accept an invitation to attend an international congress of trade unions in February 1945 to discuss, among other matters, the reconstruction of the world trade union movement following the defeat of fascism.[55] It was at that point that the advisory Council of Irish Unions declared,

> that the opinions and aspiration of Irish Labour cannot be expressed by the Irish Trade Union Conference, which is controlled by British Trade Unions and that the Irish Unions affiliated to Congress occupy an intolerable and humiliating position; that we recommend our affiliated unions to withdraw from Congress and establish an organisation composed of Trade Unions with headquarters in Ireland.[56]

Having previously used the 'red scare', a particular tendency within the Labour movement was now seeking to exploit national chauvinism as a tool, aided and abetted by members of the government.[57] The split in Congress resulting from the setting up of the Congress of Irish Unions (CIU) was to last until 1959. It was not a clear-cut division between the amalgamated and Irish based unions. Larkin's WUI was now allowed to affiliate to the ITUC and a large number of Irish unions remained affiliated to it. The ITGWU dominated the CIU.[58] Thus, at a point when Labour seemed poised to advance, the twin institutions of the movement suffered severe blows. By the time the Labour party and Congress were reunited relations between government and trade unions had begun to move onto a new plane, a development to which Seán Lemass's influence contributed greatly.

In 1941 the Trade Union Act was passed and the wages standstill orders initiated which were to continue in force until 1946. Some saw in these measures a further shift to the right and interpreted them as the prelude to a general attack on trade unions.[59] The attitude of William O'Brien and the ITGWU leadership to the Trade Union Bill was ambiguous, because of a feeling that it could be exploited to the benefit of the ITGWU.[60] Lemass, who replaced the more reactionary MacEntee as Fianna Fáil's Minister for Industry and Commerce in 1941, was sufficiently pragmatic to consult the central trade union representative bodies regarding possible amendments to the Trade Union Bill and the wages standstill orders, defusing the opposition to those measures.[61] His policy became one of drawing the trade unions into a subordinate partnership with the state, one in which, in return for certain clear advantages, the central trade union body would be prepared to accept, 'responsibilities in relation to the maintenance of discipline'.[62] His desire to incorporate the unions found an echo in the dominant trend of corporatist thinking within the trade union movement itself.[63] Lemass continued his policy of consultation with the unions in bringing forward his proposals for a labour court in 1946, designed to regulate the surge of wage demands which would be made once the wages standstill orders ceased to operate. For, while the cost of living index had increased by two-thirds in the period 1939–46, the average industrial wage had increased by only one-third.[64] The labour court would provide conciliation in labour disputes and it also acted as a facilitator in the first and second national pay rounds of 1946/7–8, initiating a 'key feature'[65] of industrial relations in the Republic – voluntary centralized wage bargaining.[66]

This was also the period when the Labour party first entered into government via the strategy of coalition (1948–51; 1954–7). Some idea of the general position of the party at this time (it was reunited in 1950) can be gained from the election manifesto of its leader William Norton, 'The People's Friend, Champion of Every Good Cause', in 1951

> William Norton has been your Deputy over 25 years. He has rendered splendid service to his constituents, irrespective of their political views. He serves everybody; he imposes no political tests . . . he befriends the weak and helpless . . . whether as a Deputy or a Minister; he looks after the County Kildare as nobody else does. Vote No. 1 Norton, The Labour Candidate.[67]

There were certain limited gains for the Labour movement from the participation of the Labour party in coalitions led, in each case, by the Fine Gael party – the party with the most conservative profile in terms of its electoral base, though it was the Fine Gael Minister for Finance, Patrick McGilligan, who was to present the state's first capital budget in 1950.[68] However, by the time the second coalition came to an end in 1957, the Labour party was coming under attack from sections of the Labour movement, and from within the Labour party itself.[69] There were also stirrings to the left, outside the party. The Communist party was active again from 1948 forward as the Irish Workers' League, though very marginalized in the 'cold-war' mood of the period. The transmission of a radical/left tradition from an older generation of intellectuals to a younger was taking place via the '1913 Club', which was founded in Dublin in 1958, the same year as the birth of the short-lived National Progressive Democrats (NPD) which, in the words of Lysaght, 'became swiftly a refuge for Independent Socialists'.[70] However, much of this activity centred on Dublin, marking the dichotomy existing between a small advanced, largely urban, section and the rest of the Labour movement in a predominantly rural state.

The real challenge to established politics appeared to come from Clann na Poblachta which, however, proved spectacularly fissiparous and quickly belied its early promise.[71] The major beneficiary of coalition was the Fine Gael party, which had reached the nadir of its fortunes in the general election of 1948, gaining only 19.8 per cent of the votes cast. 'The experience of coalition . . . reinstated the party as the favoured exponent of centre-right opinion.'[72]

A short post-war boom, assisted by a government programme of capital expenditure, led to an upsurge in trade union membership, which had steadily been increasing from the late 1930s. The 1950s were, however, a dark decade in which 'confidence about the viability of the economy reached an all time low'.[73] Deflationary policies on the part of governments of the 1950s contributed to making what was a bad situation worse, and Dr James Ryan's budget of 1957 was popularly known as the 'Famine Budget'.[74] In the general election of that year, a member of the Dublin Unemployed Association, Jack Murphy, was elected to the Dáil, along with two NPD candidates, Noël Brown and Jack McQuillan. The Provisional United Trade Union Organization (PUTUO) issued a document, 'Planning full employment', which included the call for an increase in the public capital programme, the establishment of a national investment board, repatriation of external assets and *limitation* on foreign investment by tax deterrents – a radical nationalist strategy – in contrast to the emphasis which had been placed on the attraction of foreign investment by Norton, Tániste [Deputy Prime Minister] and Minister for Industry and Commerce in the coalition government from 1955 onwards.[75]

The impact of emigration, made clear in *The Report of the Commission on Emigration* of 1956, strengthened the hands of those who wished to bring about change.[76] The limited increases in industrial production under the protectionist policies of the 1930s had been largely directed to the relatively small home market. Given the limitations of the latter, it was becoming more widely felt by the 1950s that it was only through an increase in production for export that the jobs necessary to reduce unemployment and emigration could be created. Seán Lemass, deputy leader of Fianna Fáil since 1945 and Taoiseach [Prime Minister] between 1959 and 1966, was the politician who most effectively grasped the opportunity presented, securing the alliance with the working class and drawing the unions into a corporatist strategy in the process. Economic liberalization was achieved – through the dismantling of the protectionist system of the 1930s, the opening of the Irish economy to foreign investment, and entry into the European Economic Community – despite the anxieties concerning the threats to national control of the economy, inherent in foreign capital investment, within the Labour party, the trade union movement, a section of Irish capital and within Fianna Fáil itself – no small political feat.[77] Lemass and others hoped that, through a mixture of incentives and gradual exposure to foreign competition, Irish manufacturers would be encouraged to become more competitive and that, in this way, a viable domestic industrial base geared to export would ensue. Broadly speaking, this was a misplaced assumption.[78]

The increase in employment in industry and services between 1961 and 1981, and a general mood of optimism which carried into the 1970s – when the population seemed set to increase in a sustained manner for the first time since the mid-nineteenth century[79] – was a double-edged weapon. Between 1945 and 1979 trade union membership in the Republic had almost trebled, and in a league table of density of trade union membership for EEC countries, Ireland came fifth in 1960 and third in 1975.[80] White-collar union membership expanded at an accelerating rate from the mid-1960s onwards, and in the 1960s and 1970s this sector contributed substantially to the Republic's strike record.[81] The decade 1960–70 was a period of escalating industrial unrest in which a comparatively small number of strikes were responsible for most of the days lost, as well placed unions exercised industrial strength in response to rank-and-file pressure.[82] In the 1970s militant pressure on union leaderships continued, with the foundation of the Dublin Shop Stewards' Committee in 1973.[83] The comment of Charles McCarthy, ex-General Secretary of the Vocational Teachers' Association, ex-member of the Council of the ICTU and President of Congress in 1963–4, on the maintenance craftsmen's dispute of 1968–9, is indicative of the view of the trade union leadership to such unofficial action. Writing as Professor of Business Studies at Trinity College, Dublin, in 1980, he described this strike as

> conducted by some of the craft union members with unparalleled cynicism and indifference to the welfare of other workers, not to mind society in general . . . [by] a strike committee of questionable legitimacy.[84]

Just as the incorporation of the trade unions was one of the features of state policy (particularly under Fianna Fáil) since the 1940s, so has been the increasing development of the state's social infrastructure.[85] However, a recent study of social policy in the Republic concludes 'The income/taxes/transfers data is indicative of a very modest redistribution' and suggests that 'social class structures are being perpetuated by the pattern of social policies which has evolved in recent years.'[86] With regard to education, A. Dale Tussing has written

> The system of finance for education in Ireland runs against the interests of the poor, the working class and the large majority of Irish people. It is essentially a regressive system, in which the many support the few.[87]

The taxation system also contains grave inequalities.[88]

However, it is not only at the level of social class that inequalities have persisted. One of the results of the economic growth which followed the policy of liberalization was an increase in the employment of women, especially from the 1970s forward. Despite the Anti-Discrimination (Pay) Act (1974) and the Employment Equality Act (1977), and despite a reduction in the differential, women's average weekly wages remain lower than those of men, and women continue to be concentrated in less well paid occupations with poorer working conditions. Even in occupations where they predominate numerically, they tend to be concentrated in the lower reaches of the employment hierarchy.[89]

The restructuring which was taking place in the economy, especially from the 1960s, affected both the composition of the working class and the balance of classes, and class fractions, within society in the Republic of Ireland;[90] in short

> Ireland has clearly ceased to be characterised as *petit bourgeois*: the predominant categories today are those of large-scale employers and of well qualified employees.[91]

On any reductionist, economistic reading, this should have been the moment when the Labour party would come into its own; and it did appear, yet once again, as if the party was on the threshold of a dramatic advance. From the early 1960s there had been a rapid recruitment to the Labour party. The two NPD TDs were welcomed into the fold and those joining now included an increasing number from the professional middle classes, intellectuals and personalities like Justin Keating, Conor Cruise O'Brien, John O'Donovan and David Thornley, as well as trade union officials like Michael O'Leary and Barry Desmond. There were also important trade union affiliations, including the three major general unions – the WUI, the ITGWU and the ATGWU (Amalgamated Transport and General Workers' Union). In the general election of 1965 the party gained six seats and increased its percentage of the vote by 4 per cent; and in Dublin it did remarkably well.[92] Brendan Corish, leader of the party between 1960 and 1977, who had once described himself as a Catholic first and an Irishman second[93] was sufficiently emboldened to refer to the party in 1964 as a socialist party and in 1966 the party was officially declared to be a socialist party. At the 1967 party conference, Corish let it be known that 'The 70s will be Socialist'. Brendan Halligan became political director, and subsequently general secretary, and began to give the party a new and up-to-date image, with the issuing of a series of party documents on a wide range of issues.[94]

However, it has been argued that this declaration of a socialist agenda did not mark a fundamental shift of ground, rather 'Labour's acclaimed shift to the left must be viewed within the broad context of the existent national consensus.'[95] Certainly, changes in the Republic at this time made this shift within the Labour party an accommodation rather than a radical commitment to effecting a fundamental change in the political agenda. Nevertheless, the adoption of a socialist programme set alarm bells ringing in certain quarters. In 1967, Patrick Norton, the son of the previous leader, resigned from the party on the grounds that 'fellow travellers' were in control, and many of the rural TDs who remained in the party had misgivings regarding the apparent move leftwards. Both the local elections in 1967 and the general election of 1969 showed an increase in the percentage of the vote gained in Dublin and losses elsewhere. While Labour's percentage of the national vote marked a continuation of an upward trend, the Labour party had four fewer seats in the new Dáil. In response to accusations that Labour was falling under communist and alien influences, the party justified its policies with reference to Catholic encyclicals. In a by-election in Dublin South-West in 1970, the Labour vote fell by half.[96]

Gallagher has described the outcome of the 1969 general election as a 'shattering blow' to the Labour party. This was because Labour had set its sights too high and an overreaction to the outcome offered the rural right of the party the opportunity to call for a retreat from the position adopted in the late 1960s. The activities of Steve Coughlan, the TD for East Limerick, and attitudes to Northern Ireland and to reform of the laws on contraception further complicated relations within the party. The anti-Republican views now surfacing once more within the party under the impact of developments in Northern Ireland, did not, as far as the Labour party was concerned, relate to a debate over class against nation. They arose, rather, from liberal concerns. The party as a whole – as well as the left of the party – was divided on the issue of future coalition. The question of coalition was complicated by the fact that Fine Gael's policy document of 1975 – 'The Just Society' – formally committed the party to a social-democratic programme. As well as this, there was the fact that Labour was dependent on Fine Gael transfers in both Dublin and in rural areas,[97] where 'Labour and Fine Gael are in a sort of unofficial coalition'.[98]

Labour had five ministries in the coalition government, which lasted from 1973 to 1977. The Liaison Committee of the Labour

Left (LCLL) had been opposed to coalition from the start and from 1975 onwards the Administrative Council of the Labour party was increasingly critical of the performance of the party in government. The impact of the first oil crisis of 1973 coincided with the term of office of the government and there were steep rises in the levels of prices and unemployment. By 1976 relations between the Labour party and trade unions had deteriorated. The fact that the Labour party was cast in the role of selling wage restraint to the unions, either to avoid legislative action on pay restraint or as part of a strategy for economic growth, did nothing to improve its standing with its constituency. In 1976 the LCLL, Official Sinn Féin, the Communist party and trade unionists came together as the 'Left Alternative', publishing a joint document critical of government economic policy and of Labour's complicity in it.[99] Robert Hannon, assessing the achievements of Labour in coalition, indicated the dilemma facing the party. 'All these actions', he wrote, 'fell far short of Labour policy, but none could have been achieved by Labour in opposition.' He also rightly identified a key mistake of Labour in coalition as the failure 'to publicly debate the gulf between Labour policy and the compromises reached at Cabinet level'.[100]

The attempt of the Administrative Council of the Labour party to block LCLL candidates in the run-up to the general election of 1977 led to the formation of the short-lived Socialist Labour party,[101] which became a focus for a section of ex-Labour party left and a heterogeneous mixture of radicals and Trotskyist left. In that election, Labour's share of the working-class vote fell to 11 per cent of the unskilled and 16 per cent of the skilled, while Fianna Fáil received 54 per cent and 47 per cent of those votes respectively; and Labour has not received more than 9.9 per cent of votes cast in general elections since that time. This is not just because the compromises in which the Labour party has been involved, in government, have been a 'turn-off' for some of its own supporters. The main thrust of government policy since the 1950s has, in fact, created a complex series of contradictory responses among sections of the working class. Commentators, for example, have noted an increase in the proportion of the skilled working class voting for a rightward-moving Fine Gael, on the basis that tax cuts and the support for cuts in public expenditure will be to their advantage. In the late 1970s and early 1980s a more equitable distribution of the tax burden, through a reform of the system, had become a major demand of the trade union movement, mobilizing widespread public support.[102]

The real economic growth of the 1960s made it seem as if change could be easily achieved. It facilitated Fianna Fáil's policy of incorporating the trade union movement and of increasing social expenditure. Growth lent plausibility to the argument that all would benefit from the processes taking place. It also allowed Fine Gael both to satisfy its bourgeois constituency that its redistributive aims could be achieved without too great a sacrifice on its part, and to increase its support among the working classes. However, the recession which was fuelled by the oil crises of the 1970s and by capital relocation has limited the choices of the main political parties. The right was strengthened within Fine Gael, and during the second of the two coalitions entered into in 1981–2 and 1982–7 by Fine Gael and Labour, the cabinet was 'beleaguered by rifts over fiscal and economic policy',[103] which eventually led to the collapse of the government.[104] By the end of the government's term there were moves within a number of unions to bring about disaffiliation from the Labour party; Labour's proportion of the working-class vote had declined even further, and the Workers' party was successfully competing for the left vote.[105] Labour, out of power, has maintained a formally left position, while the parliamentary leadership has reinforced the position of the centre-right within the party through a strengthening of its support in the administrative council and through the campaign ostensibly directed against the Militant entryists – with the current leader, Dick Spring, striking an opportunistically chauvinist note on the latter issue.[106] The choice of Mary Robinson, an ex-member of the Labour party, as the Labour candidate in the 1990 Presidential election, rather than the preferred candidate of a section of the Labour left, the veteran parliamentary socialist Noël Brown, was further evidence of the side on which the leadership comes down in 'the choice between democratic socialism and being the political wing of the Saint Vincent de Paul' – to quote the memorable phrase of Emmet Stagg. In terms of her public appeal, and the management of her campaign, this was a triumph for the Labour party; and Mary Robinson's stand on divorce, contraception and gay rights makes her victory a qualified triumph for liberal/secular views in the Republic of Ireland. The support she drew, on this basis, from economic conservatives (from the Progressive Democrats, for example), and the failure to make a connection between those demands and the values of socialist democracy, mean that her victory has limited relevance for socialism: an issue which both she and her supporters sought to sidestep – not surprisingly, in view of the importance of non-Labour, non-Workers' party votes and transfers in her election.[107]

Fianna Fáil contested the 1977 election with promises of increased government spending and reductions in taxation, and attempted to create an economic miracle on the basis of the proposals of Dr Martin O'Donoghue – running up against the consequences of the second oil crisis of 1979 in the process. With the threat which recession presented to its vision of a 'rising tide floating all boats', Fianna Fáil, under Charles Haughey, has emphasized its nationalism and its commitment to traditional values, as well as, lately, reasserting its corporatist commitment. Despite the fact that

> in the 1980s a massive decline in industrial production, dramatic rises in unemployment, sharp acceleration in employment in 'private' or 'traded services' – particularly in those sectors hostile to unionism with high levels of part-time and casual employment – as well as increased uses of technology led to a rapid decline in union membership.[108]

Haughey went out of his way in 1987 to woo the Labour movement, entering into talks with the ICTU and concluding the programme for national recovery, adopting a programme which 'proved a virtual replay of the appeal articulated by Seán Lemass in 1957',[109] and this is clearly the strategy with which Fianna Fáil wishes to continue. However, in September 1990, a widespread feeling that, while the programme for national recovery had put the economy back on course, 'the employers had got "their own way" over the past three years', led to hard talking at the special ICTU delegate conference which agreed, by a vote of 218 to 114, to enter into discussion with the government on a new programme for social and economic development.[110] The differences of approach which McCarthy indicated in the trade union response to government wooing in the 1960s still exist. One point of view is represented by the ATGWU:

> It did not believe that the Congress should try to get a consensus with the political forces of the Right, which created the unemployed problem.[111]

The union has opposed the reopening of talks with the government, which is advocated by the new giant on the Irish industrial scene, the Services, Industrial, Professional, Technical Union (SIPTU – formed from the amalgamation of the ITGWU and the F[ederated]WUI, Larkin's old union). Peter Cassells, secretary of Congress, put the choice thus to delegates at the special conference the purpose was to decide whether workers' priorities were jobs, tax reform, pay and conditions of employment and better access to social services, processed through national negotiations with the Government and the employers or whether some issues should be left for negotiations with the employers, company by company, while lobbying the Government on other issues.[112]

The latter is the position advocated by unions like the ATGWU and MSF, while the Congress leaders would prefer a ten-year economic and social strategy.[113] Michael O'Reilly, of the ATGWU, has stated that,

propping up a Fianna Fáil/PD government would do nothing to alleviate poverty, create jobs or raise living standards . . . a broad based alliance of the ICTU, left-wing political parties, the unemployed and the Church was the only way to deal with unemployment and poverty.[114]

However, despite these significant differences over tactics, corporatism still represents the dominant ideology of an increasingly streamlined trade union movement. From the point of view of the trade unions, there is a certain narrow sense in this

Over the three years of the present programme the take home pay on average male industrial earnings will have increased by between 4.6 per cent and 8.5 per cent, when account is taken of tax reduction and inflation. Between 1980 and 1987 gross pay increased by 76 per cent; yet real take home pay fell by between 7.5 per cent and 10.8 per cent because of high inflation and tax.[115]

Despite the failure of both the strategies initiated by Fianna Fáil, to date, to resolve the economic problems of the Republic of Ireland as an independent, sovereign state, the party's ability to maintain its base of support within the Irish working class and its relations with the Irish trade union movement have been quite noteworthy. There is no doubt that the integrative aspects of nationalist ideology have been of assistance here. The fact that the Labour party has largely presented a view of socialism which is 'principally one of "social unity" not "class solidarity"'[116] has helped to sustain nationalism as an integrative ideology – although the Labour party can now be counted among those forces in the Republic of Ireland sustaining a liberal, pluralist critique of Irish nationalism. The weakness of the Labour party is also relevant here. It has been beset by many difficulties since the foundation of the state: structural factors arising from the social composition of the state; ideological factors; divisions within the party and difficulties in relations with the other institutions of Irish labour; as well as the quality of leadership available to it. The modernization of Irish society in the twentieth century has failed to bring about the expected surge in the fortunes of the party.[117] In fact, not only has the Labour party failed to displace Fianna Fáil as the party which enjoys the greatest support among the working classes; but its relationship with the trade union movement is problematic;[118] and it also faces challenges from the left. From a position in 1969, where it took almost 100 per cent of the left vote, it had sunk to 58 per cent by 1987. The most serious challenge has come from the Workers' party, which, in the late 1980s, has consistently polled a higher vote in Dublin than Labour.[119] A feature of the politics of the state has been the marginalization of the revolutionary left, in the form of the Communist party and the Trotskyist left; although Militant had built up a position within the Labour party until its recent expulsion. On the face of it, the Workers' party looks like a more serious contender, though the extent to which it could be described as a revolutionary socialist party is questionable. Provisional Sinn Féin, with a revolutionary nationalist profile which is now more recognizable outside Europe and the 'developed' capitalist area, has little impact in the Republic. If pre-1970 Sinn Féin was the party of sections of the urban and rural *petit bourgeoisie*, Sinn Féin today is largely the party of the marginalized urban population.

The challenge presented by the Workers' party to the Labour party, and the split in Fianna Fáil leading to the emergence of the Progressive Democrats has led commentators to identify the current period as yet another of those periods of flux in Irish politics, containing the possibility of new openings. This view is reinforced by the impact of the current recession on the policies advocated by the two main parties in the post-war period, to which the building of an economic base to resolve the problems of unemployment and emigration has been central, as well as various elements of corporatism, welfarism and redistribution. Both Fianna Fáil and Fine Gael have had to face a situation in which the relatively easy choices of the 1960s are no longer options. But Peter Mair's illustration of the way in which the fact that the politics of the Republic appear to be moving onto a left/right axis has created new opportunities for Fianna Fáil as the party of the centre,[120] offers a salutary warning against facile analyses. It is true that the changes in the balance of the classes in the Republic has created the possibility of a kind of politics other than that laid down in the 1920s, 1930s and 1950s; as does the current pressure on the political parties. Equally, the Catholic Church is no longer the conservative monolith it was up to the 1960s, but contains strains of liberalism and radicalism within it. However, past experience has shown that the outcome of such a period of flux is dependent on the effectiveness of the responses of the various political groups.

The weakness and essential reformism of the Labour movement helps to explain the relative lack of tension between it and the state; although the reaction of Unionist and nationalist employers to the threat of Larkinism before the First World War, of the infant Free State and its supporters to revolutionary syndicalism, and of Church and state to the apparent left-wing threat of the 1930s, indicate that when a threat is perceived steps will be taken to negative it. However, from the period when, in the 1940s, Fianna Fáil sought to incorporate the trade unions into the central political process, it found a willing partner in the Irish trade union movement. Fianna Fáil, rather than Labour, was the party more likely to be in power; and, equally, the corporatism of Fianna Fáil was a more workable option than the liberal statism which characterized Labour and Fine Gael.[121]

The concept of a monolithic working class, united around its objective interest, is an idealized one. The politics of the working class is complicated by the pursuit by different sections of workers of what they perceive as their immediate advantage; and some are much better placed than others to do this. State policy in the Republic of Ireland has contributed to the situation whereby a complex system of contradictions affects the way in which different classes and class fractions relate to a highly active state.[122] However, despite the fact that sections of the working class have benefited to varying degrees from the economic system in the independent Irish state, all that we know about the history of labour, and of the distribution of the burdens of underdevelopment and recession, indicates the need for a Labour movement with both a strong tactical sense and a commitment to longer term objectives based on the class interests of working people. It remains to be seen whether the institutions of Labour and the left can make more of this opportunity in the future than they have done heretofore.

Notes

1 David Johnson, *The Interwar Economy in Ireland* (Dundalk, 1985) pp. 10, 20.
2 David B. Rottman and Philip J. O'Connell, 'The changing social structure', in Frank Litton, ed., *Unequal Achievement: The Irish Experience 1957–1982* (Dublin, 1982) p. 69; on the hopes of an alliance between town workers and small farmers see Henry Patterson, *The Politics of Illusion: Republicanism and Socialism in Modern Ireland* (London, 1989) pp. 30–43 and Peadar O'Donnell, *There Will be Another Day* (Dublin, 1963) *passim*.
3 O'Donnell, op. cit., p. 11.
4 Mike Milotte, *Communism in Modern Ireland: The Pursuit of the Workers' Republic Since 1916* (Dublin, 1984) pp. 59–60.
5 Emmett O'Connor, *Syndicalism in Ireland 1917–1923* (Cork, 1988) p. 186.
6 James Meenan, *The Irish Economy Since 1922* (Liverpool, 1970) pp. 303–5; J. J. Lee, *Ireland 1912–1985: Politics and Society* (Cambridge, 1989) pp. 107–17.
7 D. R. O'Connor Lysaght, 'The Munster creamery soviets', *Irish History Workshop* 1 (1981) p. 45; Dan Bradley, *Farm Labourers: Irish Struggle 1900–1976* (Belfast, 1988) pp. 65–9; Milotte, op. cit., p. 62.
8 Charles McCarthy, *Trade Unions in Ireland 1894–1960* (Dublin, 1977) p. 70; C. Desmond Greaves, *The Irish Transport and General Workers' Union: The Formative Years* (Dublin, 1982) p. 321.
9 Arthur Mitchell, *Labour in Irish Politics 1890–1930: The Irish Labour Movement in an Age of Revolution* (Dublin, 1974) pp. 183–5; Emmett Larkin, *James Larkin: Irish Labour Leader 1876–1947* (London, 1968) pp. 238–47.
10 Milotte, op. cit., pp. 67, 74, 90, 91; Mitchell, op cit., pp. 274–6.
11 Milotte, op. cit., pp. 73–4, 77, 83–8.
12 ibid., pp. 96–8, 100, 106–7, 110.
13 ibid., p. 154.
14 ibid., pp. 154–6; John A. Murphy, *Ireland in the Twentieth Century* (Dublin, 1975) pp. 83–4, 96–8.
15 O'Connor, op. cit., pp. 189–90.
16 Peter Mair, *The Changing Irish Party System: Organisation, Ideology and Electoral Competition* (London, 1988), p. 27.
17 Rottman and O'Connell, op. cit., p. 69.
18 Ronan Fanning, *Independent Ireland* (Dublin, 1983) pp. 53–7, 103–5, 131–3, 181–5; Terence Brown, *Ireland: A Social and Cultural History 1922–29* (London, 1981) pp. 17–26.
19 Milotte, op. cit., pp. 85, 90.
20 ibid., p. 109.
21 ibid., pp. 108–9, 116–20, 167; Patrick Byrne, *Memories of the Republican Congress* (London, n.d.) pp. 8–10, 12–13; Des Guckian, *Deported: Jimmy Gralton 1886–1945* (Mullingar, 1986) *passim*.
22 Quoted in J. H. Whyte, *Church and State in Modern Ireland* (Dublin, 1984) p. 70.
23 Milotte, op. cit., pp. 117, 198, 220.
24 ibid., p. 159.

25 ibid., pp.169–70, 218–19.
26 Lynn Doyle, *The Spirit of Ireland* (London, 1935) p. 5.
27 Noël Browne, *Against the Tide* (Dublin, 1986) pp. 25–39. Two novels of Dónall Mac Amhlaigh, *Diarmaid ó Dónaill* (Dublin, 1965) and *Deoraithe* (Dublin, 1986) are perceptive on this aspect of Irish society.
28 Browne, op. cit., p. 26.
29 M. A. G. ó Tuathaigh, 'The land question, politics and Irish society, 1922–1960', in P. J. Drudy, ed., *Irish Studies, II Ireland; Land, Politics, and People* (Cambridge, 1982) pp. 180–1; Rottman and O'Connell, op. cit., p. 79; Lee, op. cit., p. 377; Mac Amhlaigh, *Deoraithe*, pp. 78–9.
30 Kieran A. Kennedy, Thomas Giblin and Deirdre McHugh, *The Economic Development of Ireland in the Twentieth Century* (London, 1988) p. 146; Lee, op. cit., pp. 374, 380–1.
31 Lee, op. cit., p. 376.
32 Mary E. Daly, 'Women, work and trade unionism', in Margaret Mac Curtain and Donncha ó Corráin, *Women in Irish Society: The Historical Dimension* (Dublin, 1978) pp. 71–2, 77; Mary E. Daly, 'Women in the Irish workforce from pre-industrial to modern times', *Saothar* 7 (1981) pp. 77–8.
33 Mary Clancy, 'Aspects of women's contributions to the Oireachtas debate in the Irish Free State, 1922–37', in Maria Luddy and Cliona Murphy, eds, *Women Surviving: Studies in Irish Women's History in the 19th and 20th Centuries* (Dublin, 1989) pp. 217–21; Eoin O'Leary, 'The Irish National Teachers' Organisation and the marriage bar for women National Teachers, 1933–1958', *Saothar* 12 (1987) pp. 47–51; *see* Eunice McCarthy, 'Women and work in Ireland: the present and preparing for the future', in Mac Curtain and ó Corráin, op. cit., p. 104, for an indication of the extent of the marriage bar.
34 Quoted in Clancy, op. cit., p. 220.
35 Daly, 'Women in the Irish workforce', op. cit., pp. 78, 79.
36 Clancy, op. cit., p. 210.
37 ibid., pp. 223–5, 231 fnn. 70, 71; Daly, 'Women, work', pp. 78; O'Leary, op. cit., pp. 48, 49.
38 Quoted in Enda McKay, 'Changing with the tide: the Irish Labour party, 1927–33', *Saothar* 11 (1986) p. 31.
39 O'Connor, op. cit., pp. 189–90; McKay, op. cit., pp. 30–1.
40 E. Rumpf and A. C. Hepburn, *Nationalism and Socialism in Twentieth-Century Ireland* (Liverpool, 1977) p. 102; McKay, op. cit., pp. 28, 32, 33, 35.
41 Lee, op. cit., pp. 190, 193, 195; Kieran A. Kennedy, Thomas Giblin and Deirdre McHugh, *The Economic Development of Ireland in the Twentieth Century* (London, 1988) pp. 40–4.
42 Lee, op. cit., pp. 185–6; Paul Bew, Ellen Hazelkorn and Henry Patterson, *The Dynamics of Irish Politics* (London, 1989) pp. 75–6; Kennedy *et al.*, op. cit., p. 48.
43 Kennedy *et al.*, op. cit., p. 236.
44 Paul Bew and Henry Patterson, *Seán Lemass and the Making of Modern Ireland 1945–1966* (Dublin, 1982) pp. 2, 7; see also Rumpf and Hepburn, op. cit., pp. 107, 137; and Peter Mair, *The Changing Irish Party System* (London, 1987) pp. 21–2.

45 McKay, op. cit., p. 35; D. R. O'Connor Lysaght, *The Republic of Ireland* (Cork, 1970) pp. 108, 120; Francis Devine 'Socialist trade unionist: Matt Merrigan's political formation', *Saothar* 12 (1987) p. 95.

46 Larkin, op. cit., pp. 269, 270; Milotte, op. cit., 191. An interesting illustration of how a young Republican trade union activist entered the party at this time is given in 'A Labour consciousness in Carlow: the young Paddy Bergin, 1916–1950', *Saothar* 6 (1980) pp. 113–14.

47 Mair, op. cit., pp. 22–9.

48 Gallagher, *The Irish Labour Party in Transition 1957–1982* (Manchester, 1982), pp. 12–13; Whyte, op. cit., pp. 83–4.

49 Mair, op. cit., pp. 20, 23.

50 Charles McCarthy, op. cit., p. 130.

51 ibid., pp. 130–1, 208–9; Larkin, op. cit., p. 269.

52 McCarthy, op. cit., pp. 251, 253–4; Larkin, op. cit., pp. 270–3.

53 McCarthy, op. cit., p. 256.

54 Milotte, op. cit., pp. 198–9; Lee, op. cit., p. 241.

55 McCarthy, pp. 120, 126, 142–8, 272–3.

56 ibid., pp. 273–4.

57 ibid., p. 278.

58 ibid., pp. 276–7.

59 ibid., pp. 209–10.

60 ibid., p. 201–2.

61 Lee, op. cit., p. 290; McCarthy, op. cit., pp. 232–3, 245–6.

62 Quoted in Bew and Patterson, op. cit., p. 31.

63 McCarthy, op. cit., pp. 194, 248.

64 Kader Asmal, 'The constitution, the law and industrial relations' in Donal Nevin, ed., *Trade Unions and Change in Irish Society* (Cork, 1980) pp. 42–5; Ronan Fanning, *Independent Ireland*, p. 156.

65 Bew, Hazelkorn and Patterson, op. cit., p. 170.

66 Nevin, ed., op. cit., pp. 160–7.

67 Quoted in Gallagher, op. cit., pp. 31–2.

68 Ronan Fanning, *The Irish Department of Finance 1922–58* (Dublin, 1978) pp. 456–8.

69 Gallagher, op. cit., pp. 29–30; Lysaght, op. cit., pp. 166–7.

70 Lysaght, op. cit., p. 167; Gallagher, op. cit., p. 34.

71 Mair, op. cit., pp. 20, 27–28, 30.

72 ibid., p. 54; *see also* pp. 22–3, 30.

73 Kennedy *et al.*, op. cit., p. 55; *see* pp. 55–7.

74 Evanne Kilmurray, *Fight, Starve or Emigrate: A History of the Unemployed Associations of the 1950s* (Dublin, n.d.) p. 36.

75 Lysaght, op. cit., p. 167; Bew and Patterson, op. cit., pp. 82, 106.

76 Bew and Patterson, op. cit., p. 13; Lee, op. cit., pp. 341, 373.

77 Mair, op. cit., pp. 54–5; Bew and Patterson, op. cit., pp. 118–90.

78 Kennedy *et al.*, op. cit., p. 72.

79 ibid., p. 141.

80 Nevin, ed., op. cit., p. 171.

81 Aidan Kelly, 'White-collar trade unionism', in ibid., pp. 69, 77–9.

82 Bew, Hazelkorn and Patterson, op. cit., p. 171; Nevin, ed., op. cit., p. 168.

83 Bew, Hazelkorn and Patterson, op. cit., p. 165.

84 Charles McCarthy, 'The development of Irish trade unions', in Nevin, ed., op. cit., p. 35.
85 Tony McCashin, 'Social policy: 1957–82', in Litton, op. cit., pp. 206–11.
86 ibid., pp. 215, 216.
87 Quoted in ibid., p. 216.
88 Richard Breen, Damian F. Hannan, David B. Rottman and Christopher T. Whelan, *Understanding Contemporary Ireland: State, Class and Development in the Republic of Ireland* (Dublin, 1990) pp. 79–82; Bew, Hazelkorn and Patterson, op. cit., p. 117.
89 Mary E. Daly, *Women and Poverty* (Dublin, 1989) pp. 36, 42–5, 118–19.
90 Breen *et al.*, op. cit., pp. 54–6, 190.
91 ibid., p. 58.
92 Bew, Hazelkorn and Patterson, op. cit., pp. 143, 147, 150; Gallagher, op. cit., pp. 52, 56, 57–9, 62–3, 75.
93 Bew, Hazelkorn and Patterson, op. cit., p. 147.
94 ibid., pp. 147–8, 150; Gallagher, op. cit., pp. 55, 60–2, 67, 69.
95 Bew, Hazelkorn and Patterson, op. cit., p. 149.
96 Gallagher, op. cit., pp. 68, 71, 77, 83–4, 96, 97, 104–5; Bew, Hazelkorn and Patterson, op. cit., p. 150.
97 Gallagher, op. cit., pp. 105–13, 165–6, 174, 177, 193.
98 ibid., pp. 179–80.
99 Bew, Hazelkorn and Patterson, op. cit., pp. 153, 156–60, 161, 165–7.
100 Quoted in ibid., p. 164.
101 ibid., pp. 153, 186; Gallagher, op. cit., p. 216.
102 Bew, Hazelkorn and Patterson, op. cit., pp. 117–18, 120, 167, 184; Breen *et. al.*, op. cit., pp. 79–82; Mair, op. cit., p. 30.
103 Bew, Hazelkorn and Patterson, op. cit., p. 190.
104 Mair, op. cit., pp. 208–13.
105 Bew, Hazelkorn and Patterson, op. cit., pp. 179, 224.
106 ibid., pp. 179, 191–3; coverage of Labour party conference in the *Irish Times* (13 March 1989).
107 Coverage of Mary Robinson's campaign in the *Irish Times* (4, 18, 27 October and 9 November 1990).
108 Bew, Hazelkorn and Patterson, pp. 174–5.
109 Mair, op. cit., p. 218.
110 'Hard words from unions for the long talks ahead', 'ICTU votes for talks on new national programme', *Irish Times* (28 September 1990).
111 'National forum sought to discuss unemployment', *Irish Times* (5 July 1990).
112 'Hard words from unions for the long talks ahead', *Irish Times* (28 September 1990).
113 '10-year plan proposed by ICTU', *Irish Times* (9 October 1990).
114 'ICTU demands for new pact outlined', *Irish Times* (22 October 1990).
115 Patrick Nolan, 'Putting a shape on a new national pay pact', *Irish Times* (22 September 1990).
116 Bew, Hazelkorn and Patterson, op. cit., p. 144.
117 McKay, op. cit., p. 29; Gallagher, op. cit., pp. 167–8, 170; O'Connor,

op. cit., p. 187.
118 Bew, Hazelkorn and Patterson, op. cit., pp. 177–8, 180–1.
119 Mair, op. cit., p. 58; Bew, Hazelkorn and Patterson, op. cit., p. 224.
120 Mair, op. cit., p. 218.
121 Bew, Hazelkorn and Patterson, pp. 176–7.
122 Breen *et al.*, op. cit., chapter 4 *passim*.

5 The Irish Constitution of 1937

Joseph Lee

The preamble to the Constitution of 1937 declared that the people of Éire – the new name of the state – adopted the document 'so that the dignity and freedom of the individual may be assured, true social order attained, the unity of our country restored, and concord established with other nations'. As a solemn evocation, however rhetorical, of the idealized self-image of the people, this preamble deserves close contemplation. It obviously sought to synthesize the various emphases within the nationalist tradition, which ranged from a classic liberal stance on the one hand, to a virtually *völkisch* sense of community on the other. It thus folded in its ample embrace values and traditions which some historians of Irish nationalism have chosen to consider mutually exclusive, and refused to concede that any conflict was necessary between them. Although there is no suggestion of a hierarchy among the four objectives, the sequence is nevertheless instructive. While much critical attention has concentrated on a handful of clauses involving claims on Northern Ireland, or dealing with issues of sexual morality, we should bear in mind that however prominently these may feature in political discourse, they are not normally the clauses that impinge most immediately on the daily concerns of the vast majority of the citizens. It is rather the clauses concerning the rights of the individual in relation to the state and society, as well as, more structurally, the clauses concerned with political institutions and procedures, that most fundamentally affect their lives.

Eamon de Valera, under whose close supervision the Constitution was drafted, was a strong believer in the rule of law, and in protecting the rights of the citizen against the intrusive and arbitrary potential of state power. Indeed, had he sought an autocratic state, the Constitution of 1922, which his new Constitution superseded, allowed him immense scope for arbitrary behaviour. As Brian Farrell has observed

In the wrong hands, Ireland could have gone the way of other European states in the dangerous Europe of the mid-thirties. De Valera by now had abolished the Senate, had an overall majority in the Dáil and a totally flexible Constitution with neither effective judicial review nor the requirements of a popular referendum to restrain his will. He could, by simple act of the single parliamentary chamber dominated by his party, make whatever constitutional changes he wished. It was a classic opportunity to establish a dictatorship. Instead his mind had already turned to writing a new Constitution for modern Ireland.[1]

Nevertheless, the 1922 Constitution expressed, in essence, many values concerning individual rights that de Valera himself cherished, however irredeemably flawed it remained, in his view, by virtue of the limitations it imposed on national sovereignty. Like the drafters of the Constitution of 1922, de Valera accepted an essentially liberal concept of individual rights. He was, in this respect, a descendant, if not a disciple, of Daniel O'Connell. Indeed, by incorporating the rights into a written Constitution, both in 1922 and, in more elaborate form, in 1937, Ireland was conferring on the citizen a more systematic protection (except 'in time of war or armed rebellion', when parliament was given virtually absolute authority) than was, or is, the case in Britain itself, deemed by many to be the model exponent of the rights of the individual.

The concept of individual rights blends into that of 'true social order'. Nevertheless, 'true social order' remains a more elusive and controversial concept than personal rights. Articles 40–3, which deal with, successively, personal rights, the family, education and private property, have provoked a wide range of divergent views on where the balance ought to be struck between individual and community. The courts themselves have had difficulties in this respect. The right to individual property conferred in Articles 40 and 43 is subject to its being exercised in the interest of the common good. But 'the common good' is a notoriously elastic concept. Elastic or not, it offers a crucial criterion for the control of unbridled, and potentially predatory, individual selfishness.[2] De Valera's own preferred social order blended Aquinas with Jefferson, his ideal being a democracy of small property owners, with the family as the basic unit of a Christian society which, governed by the precepts of natural law, derived its legitimacy from allegiance to 'the Most Holy Trinity, from Whom', as the preamble portentously put it, 'is all authority and to Whom, as our final end, all actions both of men and States must be referred'.

De Valera did not, however, seek to incorporate all his own basic instincts on 'true social order' into the Constitution in any binding way. Article 45, 'Directive Principles of Social Policy', did enunciate a series of criteria closely reflecting de Valera's own paternalist Christian instincts, which also happened to be consistent with Fianna Fáil rhetoric. The principles themselves are a collection of benign platitudes. It would be difficult specifically to oppose them – in principle. But they are only 'intended for the general guidance of the Oireachtas'. They are in no way constitutionally binding, 'and shall not be cognisable by any Court under any of the provisions of this Constitution'. The sentiments were as irrelevant constitutionally as they were attractive socially and remunerative politically. For politics in the narrow sense had to weigh heavily on de Valera's mind as he presided over the drafting of the Constitution.

Fianna Fáil won a handsome electoral victory in 1933. But it became increasingly clear as the parliamentary term progressed that the party was unlikely to repeat this performance at the next election. The new Constitution was not, of course, simply an election gimmick. De Valera had long contemplated introducing a new Constitution as soon as circumstances permitted. But the timing of the referendum on the Constitution, which he held on the same day as the general election of 1937, is unlikely to have been a mere coincidence. The Constitution could happily serve not only as a model statement of eternal values, but as a shadow election manifesto. But if de Valera may have needed the Constitution to some extent to carry Fianna Fáil, he needed not only Fianna Fáil votes, but others also, to carry the Constitution – which in the end was approved by 685,000 votes against 527,000, compared with 599,000 votes for Fianna Fáil and 725,000 for all other parties in the general election. It is improbable that the 527,000 opposing votes derived from deep philosophical reflection. It is much more plausible to assume that they reflected the gut instincts of party politics. They are likely to have been cast much more against de Valera than against the Constitution. De Valera had to be conscious of the substantial negative vote his identification with the Constitution was likely to provoke. Therefore he had to pursue every possible floating vote.

Later generations have come to consider the Constitution so integral a part of the political landscape that historians may be inclined to overlook the fairly narrow electoral constraints within which de Valera had to operate, and which he had to keep constantly in mind. He had therefore to take particular cognizance of the fact that his proposals had to be acceptable to the largest and potentially most influential pressure group in the country, the Catholic Church. Even the makers of the Constitution of 1922, who could always plead the limitations imposed by the Treaty on their freedom of action, felt obliged to pay court to episcopal sensitivities.[3] By the mid-1930s the Church had established itself as virtually a state within a state in many respects. There was no possibility that a new Constitution could be passed if it significantly offended ecclesiastical sensibilities.

De Valera took a great deal of time and trouble, as the researches of the late John Whyte, and more recently, the prodigious archival labours of Dermot Keogh, have shown, to secure a phraseology in Article 44, which dealt with religion, that would reconcile the sensitivities of all the other churches with those of the Catholic Church.[4] The wording of 44.1.2 and 44.1.3 was reached only after much verbal refinement. They read as follows

2) The State recognises the special position of the Holy Catholic Apostolic and Roman Church as the guardian of the Faith professed by the great majority of the citizens.
3) The State also recognises the Church of Ireland, the Presbyterian Church in Ireland, the Methodist Church in Ireland, the Religious Society of Friends in Ireland, as well as the Jewish Congregations and the other religious denominations existing in Ireland at the date of the coming into operation of this Constitution.

Article 44.1.2 was in one sense meaningless. What it did not do, however, was far more important than what it did. It very carefully refrained from establishing the Catholic Church, which was accorded a symbolic primacy, but no additional authority. The most striking feature of the clause is the restraint exercised with respect to the role of an institution with such pervasive influence on matters of most faith and some morals in the country. In addition, the explicit recognition of the Jewish Congregations in Ireland amounted to a notable statement of de Valera's principles in the Europe of 1937. Ireland is not devoid of potential for anti-semitism. But the Constitution gave no succour to aspiring anti-semites. One irony of the abolition of Article 44.1.2 in a referendum in 1972, intended as an obeisance to the presumed sensitivities of Ulster Unionists, is that 44.1.3 was also removed, thus eliminating recognition not only of 'the special position' of the Catholic Church, but of any position of any church.

De Valera's potential problem with the Church, in so far as it was a problem – and it must always be remembered that he shared many of the assumptions of the churchmen on the proper ordering of society – was not confined to Article 44. Many churchmen, although increasingly coming to appreciate the virtues of de Valera, had earlier strongly opposed him, and may have harboured residual suspicions about him. The Constitution might even incidentally wean some of the remaining doubters from their unworthy suspicions. Several of the social clauses, particularly those relating to the role of women and to sexual morality, were pervaded by the assumptions that dominated Catholic thinking at the time. De Valera did not, it may be reasonably presumed, insert the relevant clauses in order to win ecclesiastical support. He inserted them because he believed in them. But it was a happy coincidence that they would win enthusiastic endorsement from several churchmen.

The imputation in Article 41.2 that the proper place for 'woman' was 'within the home' roused some criticism at the time, and a great deal more in recent decades. However, the courts have often interpreted other articles on personal rights in a manner sympathetic to women, so that 'Irish women now have many rights unavailable to, and even superior to, those of their English and indeed their American sisters'.[5]

The prohibition on divorce in the Constitution has also provoked lively controversy. The attempt by the then Taoiseach, Dr Garret FitzGerald, to have the prohibition modified in 1986, was rejected in a referendum by a roughly two to one majority. The critics naturally deplored the outcome. But the referendum is as democratic a device as can be found to amend a Constitution. Those who berated the people for their verdict were in effect conceding their failure to win the argument on the issues involved – just as some of the same people had failed three years earlier to prevent a similar majority inserting into the Constitution, in the 'abortion' referendum, a clause in which

> The State acknowledges the right to life of the unborn and, with due regard to the equal right to life of the mother, guarantees in its laws to respect, and, as far as practicable, by its laws to defend and vindicate that right.
>
> (Article 40.3.3).

There was one area, however, in which de Valera took only cursory cognizance of Catholic teaching. That was the area of political power. De Valera clung, with minor modifications, to the Westminster system already in operation in Ireland, of whose procedures he had already shown such mastery. Here again, his Constitution followed closely that of 1922. He did make obeisance to Catholic teaching on corporatism by creating a new Senate based on nominally vocational representation. As the vast majority of the members were to be elected by a restricted electorate of professional politicians, however, the genuflection to vocationalism remained symbolic.

The other innovation was the creation of the office of President. This provoked passionate criticism from opposition spokesmen during parliamentary debates. They feared that de Valera was fashioning an office for himself that would allow him to trample over the rights of Parliament, if not indeed to threaten the foundations of parliamentary democracy. That de Valera intended the President, even in theory, much less in practice, to be the creature of Parliament rather than its master, seemed improbable to them. Their worst-case scenario failed to transpire. De Valera would indeed long dominate the country – but through his command of the Dáil, not from a presidential palace. The presidency, although invested with some residual authority that might prove significant in situations of sustained parliamentary instability, was intended as, and remained, an essentially ceremonial office.[6]

The President was, it is true, to be elected by the people. But he could only be nominated in the first instance by members of the political class, whether in the Dáil or on county councils, thus giving, for practical purposes, the political parties a monopoly on the selection of candidates. Political parties would remain the prime sources of political power, though the word party does not actually occur in the text, an irony in a Constitution devised by the outstanding Irish party politician of the century, and designed to ensure the primacy of party politics. Indeed, in contrast to the restricted role envisaged for the president, the role of Taoiseach – the supreme party politician in the country – was strengthened. His powers were codified and consolidated, by transferring from the cabinet to himself the prerogative of recommending the dissolution of the Dáil, and the authority to dismiss ministers. The Taoiseach enjoys so powerful a constitutional position, arguably more powerful than most heads of governments in western countries, that it might even be dangerous to confer such powers on a single office, but for the fact that it too is subject to the discipline of a written constitution.

Articles 2 and 3, those concerned with 'the unity of our country', have provoked intense controversy in recent years. De Valera had to say something about unity. The 1922 Constitution was drafted under the shadow of the Boundary Commission. It was still possible to imagine that partition was only a short term expedient, and the 1922 aspiration to the reunification of Ireland was confined to the preamble. By 1937 the boundary was firmly in place. More than preamble comment was now required. De Valera could not avoid taking a position on the matter, even had he wished to. He had to pre-empt the inevitable accusation by the Irish Republican Army (IRA), Fianna Fáil's rival for Republican legitimacy, that he had betrayed the ideal of a united Ireland – particularly as one purpose of the Constitution was precisely to deprive the IRA of their claim to legitimacy, now that a democratically enacted Constitution could be held to represent the will of the people, in contrast to the *de facto* British *dictat* of 1922. The mechanism devised to square the circle of ultimate aspiration and current reality was instructive. Article 2 declared that

> The national territory consists of the whole island of Ireland, its islands and the territorial seas.

Article 3 immediately qualified the implications of this by insisting that 'pending the reintegration of the national territory', the Dublin government would exercise jurisdiction only over the twenty-six counties.

In view of the controversy these articles now generate, it must be insisted that they represented not extreme, but consensus, opinion at the time.[7] Even the Committee on the Constitution established by Seán Lemass in 1966, which reported in 1967, did not query the fundamental assumption of a one-nation unitary state underlying these articles. It merely proposed that the state should commit itself to achieving the inherited objective 'in harmony and brotherly affection'. The report of the New Ireland Forum in 1984 accepted the need for a new constitution for all Ireland if the North and the Republic joined together. But it did not envisage any change in Articles 2 and 3 pending that decidedly improbable development. More recently again, the Supreme Court of the Republic has held, in 1990, that working towards 'the reintegration of the national territory' is 'a constitutional imperative', whatever this may be taken to mean in practical terms (would it mean that it is 'a constitutional imperative' to revise the Constitution in a manner conducive to 'the reintegration of the national territory', given that the Forum implicitly accepted the Constitution posed an obstacle to such 'reintegration'?).

Articles 2 and 3 are based on a specific concept, the nation. Fortunately or unfortunately, this fundamental concept is nowhere defined. One searches in vain in the three articles, 1–3, which are included in the section 'The nation', for any definition of 'nation'.[8] Article 2 does contain a definition – but only of 'the national territory', not of the 'nation'. Article 1 proclaims that

The Irish nation hereby affirms its inalienable, indefeasible, and sovereign right to choose its own form of Government, to determine its relations with other nations, and to develop its life, political, economic and cultural, in accordance with its own genius and traditions.

This seems clear on the rights of the nation – if one could only discover what the nation is. Is it the people at any given time? The Irish version of Article 1 – and the Irish version takes precedence over the English version in cases of interpretative difficulty – merely adds to the uncertainty

Deimhníonn náisiún na hÉireann leis seo a gceart doshannta, dochloite, ceannasach chun cibé cineál Rialtais is rogha leo féin a bhunú, chun a gcaidreamh le násiúin eile a chinneadh, agus chun a saol polaitiochta is geilleagair is saíochta a chur ar aghaidh de réir dhúchais is gnás a sinsear.

This begins with the assertion 'the Irish nation hereby affirms' etc. But it then proceeds to affirm not 'its' inalienable etc. right, but 'their' inalienable etc. right to choose 'their own form of government'. It shifts from the singular of 'nation' to the plural. This is not, one can assume, a concealed version of 'two nations' theory. It presumably derives from the author equating 'nation' with 'people'.

But what do the phrases 'inalienable' and 'indefeasible' *mean* in Article 1? Do they mean that the Irish people cannot deprive themselves (or the Irish nation, if nation exists independently of people) of their sovereign right? Are the people subject to some antecedent right residing in the 'nation' which precludes the people at any given time from 'alienating' their right to choose their own form of government? Is this a more sophisticated version of the earlier celebrated de Valera dictum that 'the people have never a right to do wrong'? And what does 'in accordance with its own genius and traditions' mean? Who decides what these are? Can 'the people' define them at any given time? Or are they independent of the decision of the people?

Article 8, which confronted the thorny issue of language, found itself embroiled in the potential conflict between 'nation' and 'people' once more. Article 8.1 asserted that 'the Irish language as the national language is the first official language'. Article 8.2 asserted that 'the English language is recognised as a second official language'. The fact that the vast majority of the people spoke English did not apparently suffice to have it recognized as either 'the national language' or even as 'a national language'. Theoretically, Irish would presumably remain the 'national language' even if nobody at all spoke it. Does the idea that the nation exists wholly independently of reality at any given time inform the assumptions underlying this article?

It seems clear from the text that the nation exists independently of the 'national territory'. It is unclear whether it exists independently of the people. What is clear, however, is that there is only one nation and one people in the national territory. The preamble leaves little room for doubt on this score

> We, the people of Eire,
> Humbly acknowledging all our obligations to our
> Divine Lord, Jesus Christ, Who sustained our fathers
> through centuries of trial,
> Gratefully remembering their heroic and unremitting
> struggle to regain the rightful independence of our
> Nation . . .

To a historical purist at any rate, this would seem to exclude from membership of either 'people' or 'nation' anyone who refused to acknowledge their membership of this particular imagined community. (The referendum was not, of course, held in Northern Ireland. It is intriguing to speculate on the likely outcome if all those whom the Constitution claimed as the Irish people had in fact been invited to pronounce their verdict on it.)

The section on the state is relatively less problematical, though even here tension seems to exist between the concepts of state, people and nation. While Article 6 asserts that 'All powers of government . . . derive, under God, from the people', Article 9.2 proclaims that 'fidelity to the nation and loyalty to the State are fundamental political duties of all citizens'. What the difference here between 'fidelity' and 'loyalty' may be remains a matter of opinion. Who decides? The people? Suppose that the 'people' decide that 'fidelity' to an undefined 'nation' is not one of its 'fundamental political duties'; what then?

These issues are not raised in order to cast aspersions on either the integrity or the intelligence of those involved in drafting the Constitution. A constitution codifies in a certain sense the self-image of a people, but collective self-images are no more likely than individual self-images fully to reflect reality. Constitutions rightly embody aspirations as well as specifying practical procedures of governance. All peoples are entitled to cherish a self-image that is partly aspirational. In the Irish case, however, none of these reflections can refute the claim that there are manifestly two peoples on the island of Ireland (whether 'two nations' depends on the definition of 'nation'). It is precisely because there are two peoples that the Ulster question has festered for so long. Some – Conor Cruise O'Brien is a particularly prominent and accomplished representative – hold that Articles 2 and 3 promote conflict in Northern Ireland, by seeming to legitimize, if only in the abstract, the Provisional IRA.[9] They therefore recommend the deletion of Articles 2 and 3. This raises important issues, which will not go away. But the elimination of Articles 2 and 3 will not make the Ulster question go away either. For they do not invent that question. Many may find them unsatisfactory as responses to it. But the Ulster question existed long before Articles 2 and 3, and would continue if they were deleted.

There are at least three Ulster questions, only one of which is addressed in the Constitution. There is first, the Republic's claim on the whole of the North. There is, second, Britain's presence in the whole of the North. And there is, third, and perhaps more fundamentally than either, British insistence on ruling over substantial parts of the territory of Northern Ireland in which Unionists appear to be in a minority. Article 2, which remains wholly aspirational, pales into insignificance compared with the reality of British occupation of substantial areas of nationalist territory within the North – assuming that the majorities in those territories actually do want unification. That is why, in my view, the New Ireland Forum was correct both to acknowledge that a new Constitution would indeed be necessary in the event of a united Ireland, but also implicitly to accept that unilateral abandonment of Articles 2 and 3, with no corresponding abandonment of the territorial claims of other involved parties, would make no contribution to a just and enduring settlement of the Ulster question.

The fourth objective listed in the preamble was the establishment of 'concord . . . with other nations'. (Strictly speaking, this presumably means with other states.) There are two striking features of Article 29, which deals with 'International relations'. The first is its apparent vagueness in certain respects. The second is its commitment to the 'principles of international law'.

De Valera detested the 1922 Constitution mainly because of the oath of fidelity to the British Crown imposed 'in virtue of the common citizenship of Ireland with Great Britain' through Article 4 of the 1921 treaty. Michael Collins had manoeuvred desperately to try to reconcile the oath with the Sinn Féin commitment to a Republic. But he found himself trapped between the metaphysical Republicans opposing the Treaty because it incorporated the Crown, and the metaphysical monarchists of the British government threatening to abort the Treaty if it excluded the Crown. When Collins sought to evade the Treaty requirement in the draft Constitution he presented in London in May 1922 by simply omitting the oath, he was brusquely compelled to restore it.[10] To de Valera, such a Constitution, imposed by threat of superior force, and never sanctioned by the Irish people, could not be legitimate.

De Valera took advantage of various opportunities that arose after his coming to power in 1932 to abolish the oath in 1933 and to eliminate reference to the Crown in domestic matters from the Constitution during the little local difficulties of the royal family in 1936. He did not, however, entirely eliminate the functions exercised by the Crown from the Constitution. He did not proclaim a republic, but left open the question of the nature of Ireland's future association with the Crown in 29.4.2

> For the purpose of the exercise of any executive function of the State in or in connection with its external relations, the Government may to such extent and subject to such conditions, if any, as may be determined by law, avail of or adopt any organ, instrument, or method of procedure used or adopted for the like purpose by the members of any group or league of nations with which the State is or becomes associated for the purpose of international cooperation in matters of common concern.

This combination of words was flexible enough to encompass almost any eventuality that might arise involving the future role of the Crown in Ireland's external relations.

Article 29.2 committed Ireland 'to the principle of the pacific settlement of international disputes by international arbitration or judicial determination', while in Article 29.3 Ireland accepted 'the generally recognised principles of international law as its rule of conduct in its relations with other States'. Indeed, in the Irish version, 'International relations' is described as 'international friendship'. The principles underlying this section, therefore, are enunciated in terms of impeccable international responsibility.

The potential contained in the Constitution for changing, and thus renewing, itself counts among its most impressive features. There are two major mechanisms of change. The first is amendment by popular referendum. Proposals for referenda must be sanctioned by the Oireachtas, however, and may therefore easily become ensnared in the thickets of party politics. Nevertheless, the final verdict remains with the people.

The second source of revision is judicial review. In the past thirty years or so, the Supreme Court, by adopting an activist attitude towards the Constitution, and by choosing to determine particular cases not only with reference to specific clauses in the Constitution, but also with reference to the rights implied by its fundamental principles, has enormously widened the scope for reinterpretation.[11] Most judgments have established, or reinforced, the rights of the individual against the state and even arguably against society. That may not always remain the case, as circumstances and personalities change.

The Constitution does offer much potential for permanent reinterpretation, even without resort to the doctrine of 'implied rights'. Interpretation of numerous clauses can be made dependent on the interpretation of other clauses. Mr Justice Donal Barrington, a judge of the High Court, has argued, for instance, that Articles 2 and 3 must be interpreted subject to Article 29, which commits Ireland to the peaceful solution of international disputes. The Constitution thus permits regular reinterpretation through rereading and deepening of understanding.

Irish entry to the European Economic Community in 1973 has extended the scope of judicial review. The multitude of potential constitutional implications were covered by a single amendment in 1972 which simply stated that

> No provision of this Constitution invalidates laws enacted, acts done or measures adopted by the State necessitated by the obligations of membership of the Communities or prevents laws enacted, acts done, or measures adopted by the Community, or institutions thereof, from having the force of law in the State.

As it is the courts who interpret the relationship between Community obligations and the requirements of the Constitution, judicial review now extends further than heretofore into the broad area of international relations. These issues require delicate handling. Potential for conflict, or at least unease, has become greater, as in the case of the Supreme Court's highly controversial ruling that ratification of the Single European Act required a referendum.[12] It is not therefore inconceivable that tensions may occur over the coming decades on the issue of judicial review, particularly in the area of international affairs, where the concept of 'sovereignty', which features so prominently in the Constitution, is itself undergoing significant evolution in theory and practice. Tension may not, of course, be a bad thing, if it obliges us to confront some issues that we might prefer to avoid.

Specific clauses in the Constitution have provoked vigorous criticism on occasion. It is also the case, as always and everywhere, that the poorer members of society are likely to have less knowledge of, and less resources to have enforced on their behalf, their constitutional rights. That reflects on the structure of society, however, not on the Constitution itself. That Constitution has established itself in the minds, and even in the hearts, of the people, to the extent that it is now impossible to envisage the effective functioning of the State, or of the wider society, without it. For all the criticisms that may be directed at it, for all the inconsistencies that may be detected in it, the Constitution has made, in my judgment, a significant contribution to the common good, and can be counted among the most successful initiatives undertaken by independent Ireland.[13]

Notes

1 Brian Farrell, 'From first Dáil through Irish Free State', in Brian Farrell, ed., *De Valera's Constitution and Ours* (Dublin, 1988) p. 30.
2 For further elucidation see Mr Justice Ronan Keane, 'Property in the Constitution and in the Courts', in Farrell, ed., op.cit., pp. 137–51; Enda McDonagh, 'Philosophical–theological reflections on the Constitution', in Frank Litton, ed., *The Constitution of Ireland 1937–1987* (Dublin, 1988) pp. 198–9.
3 Farrell, op.cit., pp. 25–6.
4 J. H. Whyte, *Church and State in Modern Ireland, 1923–1970* (Dublin, 1971) pp. 50–6; Dermot Keogh 'The Constitutional revolution: an analysis of the making of the Constitution', in Litton, ed., op.cit., pp. 4–84.
5 Yvonne Scannell, 'The Constitution and the role of women', in Farrell, ed., op.cit., p. 134.
6 Michael Gallagher, 'The President, the people and the Constitution', in Farrell, ed., op.cit., pp. 75–92.
7 Gearóid ó Tuathaigh, 'The Irish nation-state in the Constitution', in Farrell, ed., op.cit., p. 51; p. 203.
8 *See* J. J. Lee, *Ireland 1912–1985: Politics and Society* (Cambridge, 1989) p. 205, and generally pp. 201–9.
9 For a recent exposition of O'Brien's views, *see* 'A tale of two nations', *New York Review of Books* (19 July 1990) pp. 33–6.
10 Farrell, op.cit., p. 25.
11 *See* James Casey, 'Changing the Constitution: amendment and judicial

review', in Farrell, ed., op.cit., pp. 156ff; Gerard Hogan, 'Constitutional interpretation', in Litton, ed., op.cit., pp. 178ff.
12 Peter Sutherland expresses some of this unease in 'Twin perspectives: an Attorney General views political and European dimensions', in Farrell, ed., op.cit., pp. 184–6.
13 For an example of reservations, see John Kelly, 'The Constitution: law and manifesto', in Litton, ed., op.cit., pp. 208–17. For a candid assessment of the reality of governmental decision making, *see* Basil Chubb 'Government and Dáil: Constitutional myth and political practice', in Farrell, ed., op.cit., pp. 93–102.

6 Industrial development and the unmaking of the Irish working class

Jim Smyth

INTRODUCTION

The imminent arrival of the European single market has brought about mixed reactions from Irish commentators. The initial euphoria – not confined to official sources – is gradually giving way to a more jaundiced view of the effects of economic union upon Irish society, and serious questions are being asked about the performance of the economy in particular and, more generally, concerning the type of society and social structure which has emerged since independence. It would be a mistake to exaggerate the extent of the unease, but clearly the consensus which dominated during the last twenty years about the possibility and desirability of economic growth within the European Community has grown tarnished and some sacred cows are well on the way to slaughter.[1]

It is clear that, despite the investment of massive state resources, the economic performance of Ireland has been dismal. During the twentieth century Ireland has had the lowest growth rate of Gross Domestic Product of any European country and, indeed, from being a relatively well developed economy at the turn of the century it now continues to slip down the economic pecking order. Having been recently overtaken by Spain the Republic now sits uneasily above Greece and Portugal among the member states of the European Community (EC). The failure of the Republic to attain the national dream of economic prosperity and an end to emigration has been attributed by J. J. Lee in a recent book to deficiencies in the intellectual superstructure and the possessor ethic of the Irish middle classes. Lee locates the 'causes of Irish retardation . . . in a failure to mobilize the intellectual resources of the country properly'.[2] Lee's thesis is a powerful one. He redeploys the dependency argument with some force

The incapacity of the Irish mind to think through the implications of independence for national development derived largely from, and was itself a symbol of, the dependency syndrome which had wormed its way into the Irish psyche during the long centuries of foreign dominance.[3]

The inadequacies of the Irish middle classes expressed themselves in the failure of national development. In comparison with other countries with similar characteristics, such as Denmark and Finland, Ireland has done very badly, in terms of overall economic performance. But it is here that one can question the underlying assumptions of Lee's thesis. Quite apart from the unreflected acceptance of economic development as the highest good, the question of why the Irish middle classes should have acted otherwise than they did must be faced.

In castigating the bourgeoisie for its intellectual mediocrity (the extent and depth of which Lee may even possibly underestimate) Lee misses a crucial point: they were behaving, and still behave, in a way which maximizes their collective and individual endowments. What has characterized the Irish bourgeoisie is an extraordinary homogeneity. Unlike the situation in advanced capitalist countries, there are no significant class fractions within the Irish bourgeoisie and little social mobility to disturb the traditional monopoly of privilege.[4] Nationalist movements have had a profoundly ambivalent attitude towards industrialization, blaming its absence upon colonialism while at the same time fearing the effects of social change unleashed by the process of development. The Irish bourgeoisie are no different. As a class, they have managed to defuse social conflict – with the help of mass emigration and the power of the Catholic Church – while appropriating the major share of the country's wealth. Nevertheless, their autonomy was, and remains, circumscribed by Ireland's position within the international division of labour, which, while permitting a degree of national autonomy, defined the parameters within which developments could take place. That the Irish bourgeoisie did not exploit the limited autonomy which is always open to even the most dependent nations, is clear. That it often did not understand the nature and effect of these parameters is also accepted. But it has managed to survive and indeed prosper having long since abandoned nationalism for a pseudo-cosmopolitanism and almost total subservience to international capital.

In the Irish case, the complex interrelations of cultural and political practices which form the dynamic of a capitalist economy are further complicated by a high level of outside inputs. Not only are cultural and political practice moulded by the colonial past but the spatial configuration of the world economy and its pattern of development has locked Ireland into specific relationships with the global economic system. What the British administration, and, after independence, the local bourgeoisie, attempted was the internal organization of social forces to ensure stability and an acceptable regime of accumulation.

The approach of the French 'regulation school' offers us a theoretical framework for the analysis of the complex interrelations which form the dynamic of Irish society. The two central ideas of the regulation school are the regime of accumulation and the mode of political and social regulation. Essentially, a regime of accumulation

> describes the stabilization over a long period of the allocation of the net product between consumption and accumulation: it implies some correspondence between the transformation of both the conditions of production and the conditions of reproduction of wage earners.

But for this regime to be coherent and stable the behaviour of the agents concerned must be structured in a particular way. According to Lipietz, there must exist

> a materialization of the regime of accumulation taking the form of norms, habits, laws, regulating networks and so on that ensure the unity of the process, i.e. the appropriate consistency of individual behaviours with the schema of production. This body of interiorized rules and social processes is called the mode of regulation.[5]

The use of this theoretical framework allows us to locate the process of Irish economic development within a larger framework and to discuss the effects of global changes upon the local economy. The idea of the mode of regulation helps avoid the pitfall of determinism by focusing upon the dynamic way in which the national bourgeoisie responded to changing events, within both the context of the capitalist system as a whole, and in terms of its own class interests. It also helps us avoid treating local elites as free-floating phenomena by reifing their actions and ascribing blame. Despite the relative failure of economic development, both the economy and social structure of Ireland have undergone dramatic changes since independence, particularly in the course of the last twenty years. In 1926 51 per cent of the gainfully employed population were engaged in agriculture, as compared to 19 per cent in 1979. The policy of protectionism embarked upon in the 1930s was abandoned in 1958 in favour of an open economy, thus sealing the fate of the small-scale and inefficient industrial sector which grew up behind tariff walls. People have drifted to the Dublin area where almost one-third of the population now lives. These changes have come about less through a process of rational planning than through a failure to come to terms with Ireland's position within the international division of labour and develop policies to maximize whatever advantages the country may have. The decision to abandon protectionism had far-reaching consequences and was not the subject of more than superficial discussion. The reality of a stagnant economy, high unemployment and the haemorrhage of emigration was met with a range of reactions – sullen silence, nationalist rhetoric and complacency being the most prevalent. At the level of policy formulation the problem was seen as a technocratic one: a choice between the continuation of 'unproductive' government expenditure on housing, health and education and 'productive' investment in areas which would promote economic growth.[6]

While it is undeniable that the policy of protectionism and fiscal rectitude had led the country into an economic and social backwater at a time when the reconstruction of the post-war capitalist economy was proceeding apace, the policies recommended by the crucial white paper, *Economic Development* (1958),[7] would have alienated significant sections of Fianna Fáil support among the urban and rural poor. The eventual outcome was a compromise on all fronts. Foreign industry was to be welcomed, but only if it was export orientated, and capital expenditure was to relate to political rather than economic considerations. This poses the question of the importance of policy decisions in the key area of economic growth and the influence such decision making can have in a small dependent economy. The importance of policy making depends upon careful analysis of the position of the economy within a larger international system and how weaknesses can be corrected to improve this position. The transformation of post-war France was at least in part achieved by a conscious decision to invest heavily in infrastructural projects to improve communications, transport and urban renewal. The spectacular growth of Japan after the Second World War owes much to state intervention.[8] Although Ireland had retained its subordinate position within the global economy in the interwar period and reacted in a predictable manner to changes in the world economy, non-participation in the Second World War isolated the country and its economy from post-war developments.

When it became necessary to reintegrate the country into the larger system this was not carried out on the basis of systematic analysis of Ireland's potential within the system and how this potential could be maximized. The debate centred simply upon economic policy and decisions were shaped and modified by electoral and political considerations, without any thought to long term consequences. Although one can agree with J. J. Lee's criticism of the intellectual calibre of the Irish administrative, academic and political elite, and lay some responsibility for the country's poor performance at their door, the intelligentsia cannot be treated as a free-floating phenomenon. Ignorance and narrowmindedness were functional qualities in post-independence Ireland as the country sank into a bog of self-congratulatory isolationism – just as a superficial cosmopolitanism is *de rigeur* in the contemporary scene.

IRELAND AND THE GLOBAL ECONOMY: THE HISTORICAL ROUNDABOUT

It was an article of faith of nationalist commentators that the economic underdevelopment of Ireland could be attributed to British rule and that independence – even Home Rule – would signal a changed situation and the possibility of economic prosperity. Equally, commentators of a Unionist persuasion were convinced that independence would not be in the interests of the industrial north east of the island which by the turn of the century was an integral part of the imperial economy. This pattern of uneven development, characteristic of capitalist development in general, was seen to be a product of political conditions and open to reversal, given independence.

Independence did not herald the immediate introduction of protectionism, as proposed by Sinn Féin. The government and administration of the Free State were cautious and unwilling to disrupt the economic *status quo*, particularly as the larger enterprises were opposed to protectionist measures. The gradual introduction of protectionism was as much a result of general global economic conditions as a product of internal pressure. The coming to power of Fianna Fáil in 1932 coincided with the intensification of global recession, and the new government moved swiftly to turn Ireland into one of the most heavily tariffed countries in the world.[9] The shift to protectionism not only reflected a general response to the global economic crisis but was in the interests of the class alliance which Fianna Fáil represented: the embryonic national bourgeoisie, small farmers and the working class. Hence the political and economic objectives of protectionism were limited. Local manufacture was to be protected and the size of the industrial work force increased. The policy had some success: the industrial work force grew by 50 per cent between 1926 and 1956, though from a very small base. There were structural reasons why protectionism failed to lead to sustained economic growth: a small internal market, unfavourable terms of trade and a work force with limited industrial experience.[10] Of greater importance were the political constraints. Risk-taking was anathema to the Irish financial elite and their clients – the country's financial assets were predominantly invested in foreign banks and government stocks.[11] The radical populism of Fianna Fáil did not extend to mobilizing this capital in the interests of national development, which would not only have meant incurring the ire of the rich, but of the Catholic Church, which was involved in one of its periodic crusades against the evils of communism at the time.

In the aftermath of the Second World War, Ireland was in no position to participate in the economic boom experienced by other western economies. Agricultural production was still geared to the export of live cattle to Britain, and other natural resources, such as fishing, were at a primitive stage of development. Industry was inefficient and geared to a stagnant home market. The population was declining due to massive emigration, and there was considerable political unrest, expressed in the organization of the unemployed in Dublin.

Economic commentators have tended to see the development of economic policy as a result of government decisions, made against a background of rational decision making as to the best means to achieve the end of economic growth. Little attention is paid to either internal social pressures (or their absence) and the role which Ireland plays in the international division of labour. Given the global economic situation in the 1930s, the introduction of protectionism was less a product of political ideology than an inevitable response to the reality of world recession. Protectionism did not alter the primary role of Ireland within the international division of labour, that of supplying unskilled labour to the British economy. If the world economy can be seen as the interaction of national social formations[12] then a primary role of Ireland within this system has been, since the nineteenth century, a supplier of surplus labour to the British, and (in a more uneven fashion) the United States economy.

Presenting the changes in economic policy after the Second World War – the shift from protectionism to integration – as the result of government policy[13] ignores both the underlying logic of a changing global division of labour and the effect of social change upon the indigenous class structure. The advent of Fordism/Keynesianism after the war assisted the reconstruction of the western economies around the axis of mass production/mass consumption, aided and abetted by an interventionist state. Economic growth could only take place if new mass markets could be created and consumption made the dominant norm of social relations. Ireland could not remain outside this process, as its economy had no other choice but to react to change. Given the weakness of the economy, this reaction could only be one of dependence: integration within the terms of the dominant mode of regulation. The demand for unskilled Irish labour had grown in the context of post-war reconstruction in Britain. Being a capitalist country, even if an insignificant one, meant that Ireland had no choice but to align itself with the dominant mode of regulation.

The crisis of the Irish economy in the mid-1950s was a crisis of growth and profitability. It had become abundantly clear that local capital had failed in its historic mission to create employment and stem emigration, and failed miserably. To locate the crisis as one of emigration is to confuse cause and effect. As Lee points out with devastating clarity, the tendency of Irish commentators to blame emigration on cultural and social habits merely served to deflect attention from the failure to modernize agriculture and the industrial structure. The country faced an acute dilemma. For the working class it was probably irrelevant where the jobs came from as long as they were there. For the bourgeoisie, foreign capital posed a threat to their comfortable existence and the coherence of nationalist ideology. On the other hand, the stagnation of economic growth posed a potential threat of existential proportions.

The crisis did not lead to any widespread self-scrutiny and what debate there was confined itself to the relative merits of different economic policies. Given the reality of the so called 'culture of dependency' it was not surprising that the solution to the problem was seen, not in internal reform, but as coming from outside: foreign capital was to be used as the locomotive of economic growth. Effectively this meant that Ireland was to be belatedly reinstated into the global economy, but under conditions and circumstances which were not understood.

REINTEGRATION: DEVELOPMENT WITHOUT JOBS?

To understand the relationship between a social formation and the global division of labour it is necessary to theorize this relationship.

It is not sufficient to attribute failure to the deficiencies of the local bourgeois, since the room for manoeuvre is circumscribed by the location of any given nation within the international division of labour. That the Irish bourgeoisie was lacking in imagination, vision and even generosity is undeniable but it still had to operate within a system over which it had little influence, and of which it was an insignificant part.

The pattern of development undertaken by Ireland after 1932 – protectionism – was in line with the response of many countries to the economic crisis. The protection of local industry meant the temporary abandonment of growth in favour of the preservation of the mode of social and political regulation. In Ireland the habituation of the poor to the necessity of emigration was necessary since a collective decision to remain would have had negative social consequences for the process of accumulation and the stability of society. This is not to say that there were no alternatives, but this was the path chosen within the context of a given division of labour, i.e. the willingness of other countries to accept Irish unskilled labour. In other economies the decline of agriculture and the release of labour reserves signalled a growing capacity to accumulate by expanding the numbers of wage earners and reducing the social cost of the reproduction of labour power. In Ireland emigration reduced the overall social costs of the reproduction of labour power but also condemned the economy to stagnation. The persistence of the post-1932 regime of accumulation well into the period after the Second World War can only be partly attributed to the policy of neutrality. Other neutral countries such as Sweden did not follow the Irish path of cultural and economic isolation but swiftly integrated their economies into the new post-war economic order.

The restructuring of capital after the Second World War involved the replacement of national industrial capital by global capitalism. Global capitalism is characterized by the emergence of a small number of giant transnational enterprises with turnovers which exceed the Gross National Product (GNP) of most countries. These corporations tend to concentrate administration and research and development in a central, core state and develop spatial strategies for using high levels of labour productivity and low wages. This strategy brings with it a new division of labour on an international scale. The crisis of Fordism accelerated this process.

The model of development adopted in the post war capitalist world has been characterized as Fordist.[14] Attempts to increase productivity through the separation of management, conception, control and task execution has a long history[15] and found its initial expression in Taylorism – or scientific management. But while Taylorism, or scientific management, is a prerequisite of Fordism, the latter is more all embracing involving, in the words of Harvey

> explicit recognition that mass production meant mass consumption, a new system of the reproduction of labour power, a new politics of labour control and management, a new aesthetics and psychology, in short a new kind of rationalized modernist and populist democratic society.[16]

The Fordist regime which emerged in the post-war world did not just consist in an upsurge in accumulation but linked the latter to consumption by transforming the consumption patterns of the working class. The extensive use of Taylorist scientific management techniques transformed the social organization of labour and intensified the mechanization of production. The expansion of assembly-line production allowed the manufacture of cheap, standardized commodities for a mass market, thus extending consumption to the working classes. The reorganization of the labour process brought about tensions and struggles which were partially controlled by the expansion of the Keynesian welfare state and the institutionalization of collective bargaining. Both collective bargaining and the welfare system stabilized patterns of consumption by maintaining a sufficient, if stratified, level of consumption among both employed and unemployed.

While the structure of European society was being transformed, Ireland was still locked into a regime of accumulation which was based upon family-owned firms, and criteria such as family ties, loyalty, religion and other such factors were paramount in defining relationships within the industrial hierarchy. For example, until the late 1950s, the main criteria for gaining employment with the country's largest private employer, Guinness, were, at management level, religion and, at the manual level, a family tradition of employment. While the bourgeoisie seemed impotent and unwilling to transform this antiquated system of communal paternalism, the working class was increasingly aware of the widening gap between living standards in Ireland and England, not to mention the increasingly obvious relative prosperity of the North of Ireland. Attempts to mimic the increasingly comprehensive welfare provisions in Britain – such as the Mother and Child Bill – were not only opposed by the Catholic Church (which had a vested interest in the preservation of the old order) but were inconsistent in terms of the absence of a regime of accumulation which would have made such reforms necessary.

Ireland did not participate in the first phase of Fordist reconstruction. Local industry was structurally and ideologically incapable of change, the state administration was equally deficient and the new regime of accumulation in Europe (and its expansion and consolidation in the USA) had not yet reached the limits of internal accumulation which was later to lead to spatial expansion, first within the European periphery and then to the Far East.

By the late 1950s rising wages, increasing state expenditure and a shortage of both skilled and unskilled labour, were causing difficulties in the advanced capitalist countries. A falling rate of profit was countered by the regional dispersal of industry at a time when Ireland was trying to renegotiate its relationship with the global economy. The Fordist organization of the labour process allowed a radically novel and differentiated pattern of geographical dispersal. In terms of the labour process, Fordism is distinguished by a division of economic activities on three levels

1) Conception, organization of production, and engineering
2) Skilled manufacturing
3) Unskilled assembly.

Under pressure of falling rates of profits the possibility of articulating these levels in a new spatial dimension was extremely attractive. The first level, which involves the organization of knowledge as a force of production, would be retained in the home country (thus keeping the crucial element of the labour process separate and under tight control) and the dispersal of the skilled manufacturing element would be limited by the availability of skilled labour in the periphery. Third-level activities, however, could be profitably located within a new horizontal division of labour with the added bonus of generous grant aid and tax benefits from the host country. The first wave of dispersal took place within the centre but soon shifted to the intermediate outer periphery – Spain and Portugal within Europe and, later, to south-east Asia. Some of these countries managed to develop Fordist sectors on the basis of an industrial tradition and a skilled labour force; the Spanish automobile industry is a prime example. Other areas (South Korea, Singapore) with no industrial traditions compensated for low productivity with wage levels far below those in the centre. Authoritarian and military regimes imposed discipline upon the work forces.[17]

The position of Ireland within this new division of labour was (and remains) anomalous. Lacking a skilled and disciplined work force it was not an attractive location for skilled fabrication and assembly and relatively high wages rendered it unsuitable for large-scale unskilled assembly, such as the mass production of consumer durables, a sector which shifted to Spain and southern Italy. Those industries which did locate in Ireland, particularly in the chemical, pharmaceutical and computer industry tended to follow the spatial division of the labour process outlined above: of thirty-two pharmaceutical and chemical operations surveyed by the Telesis team, only two carry out research and development in Ireland and none manage the distribution system from Ireland.[18]

The case of the Irish textile industry encapsulates the subordinate place of Ireland within the international division of labour and the inability of the local elite to find a profitable niche within the industry. The West German textile industry employed 357,000 people in 1968: a figure which had fallen by 37 per cent by 1976. This fall was not accompanied by any fall in output or market share. Faced with problems at home, German industry relocated abroad to take advantage of cheap labour and financial inducements. In contrast, the Irish textile industry declined dramatically after the phasing out of protection. Total output fell from an index of 100 in 1973 to 54 in 1980. Numbers employed in the industry have shown an equally dramatic decline. Given the inability of Ireland to compete with countries where wage levels are kept at a level sufficient for the day-to-day reproduction of labour power and no more, it is interesting to analyse the following German assessment of the investment potential of Ireland, written after the inauguration of a German textile plant in Waterford in 1975

The Republic of Ireland, with only 3 million inhabitants and a labour force of potentially 1.2 million, still has 9 per cent unemployment; the country is mid way through a process of restructuring from an agricultural country to a land which is also industrial. . . . His [Mr Swann, then Chairman of the Industrial Development Authority] Authority, the IDA, has therefore had no difficulty in convincing the influential Church that Nino ought to work twenty-four hours a day, seven days a week: this means a four shift operation with a total of 168 hours a week. . . . By contrast the plant could only be worked with three shifts in Nordhorn, giving 120 hours a week, or 126 at most with overtime. One particularly powerful argument which the IDA can bring to bear in attracting foreign investors, in addition to investment grants which are either measured according to the number of jobs created or the amount of capital invested (which in the case of Nino may not be less than if the company had built in a German development area with state support), is tax exemption for export profits – which applies for fifteen years.[19]

Of particular interest here is the emphasis on the advantageous nature of Ireland for capital intensive production because plant can be worked twenty-four hours a day. The recent failure of the EC countries to achieve agreement on a social charter is interesting in this context. The attitude of the Irish government towards the social charter was ambivalent, expressing a conflict between political pressures and the demands of foreign capital. While the IDA stressed the problems a social charter would present in attracting foreign investment, the government gave out contradictory signals. Clearly, adoption of the charter would have weakened Ireland's position within the division of labour by restricting working hours, shift work and other elements of capital intensive production.[20] It is clear that Ireland's position within the international division of labour is a marginal one and thirty years of effort have failed to find a combination of factors capable of attracting foreign capital on a large scale.

THE FAILURE OF INDUSTRIALIZATION

No country has ever industrialized on the basis of foreign industry alone. The purpose of attracting foreign investment is to create linkages with indigenous industry, leading to increased production and employment. The impact of foreign investment on a national economy cannot be accurately assessed because of the counterfactual question which will inevitably be posed: without foreign investment, would things have been better or worse? With respect to the Irish experience, there are some who would emphatically claim that Irish economic policy was (and is) an unmitigated disaster[21] while even semi-official reports are critical of the results.[22] Although the IDA was reasonably successful in its efforts to persuade foreign industry to locate in Ireland – there are now around 80,000 people employed in such industries, making up 34 per cent of the industrial work force[23] – the basic problem remains unresolved: foreign industry did not act as a locomotive for the development of indigenous industry. Although the country showed rates of economic growth in the 1970s higher than the EC average and the structure of exports changed from primary to manufactured products, the effect upon employment levels has been less than spectacular. The numbers employed in industry rose by 19,000 between 1973 and 1981 but by 1986 there were 43,700 fewer jobs than in 1980, leading to the return of emigration on a massive scale.[24] Of equal interest is the turnover of jobs in foreign industry. The 'defensible' nature of these jobs is questioned by the fact that 29 per cent of the jobs in existence in 1973 were gone by the end of the decade. Despite the vast effort and expenditure there are now fewer people employed in manufacturing industry than in 1950, a reality common to most western countries. The Irish case is significantly different because of the initial size of the agricultural sector and the failure to absorb the labour surplus which followed its contraction, and the inability of indigenous industry to expand in concert with foreign industrial investment.

The limited and uneven success of industrial development can in part be explained by the nature of Fordist spatial dispersal. Processes chosen for overseas location tend to be those manufacturing products which have passed, or have just reached, maturity in the production cycle. These are products which have gone through the process of conception, design, initial manufacture and modification in the core manufacturing plants and can now be mass produced without further input of research and design. Such products have begun the process of 'dematuring', since research for their replacement will already be underway. The main cost of production, at this stage, is the cost of labour. It makes sense therefore to locate such plants in areas of low wages and where government incentives will underwrite capital costs. There is strong evidence – lack of research and development activities, product type, rapid obsolescence, etc. – that it was this type of productive activity which was attracted to Ireland, producing commodities with a limited lifespan and a shrinking market share.[25]

The 1972 white paper, *Accession of Ireland to the European Communities*,[26] contained unambiguous projections concerning employment in manufacturing industry in the eight years after 1970. The projected average annual net job-creation was put at 6,000 and the annual growth rate in manufacturing output was put at 8.5 per cent. The reality was disappointing. Instead of 50,000 jobs, there was an increase of 20,000 and manufacturing output grew at 5.2 per cent annually. Unemployment, which the white paper predicted would fall, rose from 65,000 to 100,000 during the same period and has now reached 234,467.[27] Instead of narrowing, the gap between Irish living standards and those of the other EEC countries is tending to widen. The National Economic and Social Council (NESC) report, *Ireland in the European Community* sums up the effects of EEC membership in the following terms

On surveying the period since Ireland joined the Community it emerged that, overall, Ireland's economic performance compares unfavourably with that of other member countries. Both income and consumption have grown less than the average for the Community. Taking account of the job requirements of each country it is seen that Ireland has done very badly – the increase in unemployment between 1973 and 1985 was the second highest in the Community and Ireland now has the second highest unemployment rate. Ireland's relative employment rate is somewhat better – being slightly above average for the EC. Finally, this poor relative performance – in every area except total employment – has only been achieved at the cost of a very serious build up of the national debt.[28]

CONCLUSION

The structural position of Ireland within the global division of labour set parameters upon the process of economic development which the country has undergone since 1958. Ireland was unable to take advantage of Fordist methods to revitalize indigenous industry because of the resistance of local capital and the attempt to overcome this deficiency by a policy of attracting foreign industry had only limited success. The crisis of Fordism in the core states was only of marginal benefit to Ireland in terms of the relocation strategies of capital, and in the long run has destroyed the economic basis of the classic nationalist class alliance of small farmers, unskilled workers and the petit bourgeoisie, without putting anything in its place. In an attempt to compensate for falling rates of accumulation and the limited success of industrial policy, the state embarked upon deficit spending in the 1970s and provoked a fiscal crisis. Cuts in public expenditure, in response to the failure of deficit accounting, fell hardest upon the rural and urban poor and, combined with the collapse of industrial employment, led to a new wave of emigration.

The Irish state, therefore, faces twin crises: massive state deficit and unemployment. The policies pursued by the state in the search for economic growth have been spectacularly unsuccessful. The indirect approach to industrial development has brought about a situation where vast sums have been spent for dubious returns. Low corporation tax, and the repatriation of profits by multinationals – in 1986 the total outflow of profits, dividends and royalties was £1,346 million, some 7.6 per cent of GDP – has meant that expenditure on industrial development can never be self-financing. Whatever the global prospects for Fordist type industries it is becoming increasingly obvious that the problems facing Ireland are increasing: due to changes in production processes the cost of creating jobs has increased dramatically in the last decade without any evidence that industrial jobs are becoming more defensible. All the evidence indicates that after an initial period of expansion, jobs in foreign-owned industries either stagnate or contract.[29] The attempt to promote industrial development has had important social consequences. The class structure has become more polarized. The capitalist class is heavily subsidized by low corporation tax, massive subsidies and relatively low levels of personal taxation. The middle classes have managed to preserve their position by a near monopoly of access to higher education and the professions. The skilled working class is declining in size and many are being pushed into an increasingly marginalized 'underclass' of those dependent upon welfare benefits for survival. While the percentage of male unemployment in the middle classes (service class) stood at 3 per cent in 1981 the figure for the skilled manual sector was 15 per cent and the unskilled manual 49.4 per cent.[30]

It has been argued that the capitalist economy is embarking upon a new regime of accumulation, characterized by flexible accumulation. Harvey describes this new pattern of accumulation in the following terms

[Flexible accumulation] . . . rests on flexibility with respect to labour processes, labour markets, products and patterns of consumption. It is characterized by the emergence of entirely new sectors of production, new ways of providing financial services, new markets, and, above all, greatly intensified rates of commercial, technological and organizational innovation. It has entrained rapid shifts in the patterning of uneven development, both between sectors and between geographic regions, giving rise to service sector employment, as well as to entirely new industrial ensembles in hitherto underdeveloped regions.[31]

It is possible to discern, in much of the writing on the undeniable changes which are taking place, the creation of a new mythology for the 1990s[32] based upon a technological and institutional determinism. In this scenario a new localism and regionalism will be built around new types of flexible specialization and the regeneration of localities and regions. This form of utopianism underlies some of the more romantic interpretations of the impact of the single market on Ireland[33] and even hard-nosed official attempts to promote the horizontal integration of production around a core of foreign-owned computer related plants are not immune.

A significant aspect of these new developments, in the Irish context, is the impact upon the structure of the labour market. Established local labour markets, dominated by male industrial workers, are being unpicked and replaced by more flexible structures involving 'hyphenated work': part-time, self-employed, home-work, etc., and, of course, increasing participation of females in the labour force. Traditional local labour markets, in towns such as Drogheda and Dundalk, fell victim to the collapse of local industry in the face of foreign competition. The loss of 2,000 industrial jobs in Cork city in the last decade (most of them in foreign owned industries) shows that this process is continuing. While male participation in the labour force declined by 78,000 between 1979 and 1985, female participation rose by 11,000 and now constitutes over 30 per cent of the labour force. This compares with 56 per cent in Britain.

Figures from 1984 emphasize this trend. While male participation is declining, female participation is continuing to rise

Table 6.1 Irish labour force participation by gender

	1984	*1985*	*1986*	*1987*
males	922.0	917.1	915.1	911.5
females	384.9	385.2	393.3	407.7
persons	1,306.9	1,302.3	1,308.3	1,319.2

Source: *Central Statistics Office* 2 (1988) p. 7

In the United Kingdom over 40 per cent of the work force on non-regular work contracts and the number of part-time workers has risen by 3 million (to 5.9 million) since 1980. Similarily, in Ireland, some 15 per cent of female employment is part-time. The rhetoric of Irish industrial development policy is still directed at the promotion of 'defensible' male industrial employment and as such is out of tune with the shifting pattern of global accumulation. Nevertheless, the logic of capital is enforcing far-reaching changes in the Irish economy. The bitter debate and conflicts over 'dirty' industry is one aspect: fish farming and chemical plants[34] are two examples of industries which exploit a relatively unpolluted environment with the help of inadequate legislation. Popular resistance to these developments presents a dilemma for the state and in the finely balanced world of Irish electoral politics it is a dilemma not easy to resolve.

It is becoming increasingly obvious that the new international division of labour thesis, which links the development of industry in peripheral areas of cheap labour with the deindustrialization of the west, is no longer valid.[35] The classic Fordist model of accumulation, where long production runs of standard products for mass markets were typical, is being replaced, in some areas of production, by a more flexible system where product innovation and niche marketing is crucial. Long production runs are also involved, but of a changing variety of products in response to market demands. In large areas of production products no longer 'mature' but are subject to constant design innovation and production switches. The use of microprocessors is the technical basis for this shift. Because of the close interaction between research, design, marketing and production there is little incentive towards spatial dispersal of production. Indeed, the tendency towards territorially integrated production is visible in France, Germany and Italy.[36] There is little evidence, despite increasing awareness of change,[37] of a concerted response on the part of the Irish government to the rapid undermining of their industrial policy.

While these tendencies are visible it is important to stress that there has not been a fundamental shift from one regime of accumulation to another. If there is a post-Fordism, it is based upon the extension and intensification of many elements of the old order[38] as well as introducing new forms of accumulation. The Japanese system of partial decentralization – where rigid and centralized control goes hand-in-hand with complex subcontracting – retains and intensifies many of the characteristics of classic Fordism. Other factors, such as the decline in United States foreign investment[39] and the opening up of eastern Europe to capital will further complicate the situation.

With the decline of the male industrial worker the tendency towards a segmented labour market made up from a shrinking rigid sector (regular labour contracts, full-time work, etc.) and a flexible sector (part-time, non-regular contracts, increasing participation of badly paid female labour) will increase. This is a trend throughout the EC, which may attain a particular form in Ireland. The increasing emphasis on attracting firms in the financial services sector and the stress being placed upon the development of tourism may well increase the widening schism between well paid managerial, administrative and technical jobs and a low-paid, low-skill sector surviving, often on a part-time basis, on the 'trickle down' from middle-class consumption.

Although the changing nature of global accumulation is not under the control of any nation state, the potential influence of states upon the shifting pattern of uneven, or 'see-saw' development[40] should not be underestimated. The locational strategies of multinationals can be influenced by the policy of individual nation states, as has been demonstrated in the Irish case, however inadequate the outcome. Nevertheless, to ascribe blame for underdevelopment to the deficiencies of the local elite – as Lee does in the Irish case – is to ignore the importance of two further factors: the limited scope open to policy makers in a small dependent economy, and the fact that the various groups which go to make up the elite are in fact fractions of the bourgeoisie and as such will tend, historically, to act in concert to maximize the power and wealth of that class. It is facile to castigate the bourgeoisie for a failure to create full employment and end emigration when the interests of this class might well have been threatened by a well organized and self-confident working class. In the European context, the Irish middle class has seen fewer challenges to its hegemony – through class conflict, economic change or war – than any other national bourgeoisie. Increasing labour-market dualism may well consolidate the position of the middle classes by increasing the polarization between well paid administrative, technical and research employment and a low-wage sector, economically and socially dependent upon levels of middle-class consumption – a contemporary variant of the landlord–tenant relationship.

Notes

1 *See* J. J. Lee, *Ireland 1912–1985. Politics and Society* (Oxford: Oxford University Press 1989); R. Breen *et al.*, *Understanding Contemporary Ireland* (Dublin: Gill Macmillan, 1990). Along with these more general critical analyses of Irish society the unease about the effects of the single market is growing. *See* John O' Dowd, *Ireland, Europe and 1992* (Dublin: Tomar Publishing, 1989); Barry Brunt, *The Republic of Ireland* (London: Chapman, 1988).
2 Lee, op. cit., p. 612.
3 ibid., p. 627.
4 Breen, op. cit., pp. 101ff.
5 A. Lipietz, 'New tendencies in the international division of labour', in A. J. Scott and M. Storper, eds, *Production, Work, Territory* (London: Allen & Unwin, 1986).
6 K. Kennedy *et al.*, *The Economic Development of Ireland in the Twentieth Century* (London: Routledge, 1988) chapter 3.
7 *Economic Development*, Dublin, Stationery Office Pr 4796 (1958).
8 *See* P. Armstrong *et al.*, *Capitalism Since World War II* (London: Fontana, 1984); S. Marglin *et al*, *The Golden Age of Capitalism* (Oxford: Oxford University Press, 1989).

9   J. Meehan, *The Irish Economy Since 1922* (Liverpool: Liverpool University Press, 1970) p. 142.
10 *See* A. Lipietz, *Mirages and Miracles* (London: Verso, 1987) pp. 78ff.; D. Perrons, 'Unequal integration into global Fordism', in Scott and Storper, eds, op. cit.
11 *See* J. J. Lee, op. cit., chapter 3.
12 *See* M. Aglietta, 'Capitalism in the eighties', *New Left Review* 136 (1982) pp. 5–41.
13 K. Kennedy *et al.*, op. cit., p. 263.
14 *See* M. Aglietta, *A Theory of Capitalist Regulation* (London: Verso, 1979).
15 *See* H. Braverman, *Labour and Monopoly Capital* (New York: Monthly Review Press, 1974).
16 D. Harvey, *The Condition of Modernity* (Oxford: Blackwell, 1989) p. 126.
17 Lipietz calls this type of regime 'bloody Fordism' because of the political repression involved. *See Mirages and Miracles*, pp. 74ff.
18 National Economic and Social Council (NESC) 64, *A Review of Industrial Policy* (Telesis Report) (Dublin, 1982) p. 21.
19 Quoted in F. Frobel *et al.*, *The New Internalional Division of Labour* (Cambridge: Cambridge University Press, 1980) p. 123.
20 The social charter is, at present, no more than a statement of intent on the part of the Commission with regard to workers' rights. The first attempt to draft legislation (on the rights of part-time workers) has met with fierce opposition from some member states. *See* the *Independent* (16 April 1990).
21 *See* R. Crotty, *Ireland in Crisis; A Study in Capitalist Colonial Underdevelopment* (Dingle: Brandon, 1986). While Crotty's analysis of the impact of colonialism is convincing, he uncritically applies theories of colonialism to the contemporary situation.
22 NESC 64 (Telesis), op. cit.; NESC 88, *Ireland in the European Community: Performance, Prospects and Strategy* (Dublin, 1989).
23 NESC 64, p. 134.
24 Net emigration over the five years to 1991 is estimated at 25,000 a year. See Department of Finance, *Economic Review and Outlook*, Dublin, Stationery Office (1987).
25 NESC 64.
26 White Paper, Dublin, Stationery Office, Prl 2064 (1972).
27 CSO, *Labour Force Survey* (Dublin, 1989).
28 NESC 89, p. 524.
29 *See* D. O'Hearn, 'Estimates of new foreign manufacturing employment in Ireland', *Economic and Social Review* 18, 3 (1987) pp. 173–88.
30 Breen *et al.*, op. cit., chapter 3.
31 Harvey, op. cit., p. 247.
32 *See* S. Hall and M. Jacques, *New Times, The Changing Face of Politics in the Nineties* (London: Lawrence & Wishart, 1989); C. Sabel, 'Flexible specialization and the re-emergence of regional economies', in P. Hirst and J. Zeitlin, eds, *Reversing Industrial Decline* (Leamington Spa: Berg, 1989).
33 *See* R. Kearney, ed., *Across the Frontiers, Ireland in the 1990s* (Dublin: Wolfhound Press, 1988). *See*, in particular, the editors' introduction.
34 'Dumping poisons in our own backyard', *Irish Times* (5 December 1989); 'Smell of suspicion over Cork harbour', ibid. (26 September 1989); 'East

Cork to fight plan for toxic dump', *Sunday Tribune* (14 January 1990); 'The cheek of our "green" President', ibid. (7 January 1990).
35 *See* A. Scott and M. Storper, eds, op. cit., chapter 1.
36 *See* E. Makecki, 'Corporate organization of R and D and the location of technological activities', in *Regional Studies* 14 (1980) pp. 219–35. M. Dunford, 'Integration and underdevelopment' in Scott and Storper, eds, op. cit.,
37 NESC 88, chapters 8, 9. *See also* 'Europe isn't all free lunches', *Sunday Tribune* (17 June 1990).
38 See J. Hirsch, *Der Sicherheitsstaat* (Frankfurt/M, EVA, 1980).
39 *Industrial Policy* (Dublin: Stationery Office, PL 2491, 1984) p. 11.
40 *See* N. Smith, *Uneven Development* (Oxford: Blackwell, 1984).

7 The Protestant working class and the state in Northern Ireland since 1930

A problematic relationship

J. W. McAuley and P. J. McCormack

Over the past twenty years a common explanation of the Irish situation has dominated the debate within the left in Ireland. This position, also adopted by several revolutionary groups in Britain,[1] is one which seeks to explain the situation in terms of imperialism and colonialism. This understanding of events regards British imperialism as the cause of the situation in Northern Ireland. Consequently the starting point for any political programme is immediate British withdrawal. Furthermore, for many commentators a national liberation struggle is seen as a legitimate response and the Provisional Irish Republican Army (IRA) is seen as the vanguard of this struggle.

In discussing the contemporary crisis those who adopt this 'anti-imperialist' position regard divisions amongst Irish people as the result of 'false consciousness', the consequence of the divide-and-rule policies of imperialism. Central is the position of Protestant workers and the Protestant working-class (PWC) groups, which traditional Irish Marxism has tended to dismiss. Two themes dominate the discussion.

1) The PWC is considered a group with whom it would be foolish, if not impossible, to seek accommodation. The national liberation struggle should be pursued whatever the consequences for this section of the working class. The following statement elaborates this position

   > The structure of oppression built into the six counties state means that most social conflict takes the form of Nationalist resistance against Loyalist oppression. The Protestant working class has no existence as a class – it acts and fights as part of the Loyalist community.[2]

2) A second theme is that the PWC may be capable of participating in class politics but only after the advent of national liberation.

The guarantee of the link with British imperialism, provided by the British state and its military presence, locks the PWC into a position of false consciousness. The following statement from Sinn Féin members makes this position clear

> Over the centuries, Protestant workers and farmers have been taught that loyalty to the British Crown guaranteed them marginal privileges over their Catholic neighbours. Loyalism has thus become hopelessly entangled with the British state's military presence in Ireland, creating a colonialist aristocracy of labour dependent to a degree on the British military machine for employment.
>
> Before Loyalist workers can ever discover their real class interests, that military machine must be destroyed. Any attempt to delay struggle until the majority of Loyalists allow the scales of imperialism to drop from their eyes is misplaced.[3]

The theoretical bases of this conception can be expressed in a number of propositions

1) Working-class Unionism is a creation of the bourgeoisie and functions to further the interests of the capitalist class. Arising from an external source, the ideology of working-class Unionism is essentially the by-product of manipulation.
2) The internalization of this ideology leads inescapably to false consciousness. To the extent that Unionism involves class collaboration, to that extent it denies the basic contradictions and antagonisms between classes.
3) There are three major consequences

   (a) Because of false consciousness the PWC cannot be mobilized to challenge the hegemony of the capitalist class: the grave diggers of the bourgeoisie become the gate keepers.
   (b) The social structure ossifies. Since in capitalist society the class struggle is the catalyst for social transformation, the possibility of progressive development in the context of Northern Ireland is minimized.
   (c) There is a permanent division between the PWC and other sections of the working class.

Although it is not true to say that there is a definitive position on Ireland to which all Marxists subscribe (indeed a close reading reveals contradictory perspectives), nevertheless a large majority would accept all or most of the above.[4] Further, there is little doubt that it is a seductive and coherent analysis. However as it applies to Northern Ireland it raises a number of problems.

First, it would not be historically accurate to describe Northern Ireland since the 1930s as divided into two groups – a small capitalist class and a mass of proletarians. The large proportion of the population who live in rural areas and in small towns, independent traders (there are no 'tied pubs' in Northern Ireland), small farmers, artisans and rural labourers, constitute an important intermediate grouping or groupings in the stratification system and are interwoven into it.

Second, powerful reasons for class collaboration exist, and have existed in Northern Ireland. Nor is Northern Ireland unique in this context as a study of the miners' strike in Britain in 1984 would confirm. Given the historically high unemployment rates and the state of almost permanent economic crisis, the PWC, due to chronic deprivation and class fragmentation, had a perceived vested interest in the *status quo*.

Third, it is assumed, without sufficient evidence, that the PWC delivered its support with willing consent.[5]

In challenging the type of Marxist analysis mentioned at the outset, we will attempt to describe the nature of loyalist, urban, working-class communities; and to uncover the origins and types of resistance to hegemonic rule. At the same time we will try to make sense of the socio-political world of these communities – characterized at the national level by the fragmentation of Unionist politics, and at the ground level by the emergence of loyalist paramilitary groups.

The version of Marxism which has dominated in Ireland for a number of decades suggests that the political struggle and social ideologies of the PWC can be explained largely in terms of its defence of ancient privilege(s). Thus the existence of the Northern Ireland state is predicated on the material deprivation of Catholic workers, manifesting itself in an unequal distribution of scarce resources such as jobs and housing. It is largely because of the relationship of the Protestant masses to the state that Northern Ireland is deemed irreformable. Farrell[6] uses the term 'labour aristocracy' to refer to Protestant manual workers. This concept has a central place in traditional Marxist analysis of Northern Ireland. The analysis is, however, simplified. Protestant skilled workers are juxtaposed to Catholic unskilled workers. This has the consequence of abolishing Protestant unskilled workers from the analysis, hinders the search for evidence of differentiation in the class situation of different groups of manual workers and suggests a monolithic structure where none exists. In addition it is among the most skilled sections of the working class in Northern Ireland, as in Britain, that progressive, albeit reformist, ideas fall on most fertile ground. Militant loyalism was and is located primarily among the poorer and unskilled sections of the Protestant masses (but is not exclusive to them).

Labour aristocracy theory undoubtedly rested on incontrovertible differences between the Protestant and Catholic communities. There is, however, the danger of abstracting the notion to a level where it relinquishes its analytic utility and simply becomes an all-embracing label which conceals a complex phenomenon. As several writers[7] have shown, if the notion is to be of utility it must be used with the greatest precision. In the Northern Irish context it is necessary to avoid the danger of conflating the position of the aristocracy of labour (who remain after all, manual workers) with political elites. Nor must we forget that Foster's intention was to locate the concept as a product of a particular phase of capitalist development. The study of the periodization of capitalist development in Northern Ireland is far from advanced. Indeed there is a tendency by some writers within the anti-imperialist school to take the social structures of the 1890s and transpose them onto the 1990s. While the aristocracy of labour produces institutions and ideologies tending towards adaptation to the capitalist system, and this seems to be true of all societies, it is also the case that in mobilizing for struggle they assist other sections of the subordinate class who have their interests catered for at some level. It is this latter tendency which is ignored in the case of Northern Ireland.

Another non-Marxist outcome of some Marxist analysis of Northern Ireland is to see Northern Irish society as unique. This is particularly the case in discussions of unemployment. In the past twice as high as other parts of Britain, unemployment in Northern Ireland is now not all that different from some regions in Britain (e.g. the north east), and has to be seen as an outcome of global patterns of capital accumulation.

It is clear that labelling a whole section of the working class as 'unreformable' is only possible if we omit much working-class experience. To claim further that the 'Irish problem' flows simply from British imperialism manifesting itself in colonialism in the north and neo-colonialism in the south, is to underestimate the role of indigenous social actors. Even if we accept that working-class Unionism has its origins in ruling-class attempts to manage class relations, such efforts would hardly have been necessary if these relations had not been threatening in the first place. We therefore reject the view of

Protestant workers as 'pawns' to be manipulated at will by a ruling class. Our position is that hegemonic control was never total, was and is inherently unstable and cannot be taken for granted. Further we would like to get away from static views of the problem and to stress the dynamic nature of the situation.

Two processes characterize the present condition in Northern Ireland: hegemonic decline and a rapidly deteriorating economy. Some commentators assume that the involvement of the PWC in the state is a normative one: others see it as calculative. Given the deepening crisis in the economic and social spheres this involvement could become alienative. At the level of power an index of this would be a movement from remunerative power (the attempt to 'buy off' dissent) to coercive power (increased confrontation between the PWC and the 'security forces').

The Northern Ireland government, true to its conservative traditions, was always suspicious of large-scale interventions.[8] By the mid-1950s however, it had become clear that the traditional industrial base of shipbuilding, textiles and engineering could not guarantee a viable and prosperous economy. At this stage a policy of reindustrialization was adopted and external mobile capital was canvassed with large-scale grants. This policy was successful, for example, in attracting the largest concentration of artificial fibre capacity in Europe, a new rubber production industry and an important share of the rapidly growing telecommunications industry. These developments were organized around predominantly transnational firms which were looking for a strategic location in Europe and which were in addition keen to take advantage of the high levels of grant aid to 'top up' investment. Consequently unemployment, which had hovered around 90,000 in the interwar years, fell to 31,980 in 1961 and did not rise above 38,000 for the rest of the decade. However the boom was transitory and was undermined by the oil crisis of 1973. The transnational companies which had provided the engine of Northern Ireland's economic growth transferred production to minimal-labour-cost economies. Entire sections of industry closed down and, in their wake, small local supply firms shrank or went out of business. This was largely the case with synthetic fibres and rubber production. The flow of mobile capital dried up and, to make matters worse, the only major concerns attracted in recent years – namely Delorean and Learfan – proved to be economically disastrous.

In the unsettled economic conditions of Northern Ireland this was deindustrialization with a vengeance. Since 1979 it was the most highly capitalized and advanced sectors of industry which were devastated.

At the same time the decline of traditional industries continued apace. Since the end of the Second World War, Northern Ireland has been a fragment of an advanced capitalist economy, but its special characteristics, such as a high dependence on transnational capital, has made it extremely vulnerable to global operations. The task of reconstructing the Northern Irish economy is not simply an internal one but is comprehensively locked into the strategies of capital itself.

Differential access to power and privilege are crucial concerns in the analysis of Northern Irish society. It would, however, be a mistake to overestimate the direct effect of economics. The capital –labour relationship within the mode of production is not the only significant material relationship which acts as a determinant of political consciousness.[9] In Northern Ireland a social class identity has to compete with a religious one for saliency in the lives of individuals. The working class in most societies is internally differentiated in ways not directly attributable to economic interests. In advanced capitalist societies dual and segmented labour market theories have emerged to account for racial and sexual discrimination. The application of such an approach in Northern Ireland might explicate some of the issues involved in dealing with differences both within and between the two communities.

Any assessment of the current state of Irish society must be concerned not simply with 'macro' issues but also with 'micro' ones. It is necessary to examine the relevance of the religious identity to the way in which people experience the conditions of everyday life. In this context Allen has this to say

> Class analysis based on the concrete reality of capitalism should tell us about the formation and distribution of political allegiances not simply through voting patterns but through identification with policies over everyday affairs.[10]

It is in this way that contradictions within classes, for example racism, sexism or sectarianism can be exposed. Such contradictions may act on classes to alter their composition and determine experience. An examination at the micro level of analysis should explicate where, when and how divisions are made relevant in the context of political, economic and social action and lay bare the mechanisms involved in socialization and the transmission of subcultures.

First it is necessary to understand the degree of physical segregation in Northern Ireland and especially in Belfast, resulting from population movements and conflicts over territorial boundaries. Although physical boundaries have become much more clear-cut since the early 1970s, such divisions are far from new in the history of Belfast. The working-class neighbourhoods in Belfast took on a recognizable form as the city industrialized rapidly around the 1880s. This resulted in the development of distinct local social structures and segregation between Protestant and Catholic workers.[11] The values of this culture impose themselves at the material and social levels; physically, in the networks of streets, houses, pubs, etc., and socially, in the networks of kin, work, neighbourhood and recreation patterns.

These institutions are of course cross-cut by external forces. The structure of work and workplace links the local labour force to wider economic institutions. The overall effect of these cross-pressures is to create conditions which are socially very complex. Williams[12] has called this process 'bonding', and goes on to say that

> the institution of modern industry, especially in the most aggregated forms of factory, mill, mine, docks, shipyard, has produced in otherwise diverse cultures and societies, the characteristic forms of unionisation and some regular minority association of these with socialism.

It would seem strange to argue that this process has completely bypassed Belfast and the PWC. In Belfast as elsewhere, spatial unevenness of production combined with local particularities such as relationships with fellow workers, neighbours and kin generated characteristic forms of expression. It is necessary to highlight the political effects of location on the class structure. Quiescent political forms have developed among specific groups of workers, their vulnerability being structurally determined by particular conditions. An important consideration is how members of such groups perceive their own vulnerability. The relations of production which they experience are mediated by the manner in which they are socially constructed. Often the resultant situation prevails, not because the class is necessarily passive to ruling-class ideas, but because its perspectives are bounded by other immediate and practical concerns or limited to concrete situations.

The neighbourhood is thus bounded socially and economically. At one level, the horizontal, there are the ties which bind spaces and institutions to the neighbourhood, such as local culture and tradition. At the vertical level are those structures which lock it into the dominant institutions and culture.[13] Much attention has been given to the way in which the two religious communities have become polarized. Developments within each community are less well understood. In the urban Protestant community this period has witnessed the growth of self-help and support groups concerned, among other things, with loyalist prisoners. These groups not only create alternative institutions for the PWC, but at the same time establish an organizational platform to challenge the power of the dominant order. The emergence of these local organizations coincided with the fragmentation of Unionist politics at the national level. The relationship between the PWC and mainstream political parties could no longer be taken for granted but became a matter for negotiation. The Democratic Unionist Party (DUP) was to play an important part in filling the vacuum left by the demise of older allegiances.

It is easy to forget that it was not until 1979 that the DUP first won a seat in the heartland of the PWC – East Belfast. For half a century the Unionist leadership have not permitted economic or social issues to divide the party, although on some occasions dissension was just below the surface. East Belfast has a strong tradition of both Labour and Independent Unionist candidates. While the fragmentation of Unionism has been well documented, it is worthy of note that in addition to the main split in Unionism were others, flowing from working-class dissatisfaction. Some of the dissatisfied perceived the traditional leadership as being weak in the battle against the IRA. For others the leadership was completely distant from the needs and concerns of the PWC. Underlying both concerns was a widespread fear of betrayal by Britain. In this context the DUP has been to some extent a radical force within Unionism, articulating the feelings of distrust voiced by the PWC. While 'Paisleyism' has been characterized as ideologically middle class and politically proletarian, it is the latter which gives the DUP its momentum. Having split Unionism on a class basis an attempt was now made to reconstruct Unionist hegemony around the DUP. Historically, fissures within Unionism articulating such social grievances produced nothing more than short-term programmes. Most were easily absorbed by the adoption of more strident anti-Catholic posturings, which gave the Northern Irish state its specifically sectarian character. It was through the exercise of a special kind of power, that of being able to frame alternatives, and to win and shape consent, what Lukes has called the power to shape the agenda[14] that Unionist hegemony was maintained. One of the most enduring ideological effects of this among the Protestant masses has been the identification of their security with a particular type of control and repression, and the defence of the existence of the state.

As Northern Irish society split along communal lines in the early 1970s conflict and violence appeared at many levels. The dominant class still retained power but its range of options was reduced. The most striking example of this was the shift in the exercise of control from the mechanisms of 'consent' to those of 'coercion'. On the one hand there was the increasing use of the police, army and Ulster Defence Regiment (UDR), and on the other the use of 'legal repression' the most recent expression of which is the 'supergrass' system. It is this response which marks the real crisis of Ulster's ruling class. The DUP has been in the forefront of calls for stronger 'security' measures. It is because the agenda can be defined as centring on 'law and order' that support can be maintained from substantial sections of the PWC whose fear is that the Union is increasingly under threat.[15]

The relationship between the DUP and the PWC is not, however, a direct one. The DUP is quite capable of calling for increased state repression while at the same time organizing protests against closures and lay-offs in industry. Many DUP politicians and local councillors also have excellent records in pursuing day to day issues important in working-class areas such as housing, health and welfare matters. Here as elsewhere, 'anti-imperialist' commentators have tended to underestimate these aspects of PWC consciousness.

In the course of the present crisis not all sections of the PWC have been content to express grievances through parliamentary political parties. Those who can be classified as extra-parliamentary range from paramilitary groups to the plethora of community groups and housing associations that have grown up since the demise of Stormont. At first sight the Ulster Freedom Fighters and the East Belfast Housing Association may seem strange partners. Without wishing to deny the sectarian nature of their military activities it should be remembered that the Ulster Defence Association (UDA) also engages in non-military activities. Deriving from a common root, the social world of the PWC, it is hardly surprising to find in these organizations a tendency, however muted at times, to challenge the dominant culture. Before 1969 the PWC had been encouraged to believe that its right to exist and its livelihood were guaranteed by the existence of the Stormont parliament, the Unionist party and the Orange Order.[16] Thus to oppose or even criticize the state was to display evidence of 'disloyalty'.

However the traditional, densely populated, urban PWC communities did provide some sort of supportive environment for protest. These communities based largely on neighbourhood values and organized around extended family and friendship networks were geographically stable. They displayed a great deal of cultural homogeneity and welded all age groups into a morally dense collectivity. The UDA emerged from these communities and their initial programme was a bloody campaign of sectarian murders. In time a gulf arose between sections of the loyalist paramilitaries and traditional Unionist political parties. Demands for a more coherent social and political programme were now made from within the UDA. This independent line with a crudely class-conscious base continued to evolve throughout the early 1970s[17] and resulted in much internal tension and even assassinations within the organization.

These developments, however, were largely overshadowed by the events of the Ulster Workers' Council strike. Following the stoppage much of the effort of the UDA began to be channelled into other activities. The strike had seen an unprecedented mushrooming of voluntary groups involved in 'welfare' at a local level. The Ulster Community Action Group (UCAG) established itself as an amalgamation of various groupings and was closely connected to the UDA. These developments encouraged some paramilitaries to seek a more direct political role. This initiative however failed miserably and precipitated a crisis of confidence in many loyalist districts amidst allegations of 'gangsterism' and the exploitation of 'ordinary people' whom the UDA were supposedly protecting. Much of the direction taken by the UDA since then reflects these considerations and the attempts to resolve the problems of legitimation and community trust.

Since the mid-1970s there have been identifiable lines of tension within the organization. While many UDA members remain committed to a military campaign to 'terrorize the terrorists' there have also been a series of political initiatives within the organization. The UDA has consistently promoted the idea of an 'independent Ulster' as a solution to the problems of Northern Ireland. The UDA has also made an effort to strengthen its position at the community level and recently relaunched the UCAG. The latest development has been a new set of proposals set out in a document entitled 'Commonsense' which envisages a power-sharing, devolved government in Northern Ireland.

In the immediate post-Anglo-Irish Agreement period, Unionist hegemony reconstituted itself as it was always likely to do when faced with a perceived constitutional threat. It did so around the Democratic Unionist party, which best articulated Unionist resistance. As Bew and Patterson put it

Although the history of Protestant politics is replete with divisions on democratic and class issues, on the national question, even in its more humane and liberalised post-Forum form, there is no significant intra-unionist division. The liberals and the neanderthals make common cause.[18]

The Unionist political leadership clearly believed that, as in the UWC strike, it would be the paramilitaries who would provide the 'cutting edge' of loyalist protests. Key elements within the UDA quickly excluded themselves from the direct control of the Unionist leadership. This was in part because sections of the UDA leadership clearly supported a more actively military role. Signs of disillusionment emerged as early as January 1986 as can be seen from the following statement

> In view of . . . the lack of a real plan to deal with the constitutional crisis we find ourselves in, we, the Ulster Nation, are entitled to ask what our Politicians have been doing since last November and where they are going? While they dither, others wait with increasing impatience and concern.[19]

An additional source of criticism concerned the political role of the Unionist leadership. As one of the UDA leaders put it, 'What we lack is a clear and decisive leadership and a co-ordinated plan of action.'[20] The hostility of this section of the UDA was based on recent experiences with loyalist politicians, particularly on the issue of loyalist prisoners. It is here that class differences within Unionism are most acutely felt. The idea that paramilitary members were being used as 'cannon fodder' gained ground. This feeling was compounded by the reluctance of Official Unionists, and to some extent Democratic Unionists, to become involved over the issue of segregation of loyalist and Republican prisoners. The loyalist ex-prisoners association has warned of the dangers of manipulation by Unionist politicians, claiming they had repeatedly plunged the community into turmoil by their 'cul-de-sac politics'.[21] At the same time as some UDA members were active in street protests and sectarian violence, others were working in advice centres and loyalist prisoner welfare groups. The expression of politics from within PWC communities is not uniform.

The overall picture then is one in which it is no longer possible to describe PWC culture as unidimensional. By definition class conflict cannot disappear until the relations which produce and sustain it disappear. It can, however, be more or less formal, or more or less institutionalized. The position of the PWC is clearly not settled. It is not an irredeemably reactionary movement. Too often socialists have been content to look no further than the surface signs of loyalism and define the Protestant population in Northern Ireland as one undifferentiated reactionary mass, which has no part to play (except an antagonistic one) in working-class struggle. It may be more fruitful to conceive of the balance of class forces within the PWC as remaining open. As a class it is not necessarily passive to ruling-class ideas even if its perspectives are often constrained by immediate political concerns. It is this which forms much of the material base and rationality of working-class 'economism' in Northern Ireland. Part of the reason why the idea of an independent Ulster has failed to attract the support of any substantial sections of the PWC is that many in that class still regard the link with Britain as the basic guarantee of their well being. Activities by PWC organizations have created lines of resistance to the dominant capitalist hegemony, although they are somewhat constrained by the continual search for an alternative basis of legitimacy. The latter is crucial if one is fully to understand the importance of loyalist paramilitary groups in loyalist politics.

Given the different range of experiences within the PWC, a serious analysis of its politics and ideology must incorporate all of these concerns. Ideology marks out the framework of thought through which Protestant workers make sense of and give meaning to their social and political world. It is this framework which imposes a certain logic in looking at the world and which structures and confines the concepts, ideas and language used to explain that world. Social and political thought is not open ended. Although there are a diverse range of views within the PWC, each member constructs his or her own world-view out of the limited range of ideas to which he or she is exposed. It is necessary to try to construct the broad contours of social thought which dominate the Protestant working-class world.

Northern Irish society has, since the outbreak of the current phase of the conflict, experienced complete destabilization of political and ideological relations. The shattered hegemony of the Unionist ruling class allows Protestant workers to intervene in political struggle, even if such intervention remains confused and contradictory.

To account for the internal construction of loyalism as an ideology, and the logic which shapes its contemporary direction, it is necessary to give a detailed charting of the limits of that ideology; of what is included and omitted from the formulation of that ideology. Marxists writing from an anti-imperialist perspective simply do not provide the necessary tools for this. These analyses project Protestant working-class consciousness and politics as stable and homogeneous. However, an adequate construction of the ideology of Protestant workers involves some attempt to account for their everyday values, everyday beliefs and everyday conceptions of the world. Protestant working-class ideology, like many actually experienced class ideologies is fragmentary, internally contradictory and constituted from incomplete forms of thought. It is within this framework that everyday 'commonsense' political decisions are made. This thinking is based on a set of common historical reference points, diluted and confused ideologies, sectarian prejudices and inherited values and ideas. It is this which enables working-class supporters of the DUP to talk on the one hand of 'upholding democracy' while on the other refusing to work with elected Sinn Féin councillors. It also explains why they can simultaneously promote stronger 'law and order' policies and campaign against 'Thatcherite cuts'. It is this direct link into a strong collective identity and its ability to express the broad set of ideas commonly held within the PWC community which partly explains the success of the DUP. It also partly explains the political failure of the UDA. In trying to construct a new 'independent' identity, the UDA is at variance with the self-conception and everyday ideology of the PWC.

It is at this level that the politics of the PWC is best understood. By focusing in detail on the construction of PWC ideology it is possible to move away from the cruder forms of historical materialism adopted by those anti-imperialist analysts who conceptualize PWC political action as a reflection of material interests. This position reduces PWC ideology to a wholly dependent status, a deliberate cover for sectional interests. However a proper understanding of activities at the community level should facilitate a reopening of the agenda. Marxists should be interested in the outcome of research at this level and resist any temptation for a premature closure of the debate. An effective analysis of class formation must not make presuppositions about its form. In addition it must incorporate all those aspects of behaviour which sustain the social structure. To do otherwise is to dismiss a huge range of working-class experience. The politics and ideology of the PWC clearly remain problematic. However it is only by examining the full range of PWC experience and the social construction of its ideology that the politics of the PWC can be fully understood.

Notes

1 This traditional 'anti-imperialist' analysis is best represented by works such as L. De Paor, *Divided Ulster* (Harmondsworth: Pelican, 1970), M. Farrell, *Northern Ireland: The Orange State* (London: Pluto Press, 1976), E. McCann, *War and an Irish Town* (London: Pluto Press, 1972) and G. Adams, *The Politics of Irish Freedom* (Kerry: Brandon, 1986). It also links these works with most of the leading Trotskyist groupings in Britain and with organizations such as Troops Out and Time to Go.

2 Irish Freedom Movement, *An Anti-Imperialist's Guide to the Irish War* (Belfast: Junius Publications, 1983) p. 85.

3 Sinn Féin members, 'open letter', cited in Communist Party of Ireland, *Armed Struggle* (Belfast: Unity Press, 1988) p. 7.

4 There is of course another 'school' of Irish Marxist thought which can loosely be termed as 'revisionist'. Although by no means coherent, revisionist positions are represented in the British and Irish Communist Organization: *Ireland Two Nations* (Belfast: Athol Press, 1971), *The Economics of Partition* (Belfast: Athol Press, 1972), *The Birth of Ulster Unionism* (Belfast: Athol Press, 1984), A. Boserup, 'Contradictions and struggles in Northern Ireland', *Socialist Register* (1972), B. Probert, *Beyond Orange and Green* (London: Zed Press, 1978), T. Nairn, *The Break up of Britain* (London: NLB, 1981), P. Bew, P. Gribbon and H. Patterson, *The State in Northern Ireland, 1921–72* (Manchester: Manchester University Press, 1980), P. Bew and H. Patterson, *The British State and the Ulster Crisis* (London: Verso, 1985) and H. Patterson, *The Politics of Illusion: Republicanism and Socialism in Modern Ireland*, (London: Hutchinson Radius 1989). Although it fits most comfortably within the 'anti-imperialist' school the work of L. O'Dowd, B. Rolson and M. Tomlinson, *Northern Ireland: Between Civil Rights and Civil War* (London: CSE Books, 1980) represents another alternative analysis. They argue that sectarian divisions are a class phenomenon, hence the British state must recognize and work within pre-existing divisions in society. To do otherwise would be to involve the state itself in the impossible task of transforming class divisions (ibid., pp. 24–6).

5 Bell, op. cit., p. 15.

6 Farrell, op. cit., p. 11 and pp. 16–17.

7 See for example the works of E. J. Hobsbawm, *Labouring Men* (London: Weidenfeld & Nicolson, 1964), J. Foster, *Class Struggle and the Industrial Revolution* (London: Weidenfeld & Nicolson, 1974), R. Q. Gray, *The Labour Aristocracy in Victorian Edinburgh* (Oxford: Oxford University Press, 1976), *The Aristocracy of Labour in Nineteenth Century Britain* (London: Macmillan, 1981).

8 See for example Probert, op. cit., p. 71, Farrell, op. cit., pp. 81–120, Bew *et al.*, op. cit., pp. 102, 128.

9 As O'Dowd *et al.* argue, sectarian divisions are themselves a material reality 'which has been constituted and re-constituted throughout the history of capital accumulation and class struggle in Ireland as a whole', op. cit., p. 25.

10 V. Allen, 'The differentiation of the working class', in A. Hunt, ed., *Class and Class Structure* (London: Lawrence & Wishart, 1977) p. 64.

128　*J. W. McAuley and P. J. McCormack*

11　P. Gibbon, *The Origins of Ulster Unionism: The Formation of Protestant Politics and Ideology in Nineteenth Century Ireland* (Manchester: Manchester University Press, 1975).

12　R. Williams, *Towards 2000* (Harmondsworth: Penguin, 1985) p. 166.

13　S. Hall and T. Jefferson, eds, *Resistance Through Rituals, Youth Sub-Cultures in Post-War Britain* (London: Hutchinson, 1977) p. 43.

14　S. Lukes, *Power: A Radical View* (London: Macmillan, 1975) pp. 23–4.

15　Bell, op. cit., p. 47.

16　H. Griffiths, 'Community action and voluntary involvement', in J. Darby and A. Williamson, eds, *Violence and the Social Services in Northern Ireland* (London: Heinemann, 1978) p. 166; Probert, op. cit., p. 58.

17　For detailed accounts of loyalist paramilitary politics at this time *see* D. Boulton, *The UVF: 1966–73* (Belfast: Torc Books, 1973), S. Nelson, *Ulster's Uncertain Defenders* (Belfast: The Blackstaff Press, 1984), Probert, op. cit., pp. 137–41.

18　Bew and Patterson, 1985, op. cit., p. 45.

19　Editorial in *Ulster Magazine*, January 1986.

20　John McMichael, *Fortnight*, March 1986, p. 5.

21　Sunday News, 1 February 1987.

8 Tearing the house down
Religion and employment in the Northern Ireland Housing Executive

Donald Graham

The Northern Ireland Housing Executive (NIHE) was created in 1972 by the British government, with the objective of taking public-sector housing provision out of the hands of local government, which was dominated by Unionists. It inherited 146,000 dwellings and 2,200 staff who had been employed in the various housing authorities. The executive board is primarily composed of government appointees. As such it is a body wholly controlled by the Department of the Environment, accountable only to government ministers for both its housing management policies and its employment practices. The direct responsibility for employment is therefore inescapable. The authority's often patronizing and ill informed housing management practices are only over-shadowed by its recruitment policies at the individual and general level. The merits of this statement may be evaluated by beginning with an examination of its personnel department.

THE MAN AT THE TOP

Oliver Kearney is a Catholic and a nationalist. Although not unusual traits for an Irishman, they can sometimes mark people out for special treatment. As the executive's personnel manager with responsibility for recruitment, his religion placed him in an exposed position. The Ulster Volunteer Force's journal *Combat*[1] accused him of discriminating against Protestants during his long service at the executive. *Combat* further noted, 'he was seen walking behind the tricolour-draped coffin', of the brother of Peter Shevlin, his colleague in the personnel department. The UVF warned 'all concerned that the loyalists are not going to take this lying down'. This direct warning, combined with a series of internal manoeuvrings by senior management, led to Kearney's resignation on 30 November 1982. He also ended up in Belfast's Recorders Court, suing the late Unionist MP Harold McCusker for libel.

As Oliver Kearney was personnel manager from the NIHE's inception until 1982, his case merits particular attention. The problems arose from an exchange of correspondence between McCusker and then chairman of the executive, Charles Brett, at the height of the 1981 hunger strike by the Irish Republican Army (IRA) and the Irish National Liberation Army (INLA). McCusker began by alleging that housing policies were undermining the safety of his constituents. He was extremely concerned that areas formerly 'safe' for members of the Royal Ulster Constabulary (RUC) and Ulster Defence Regiment (UDR) to live were no longer safe. He further complained 'numerous estates [are] Roman Catholic but none of any size 100% Protestant'. McCusker also asked why it was that 'in my constituency 4 out of 5 district managers are Roman Catholic', and 'why in the Newry district where there are approximately 100 Housing Executive employees are they approximately 100% Catholic'. He added, 'Why when the Executive recently recruited graduate trainees were 75% Roman Catholic. . . . Should I be surprised when your Personnel Manager and his Deputy are Roman Catholic and when the interview panel for Manager Trainees are predominantly Roman Catholic if not 100% so.'[2]

The late Robert Bradford, MP, pursued the issue in the House of Commons. He accused the executive of having 'a dreadful record in discriminatory' acts against Protestants, and firmly laid the responsibility at the door of the personnel department. Bradford further suggested that discrimination also included its building programme, because it had 'swallowed the lie that persistent and systematic discrimination in housing existed in Northern Ireland [against Catholics]'.[3] The DOE was urged to instruct the local Fair Employment Agency (now Commission), to conduct an immediate investigation.

Against this hostile background, Kearney's libel case was heard in Belfast during April 1983. Judge Ian Higgins found that McCusker's allegations were 'false and injurious' and 'that the words complained of are defamatory'. He added that McCusker's 'conclusions owed more to prejudice than to reason or logic'. Despite this, the judge dismissed the case on the grounds that the comments were covered by parliamentary privilege, as McCusker had used House of Commons headed notepaper. Higgins concluded that as McCusker had believed 'in the truth of what he wrote', 'malicious intent was absent'.[4]

Oliver Kearney may be forgiven for not sharing the judge's learned opinion. While this very public affair was being pursued, Kearney had come under intense pressure from within the organization.

When his own immediate director, Mr Mander, advised him he was 'politically unacceptable', because of McCusker's allegations, he resigned. During the libel case McCusker declined to name the informant who had provided personal details about Kearney, on the grounds that to do so would jeopardize the career of one of the executive's most senior managers. At a later industrial tribunal over constructive dismissal, Kearney expressed his belief that this source lay in the chief executive's office.

Although a senior manager's professional and personal integrity had been seriously maligned by an unknown informant, the housing executive did not conduct any internal inquiry, nor did it question its most senior managers. The political nature of this may be gauged by the advice given by Mander to Kearney in 1982, before his resignation. He warned of the possible inflammatory consequences of McCusker's letters during the forthcoming Assembly elections, and directed Kearney to 'correct' the proportion of Catholics in the personnel department by taking disciplinary action against specific individuals named by McCusker. A transfer to the Eastern Health and Social Services Board was also suggested.

A further twist in the intrigue occurred in the year after Kearney's resignation when PA Management Consultants in Belfast advertised for a manpower services manager, for an unnamed client. Kearney applied and was interviewed on 28 October. On 7 November, PA confirmed his place on the short list. But he heard nothing more. The employer turned out to be the housing executive: no appointment was made. Kearney lodged a formal complaint with the Fair Employment Agency (FEA) on 30 January 1984. Three and a half years later this lethargic body concluded that no unlawful discrimination had occurred.

Another *cause célèbre* was the case of Paul Shevlin, a colleague of Kearney in the NIHE personnel department. Charles Brett, former chairman, advised Kearney on 18 August that the 'Board still harbour deep suspicion of your association with Shevlin'. McCusker had included Shevlin in his public diatribes. The individuals felt that their personal association was one of the reasons for the concerted campaign against the personnel department. Mander had attempted summarily to dismiss Shevlin in July 1983. This followed an auditor's report alleging corruption over the recruitment of a training consultant, and a newspaper article in the *Andersontown News* which alleged that three Catholics in personnel were being discriminated against. Only Charles Brett's direct intervention prevented Shevlin's dismissal. He was, however, suspended and subjected to the humiliating experience of being supervised by a senior security officer while clearing his desk before being publicly escorted from the building. Brett stressed his 'confidence in the integrity' of Mander and referred to staff suffering from an 'incurable chips' syndrome.[5] Shevlin in turn submitted a fourteen-page document alleging political victimization of himself and three others, including Kearney.

Brett rejected the submission, calling it 'a farrago of half-truths, false inferences and malicious innuendo'. Shevlin later won a case of unfair dismissal at an industrial tribunal in April 1984. Mander's actions were criticized as 'unreasonable and unwarranted'. But the executive refused either to reinstate Shevlin or to give reasons for failing to do so.

PATTERNS OF EMPLOYMENT

Amidst this chaos, the Environment Minister gave Unionists an assurance that he would direct the FEA to conduct an inquiry with specific reference to Protestant claims. Brett, for his part, welcomed any proposed investigation. However the FEA chairman advised Brett, 'There has as yet been no contact from the Minister. . . . The agency is not therefore in a position at the moment to determine what action should be taken.' Instructions arrived in July and the FEA finally issued a notice of investigation on 29 March 1982.

In the interim, Brett had maintained correspondence with McCusker. Brett advised him that although 'he should regard (it) as a highly retrograde step', if the religious affiliation of job applicants were recorded, some 'trial balances', 'so to speak' had been recorded. These secret trawls revealed 'the total staff of the executive divides somewhere between 66:33 and 50:50 in favour of the Protestant community'. A 'preponderance of Protestants' in certain areas was attributed to the numbers of staff 'inherited' by the executive from those local authorities previously responsible for housing provision. In addition, Brett provided McCusker with the religious breakdown of the staff in his own constituency.[6] Six days later Brett advised McCusker that any absence 'due to voluntary participation in political activities (attendance at marches or funerals in support of Hunger Strikers) will be reported with a view to possible disciplinary action'.[7] Declining this palliative, McCusker replied by further criticizing Brett for suggesting that only in some areas 'there may be a preponderance of Protestants – in fact there should *always* [his emphasis] be so if your employment practices are in keeping with the objective of the FEA'.[8]

The investigation by the FEA took over three years to complete. Although ready early in 1985, its issue was delayed until October, well after the marching season. With a legendary reputation to sustain, the FEA firmly concluded that 'by and large equality of opportunity in employment is being provided by the Northern Ireland Housing Executive for both Protestants and Roman Catholics . . . further detailed investigation of recruitment and promotion was not necessary'.[9] 'By and large' – what this concept means in terms of equal opportunities is not amplified. The inside story, supplied by Unionism's informant in the higher echelons of the executive, claimed that the draft report had been sent to the Northern Ireland Office (NIO) for final vetting and alteration. No attempt was made in the report to address the specific issues raised by the Kearney case, McCusker's allegations or the replies given by Brett. In place of a rigorous examination, the FEA merely recommended that the executive adopt the government's voluntary guidance code on equal opportunities. No targets were set nor were the executive required to submit regular monitoring reports. The FEA simply washed their hands of the affair.

AN INVESTIGATION IN MOTION

The FEA's investigation was limited to 3,500 non-industrial workers, thereby excluding 1,500 of the executive's employees. In the preface to the final report, the FEA recorded its mandate. They said the inquiry was a direct response to 'problems in the Executive which suggested that in some areas there was discrimination against Protestants'. It was a full year before the FEA sent out a (voluntary) questionnaire to executive staff. All parties involved knew that this was a futile approach. However it was not until June 1984, two years after the original notice of inquiry, that the elementary task of examining personnel records to establish religious affiliation was embarked upon. Even then only the most general and uninformed approach was adopted. For example, the housing executive is divided into six major administrative regions, and appears to offer reasonable access to employment for the whole population. The opportunity for examining employment practices at the local and province-wide level thus presented itself. Some district offices had well established reputations for sectarianism in housing circles. For example, local management at the Shankill district office combined their contempt for the local Protestant population they served with hostility towards any Catholic employee unfortunate enough to be seconded there.

Membership of the Orange Order was almost a condition of employment. Situations such as this were common knowledge, yet management failed to take any positive action.

The FEA determined that detailed investigation 'was not necessary'. In overall terms the composition of the work force examined turned out to be 61.9 per cent (2,172) Protestant and 36.6 per cent (1,284) Catholic, with 1.6 per cent (55) others or unidentified. In the primarily Catholic southern and western regions, the proportion of Catholics, at 7–10 per cent, was lower than the population figures would lead one to expect. In the south the 410 staff were 45 per cent Catholic (55 per cent population); in the west, the 246 staff were 50 per cent Catholic (the population 57 per cent). In terms of occupational patterns, the FEA expressed its satisfaction with 'the single exception of technical services'. Of 354 staff, 71.2 per cent were Protestant, 26.3 per cent Catholic and 2.2 per cent others. When further analysed by region, serious patterns of inequality were apparent with Protestants outnumbering Catholics by a factor of anything between two and seven.[10]

The reasons for this disparity were not explored. No questions were asked or recommendations made. The concept of targeting, or developing specific employment programmes, was not raised: surprising perhaps for a body which had been established with a brief to eliminate discrimination in housing. Only for the north west, as a result of 'particular allegations about over-representation by Roman Catholics in Londonderry' by loyalists, was a specific analysis presented. The overall figures for the region were 52 per cent Catholic, 45 per cent Protestant and 7.6 per cent others. The population in the region was 56 per cent Catholic. In the Protestant north east Protestants held 81 per cent of the jobs and represented 77 per cent of the population. In the north west the only comparable figure for Catholics occurred in the Derry district office. There, 72 (69.9 per cent) of the work force were Catholics as compared to 31 Protestants. Within the north-west region, only in Strabane did Catholics exceed the number of Protestant workers (18 RC; 15 P). In the three other district offices, Magherafelt, Coleraine and Limavady, Protestants accounted for 66 per cent (60) of the 91 staff. In the north east, by comparison, it was only in the tiny Ballycastle office where Catholics exceeded Protestants (8 RC; 5 P). In the other seven offices the proportions ranged from a high of 25.5 per cent (11) in Antrim to a low 9 per cent (6) Catholics in the two offices at Newtownabbey. The majority of Catholics employed, 958 of a total of 1,284, in the executive occupied administrative and clerical grades. Of the employees inherited by the executive, 607 (17.3 per cent) were still employed. This group alone filled 3.5 per cent (86) of senior management positions. Seventy of them were Protestants. From the pool of 224 managerial staff (i.e. Principal Officer 1 and above), 67 (27.5 per cent) were Catholic.

In one year, 1980, more Catholics were recruited than Protestants. The executive explained this was due to the appointment of 226 supernumerary staff who later became permanent. Furthermore, contrary to Brett's claims that religion was never monitored, it was revealed that the executive board were so concerned at this phenomenon that they instructed that the recruitment should be investigated. This showed that 55 per cent of the recruits were Catholic, but 'no improper discrimination' had occurred. Why the recruitment of Catholics should be a cause for concern was not questioned. But the FEA failed to follow it up. Instead it opted for the safe conclusion that discrimination had occurred, but only in the past, particularly in the group inherited by the executive from local councils and the former housing trust. The apparently sectarian machinations at senior management level and the public scandal of the Kearney and Shevlin cases indicates at the very least, that the FEA's platitudes were not sufficient.

In general terms, the management problems can be demonstrated by the fact that the executive regularly tops the league of grievances to the Commissioner of Complaints, accounting for 60 per cent of its annual workload. In January 1986 the policy of adjournment in protest at the Anglo-Irish Accord was implemented by the loyalist dominated executive board. In December 1986 two executive officials who were founding members of the Fair Employment Trust, a body set up to promote equal opportunities and the MacBride Principles, were advised that their duties 'were incompatible with membership of the Trust on the grounds that the MacBride principles are contrary to the employment laws of Northern Ireland'. The Trust declared of this 'legal' opinion was no more than an attempt to 'subject our members to political intimidation in its most sinister form'.[11] Formal protests were registered by Irish-American groups, the Labour party, Sinn Féin and the Social Democratic and Labour Party. The Trust also asked pertinent questions about what the executive had done about employees who were members of 'the Masonic Order, the Orange Order, the Ulster Clubs' and other political groupings. During 1987, the Trust claimed that its members were threatened with the sack and denied internal promotion. Their trade union, the Northern Ireland Public Service Alliance (NIPSA), condemned the executive's action and accused it of breaking its own code of conduct. NIPSA asserted the rights of its members to 'belong to any legal organisation'. It is perhaps worth recalling at this point the chairman, Charles Brett's confidence in the integrity of his management team and his belief that 'we have established a reputation for fairness and impartiality' and his pleasure that board members 'leave their prejudices outside in the umbrella stand'.

In Northern Ireland, loyalists carry their prejudices under their black marching bowlers. One feels there should be a law against it, but of course there is, 'by and large'.

FUTURE PATTERNS

In April 1989 the executive announced the introduction of a database to monitor its work force. Taking 3 July 1988 as its starting point, the work force was found to be 54.5 per cent (1,788) Protestant and 41.6 per cent (1,366) Catholic, with no religions assigned to those educated outside the north.

The technical services division remained dominated by Protestants (60 per cent, 599 Protestant; 34 per cent, 377 Catholic). At the regional level inequalities persisted in the north east and south east. Protestants accounted for 76.2 per cent (304) and 70 per cent (305) of the staff respectively. In the two regions where Catholics form the majority, the west and north west, the respective figures were 55.9 per cent (133) and 60.2 per cent (241). The analysis by grades confirmed that Protestant representation was higher at middle and senior management levels than their overall percentage in the work force (63.4 per cent, 473), Catholic proportions were correspondingly lower (30.6 per cent, 228). Above Principal Officer 2 level, the religious composition was 53.8 per cent (28) Protestant and 21.2 per cent (11) Catholic. The longer service record for Protestants was reflected in their seniority and higher rates of wastage through retirement.[12]

This database, which anticipated the new Fair Employment Act (NI) of 1989, offered a distinct improvement on the FEA's efforts. No excuse can now be given for being unaware of the effects of recruitment and promotion practices.

AROUND THE HOUSES

In 1968 the Cameron Report[13] concluded that 'Council housing policy has also been distorted for political ends in the unionist controlled areas . . . houses have been built and allocated in such a way that they will not disturb the political balance'. The government of the day accepted the charges of discrimination were 'justified in fact'. This led to the creation of the NIHE some four years later. The transfer of 2,200 staff and housing responsibilities took place between 1971 and 1973. The 'democratic' input to housing was to be provided by the Unionist controlled Housing Council: it was allowed to nominate three persons to join the six other government appointees to form the executive board. As an advisory body representing the twenty-six district councils it has yet to nominate a non-Unionist. The NIHE's current stock is approximately 177,000 dwellings and 3,515 staff. In 1972–3 it was left to pick up the tab for twenty years of public neglect by the Stormont regime, which had placed public sector provision at least twenty years behind Britain. One in five, or 19.6 per cent of the total housing stock was statutorily unfit (89,370 dwellings); 60 per cent of these were in Belfast, with over 40,000 in need of urgent repair.

If the physical problems were not daunting enough, the whole planning process was tainted by the sense of acute Unionist paranoia. In Dungannon, for example, which was one of the major starting points of the civil-rights movement, housing was a contentious issue. In 1963, Dungannon had approximately 300 families on the waiting list, some had been on it for as long as twelve years, yet not one new Catholic family had been allocated a permanent house for thirty-four years. Of the 204 houses built since 1944 in the area of the Dungannon Catholic parish, two had been allocated to Catholic families.[14]

This legacy is also evident in the much larger example of the creation of a new town, Craigavon, and the location of a new university at Coleraine. Controversy over these decisions raged, as many felt the north's maiden city, Derry, to be the obvious choice as an area in desperate need of investment and with the opportunity to build on the historical educational centre in the town. Derry, however, is Catholic, with Unionists then holding power only through skilful gerrymandering. Over £500m was spent on the new 'rainbow' city which was to cover 100 square miles with a population target of 100,000. As with most Unionist grand designs it proved to be an expensive failure: whole public sector estates had to be demolished because of poor design, the inability to persuade people to live in Craigavon because it was so isolated and lacked a proper infrastructure around the estates. With eleven roundabouts, it rapidly became known as the place where people 'went round and round in a futile search for an escape route'.

The English architect appointed to design the new city publicly resigned, making a 7,000 word statement. He said he had been 'asked to engineer propaganda rather than a new city', and that Derry was the most obvious choice as a centre for industrial development and higher education.[15] Like Craigavon, the university failed. In 1985 it was obliged, in order to survive, to merge with the Ulster Polytechnic and Magee College in Derry. The alternative presented by government was closure. Craigavon's unemployment rate averages 26 per cent and its population targets have never been reached. The local council actively participates in measures which enhance its reputation for sectarianism. These include employment practices, attempts to prevent facilities for what are deemed Catholic sports being provided, closing play areas on Sunday, and so on. The experience of the executive has proved that it has not been up to the challenge of overcoming Stormont's structural and ideological inheritance, nor has it actively sought to do so. Instead the executive has directly assisted in the reproduction of sectarian ghettos, and passively accepted, and indeed promoted, military planning objectives.

The 1987 House Condition Survey[16] indicated that unfitness was down to 42,900 dwellings (8.45 per cent), with 114,920 (22.5 per cent) still requiring repairs in excess of £3,000 each. The majority of these were owner-occupied dwellings built before 1919. Thus, in physical terms, through the processes of slum clearance, redevelopment and rehabilitation, significant physical improvements have been made, compared with the first survey in 1974. Between 1984 and 1987, 38,650 sound properties fell into disrepair, while 36,060 dwellings were made sound. The physical challenge remains great and is one with which the executive is unable to keep pace. Part of the reason for this has been the reliance on public-sector house sales as a major source of revenue, which in turn led to subsidy cuts by government as greater emphasis was placed on capital receipts. When capital receipts fall, the budget cannot be supplemented from other sources. In 1985 a total of £44m was cut in real terms from its budget. In its seventeenth annual report, the executive expressed the view that, 'If present trends continue, by the late 1990's the shortfall in public funding for housing could be more than £100m.'[17]

Apart from the direct impact on the standards of housing provision, many of the 25,000 workers engaged in the building trade who rely on executive grants will find their employment in jeopardy. This will have a more direct impact on Catholics than on Protestants, due to the former's historical preponderance in the building trade. In the immediate term, 1989–91, government cuts have left the NIHE short of £51m. There is the additional burden of damage caused by riots, explosions and intimidation. Most recently much of this has been caused by loyalists protesting against the Anglo-Irish Accord. This cost £139,000 in 1986–7 and £122,000 in 1987–8.[18] General incompetence and lack of management control over expenditure have added to these difficulties. In 1984–5, the NIHE recorded an £11m underspend, followed by £6m in 1985–6. Deloitte, Haskins and Sells, the accountants, were called in to try to sort out the financial chaos. Their confidential report heavily censured the NIHE: value for money had been given little consideration and monitoring of expenditure was ignored until it was too late. Amazingly, no controls existed to prevent duplicate payments on the same contract, and widespread fraud. A number of 'curious' consultants' fees were also identified.

A prime example of such financial mismanagement led to an investigation by the Royal Ulster Constabulary. It concerned a microfilm contract for £450,000 over three years. This was increased to some £1,190,775. Such profits for individual companies have been at the direct expense of public tenants. Exceptions to this are the 147 claims in the same street from sixty-one households who managed to obtain an average of £2,000 each in compensation for tripping over paving stones: it was obviously worth the trip! The Commons Public Accounts Committee censured the NIHE for failing to identify malpractice in sums it paid out in such cases. Over 6,500 people benefited, to the tune of £13.5m with claims by 9,526, worth £19.8m, outstanding.[19]

It is fair to say, then, that over a wide range of 'normal' housing issues the executive has steadfastly pursued policies which undermine its very ability to deliver the service for which it has a statutory responsibility. But the wider dimension of sectarianism requires further analysis.

BACK TO BASICS

Although the sectarian allocation of houses was a major civil-rights issue, serious analysis of allocations during the executive's regime are remarkable for their absence. Part of the explanation for this has been the 'self-selection' process whereby people have opted for 'safe areas' according to their religion. The concept of integrated housing estates in the harsh reality of the north is no more than an empty platitude. For those active in housing campaigns, the traditional stereotyping of 'respectable' and 'not-so-respectable' tenants and applicants is commonplace. This in itself must raise some questions. In the absence of any detailed study and the proliferation of ghettos in response to the threat of violence, the points system used by the executive has been taken at face value. Rent arrears, however, are still loudly criticized by loyalists, as Republican inspired. Even the executive's own publicity recognized that debt has more to do with material and economic deprivation than political protest.

Debate heats up when questions of planning and investment are at issue. The competition for finite resources and the extent of military intervention remain significant areas of conflict. A major example is the Poleglass estate, built as an overspill for Catholic West Belfast. Because it falls within the Protestant boundaries of loyalist Lisburn at the edge of Belfast, its development produced loyalist protests and threats of paramilitary violence. The building of the estate was first mooted in 1973 but it was six years before construction started, in December 1979. The public objections, led by the leaders of the Unionist parties and the UDA, moved the DOE to adopt a much reduced scheme. The DOE had earlier declared that without Poleglass, 'the regeneration of inner Belfast could not be achieved in the west of the city'. It proposed the building of 4,000 units to cater for the needs of 18,000 people. By the end of 1989, 1,563 public-sector houses had been provided.

Even after the first tenants had moved in, one cold winter's dawn, to avoid the dual threat of squatters and UDA violence, the local Lisburn council would not allow them to live in peace. One councillor, who was also a member of the executive board, demanded that all further building should stop because some tenants were in arrears. The council refused to provide a refuse service or to support a proposed community centre and turned down permission for a public library and health centre. The DOE eventually had to make an order under the Public Health Act to force Lisburn to provide a refuse service. The Commissioner for Complaints found the council guilty of maladministration, for refusing to allow its community service minibus to be used by a Catholic school for an all-Ireland football match. Rent arrears on the estate at the time were below the average.

The NIHE's role in this affair, as the body with a statutory duty to provide housing free from discrimination, indicates that on crucial issues it will offer, at the very least, passive acceptance of sectarian planning decisions as well as a form of active support, by tolerating sectarian councillors on its board.

The Divis and Unity flats are severe examples of the worst forms of system-built flats which the 1960s planners had to offer. Many of the occupants came from areas where they had been subjected to loyalist intimidation, or simply burned out. While the Catholic residents of these blocks fought long and hard campaigns for repairs, demolition and redevelopment, their counterparts on the loyalist Shankill Road had their, equally reasonable, demands met. The 750 'Weetabix' flats were replaced by two storey dwellings. Nationalists campaigning for the same were pilloried as Republicans, terrorists and uncivilized. Divis residents also endure twenty-four hour sound and camera surveillance from a permanent British Army base on the top of Divis Tower. It took a major international campaign, led by the Divis Residents' Association and assisted by, among others, Brian Anson at the Town and Country Planning Association's Divis Planning Group in London before the NIHE was forced by the government to concede to demolition late in 1986. In this they were able to take advantage of the political disturbances caused by the Anglo-Irish Accord and the many promises the British government was making internationally, especially in the USA, as to the benefits this would bring. Unity Flats, which loyalists described as a 'cancer on the main artery of Belfast', increased their campaign and secured demolition and redevelopment, on the back of this decision, the following year. The reasons for their failure to gain the right to produce their own redevelopment plans are outlined below.

In January 1985, the DOE published its housing strategy for the Greater West Belfast area up to 1990. It included the Catholic estates of Poleglass and Twinbrook, in Lisburn. The report found that because of the preponderance of large, young families in the area, it was likely to grow well beyond its current population of 93,100. The DOE also recognized that the possibility of families from the area moving to other areas of the city 'is very small' and that 'West Belfast has the lowest level of owner-occupation of any part of the city'. Despite this, the sectarian practices of earlier administrations were effectively reinforced by the conclusion, 'any additional land to deal with housing needs of Greater West Belfast must therefore be found within the same area'.[20] Further expansion into loyalist Lisburn was ruled out, along with other Protestant areas. Instead the population are to endure further pressure in terms of services, population size, density, shortages of housing and diminished potential for employment opportunities within the area.

As the Democratic Unionist Party said, 'People do not want a ghetto line stretching from Castle Street in Belfast to Dunmurray.'[21]

To avoid this, industrial areas would be re-zoned for housing use in West Belfast, thereby terminating possibilities for significant future investments. The acceptance by statutory bodies that housing planning is to be conducted within a sectarian geopolitical framework can only blight the future for the current generation and for those to come.

THE MEN BEHIND THE MASK

Occasionally the veil is lifted from the darker recesses of the security world. Apart from the obvious scar of so-called 'peace-lines' where a temporary corrugated iron fence all too often becomes a permanent brick wall or unnecessary motorway, the security forces have always been wary of displaying their peculiar planning talents. In the case of the north, this takes the form of the Belfast Development Office (BDO), a division of the DOE. There, common interests, such as accessible estate lay-outs, the blocking of potential escape routes, the reinforcement of paths in estates for military vehicles and ramps to slow traffic are all mapped out. High-rise walls can cost as much as £240,000, be twenty feet high and run for hundreds of yards. The cost is met from the housing budget.

Intimidation is very costly. A new development in 1986 at Manor Street in North Belfast was the target of intense loyalist attacks at the peak of protests against the Anglo-Irish Agreement. Twenty-five houses previously occupied were demolished in 1989 as they proved too dangerous to let. A thirteen-foot wall, built in 1985 to separate part of the Shankill Road from the nationalist Ardoyne, makes an interesting case study. The BDO claimed that the request came from the residents. Locals however alleged that this 'need' was manufactured by the security forces with a series of bomb hoaxes and unnecessary searches by the British Army during 1984–5. It is also claimed that there was no record of these incidents being logged at the local RUC barracks. Another curious incident was the building of a wall at Springmartin, a loyalist area overlooking a British Army base.

A number of leaks from within the DOE and NIHE during 1982 revealed the degree of collaboration between the BDO's planners and the British Army. A special 'Security Committee on Housing' was created, excluding the NIHE. This exercised a veto over any development proposals. It inevitably filtered down into the day-to-day practices of the NIHE. For example, one internal memo outlined problems in the loyalist Oldpark.

The area suffers sectarian strife. Future real demand from 'Orange' will be minimal, while future real demand from 'Green' will be maximal. The problem is to proceed to public enquiry, where sectarian issues are likely to be raised since 'redevelopment' will be seen as the replacement of Protestants for more Catholic houses.

Press articles carried by the *Guardian* (13 March 1982) and a local community magazine (*Scope*, April 1982) added further confirmation of the military's role. For example, in the Catholic Ardoyne a row of houses was arbitrarily removed from the redevelopment programme without the knowledge of the NIHE. This occurred after the NIHE had submitted plans for approval to the BDO. The military regarded this as a potential security threat, due to their proximity to the loyalist Woodvale area. The head of the BDO stated to the Belfast Regional Controller

> We have in recent months sought to remind everyone concerned in DOE and NIHE of the need to involve the security forces at an early stage of proposed new works involving new buildings, road realignments, etc. We have however subsequently had several instances where it emerged that plans were afoot – and virtually at a starting date – where the proposals were unacceptable to the Security Forces and we have had to make last minute and potentially costly changes.[22]

'Costly changes' were successfully avoided during the redevelopment of the New Lodge at the junction of the Antrim Road in North Belfast during 1986. This was done in such a way as to 'turn' the corner houses to provide the permanent military post at this junction with a clear field of fire and vision as far as Artillery Flats. There, another base is perched on top of the flats conducting constant sound and camera surveillance.

Again, in 1986 when the NIHE finally gave in to the struggle by the Divis Residents Association to achieve demolition and redevelopment, a hidden agenda was discovered. The NIHE had 'commissioned' an analysis from the RUC which concluded they would favour either of two options: the isolation and partial demolition of the blocks or total demolition with replacement by two-storey dwellings. The RUC considered the latter would enhance 'security surveillance and hot pursuit of known criminals' (i.e. Republicans). The nineteen-storey tower block should stay, as it provided the British Army with a vantage point over all the city.

Ironically, this coincided with the interests of the elderly residents, as they felt more secure from the conflict on their doorsteps.

The NIHE was obliged to confirm that security considerations had swung the balance in favour of demolition in discussions with the author and residents. The RUC document specifically identifies '(a) the problems of pursuit (b) the difficulties for residents surveillance', and the 'Divis connection with over 500 stolen vehicle and joy riding incidents during 1985'. It also noted that there had been a recent conference at Downing Street on crime prevention, and mentioned 'the importance of tenant security' (a novel approach by the RUC) and 'the disappearance of the severe policing problems following demolition of the T Block in Turf Lodge' (a nationalist area).

A further critical example is provided by the Unity Flats. In July 1987, hard on the heels of the Divis decision, their demand for demolition was accepted. Informal approaches to the residents by NIHE officials had suggested that if they accepted removal to another area, the government would more readily bow to their demands. This was rejected and the struggle to demolish and rebuild on the same site pursued. However two of the prices of this victory were the loss of a hundred units and the rejection of the use of nearby derelict land for additional housing. In addition, a totally unnecessary eight-lane motorway is to be constructed along the edge of the estate, thereby sealing it in on four sides by motorways. Belfast is a small provincial city, which does not require an eight-lane motorway. Immediate access to the city centre will be denied, thereby restricting the easy flow of what is considered a nationalist population.

The point of the examples above is not to construct a scenario where military intervention occurs at all levels of planning. What is demonstrated, however, is that when military forces consider they have an interest, this becomes of paramount importance, to the detriment of the normal planning process. The housing executive, for its part in these circumstances, is no more than the passive or active agent for forces much stronger than itself.

MAY THE FORCE BE WITH YOU

In November 1985 the Anglo-Irish Accord was formally signed. Tom King, then Secretary of State declared that its purpose was to create 'a more peaceful, tolerant and prosperous society'. But in violent scenes reminiscent of the early 1970s, the Catholic population was subjected to intimidation, firebombing of homes and sectarian assassinations by loyalists. In Lisburn, for example, 114 families were intimidated or burned out. Another forty-seven demanded to be rehoused in another area. One attack at Jeremy Walk saw loyalists seal off the estate, cut the power from street lights and proceed to stone and petrol bomb every Catholic house. The mob chanted 'Get the fenian bastards.' Although the attack lasted from 10 p.m. until 1 a.m., the RUC failed to put in an appearance.

During April 1986 alone, the RUC reported 79 attacks on Catholic homes, 337 formal complaints of intimidation and 92 attacks on Catholic premises such as church halls, schools and commercial property. One factory sustained £2m worth of damage. On 12 July weekend another seventy-one families were forced out. On the edge of the Catholic New Lodge in North Belfast at Hillman Street, one family was forced to leave a newly completed house, by a group of 200 men in paramilitary uniform. This area is constantly patrolled by the British Army. Opposite the New Lodge in the newly completed development at Manor Street, twenty-two families were forced out. These houses were demolished in 1989.

A shocking attack occurred in the village of Rasharkin in County Antrim. Loyalists in paramilitary uniform, carrying sledgehammers, hatchets and iron bars systematically attacked Catholic homes, beating up anyone too slow to escape. By September the NIHE had recorded 392 requests for transfers due to intimidation and violence. Of these 228 were given priority status. No action was taken by the NIHE to terminate the tenancies of those found to be actively involved in the physical attacks on their neighbours. Frightened tenants in Agnes Street, South Belfast, after a narrow escape from their burning houses, condemned the executive for doing nothing. They demanded to know 'how much longer will you leave it before someone else is killed', as they sought refuge outside the area. One family which fled to Peterborough were granted refugee status. Local Tories criticized this as opening the 'floodgates for other Irish families'.

Petrol bomb attacks and bullets in the post became so commonplace as to attract only a passing footnote in the press. One savage attack on a Protestant family occurred at Steelstown on the outskirts of Derry: petrol bombs thrown at farm buildings destroyed family pets, thousands of bales of fodder and farm equipment. An editorial in the *Republican News* condemned 'the people who carried out this attack (and) inflicted needless suffering on a blind old woman and her family for a purely sectarian motive'.[23] Equivalent statements were not forthcoming from loyalists such as the UDA. This still-legal terrorist organization which was responsible for car bombs in Dublin killing twenty-one and a long list of sectarian assassinations in the north has no reservations about its terror campaign. Its contribution to the housing debate, apart from burning people out of their homes, is usefully captured in its views on the decision to demolish Divis. An editorial in its journal *Ulster* thundered,

> And when Divis comes tumbling down, where is the NIHE intending to accommodate these mealy-mouthed scavengers? Will Poleglass be extended or will further encroachment into Protestant areas be on the agenda. Whichever way it goes, the memory of stench-filled Divis should remain in Protestant minds as a poignant reminder that this is the way we would expect to stagnate in any future, 'All-Ireland Socialist State'. There's food for thought.

Indeed. In case anyone missed the point, *Ulster* adds, Divis should 'remain standing, gaunt against the West Belfast skyline, as a grim reminder of how Catholics can turn a palace into a human cesspool. . . . Are their filthy habits too deeply ingrained to be removed?'[24] Physical violence has not abated, it is simply not widely reported.

CONCLUSION

Eighteen years after the introduction of the Northern Ireland Housing Executive as the main provider of public housing, there is ample evidence to demonstrate its extreme sensitivity to the various forces of loyalism. The earlier objective of integrating and rebuilding communities has long since been abandoned. This was clearly beyond its capacities. The wider political crisis has however found expression in executive management and recruitment practices. For this it carries direct responsibility. Its ready accession to forces stronger than itself may be considered inevitable but if so then the more fundamental question of the contradiction between the NIO's image of 'normality' and the reality in the north needs constantly to be confronted. If 'normality' at every level, especially in relation to so basic an issue as housing provision, cannot be achieved, then solutions to these issues must lie outside, in a larger framework than that which is currently presented.

Historical and contemporary studies continue to confirm the existence of major inequalities in public-sector provision, material conditions and employment practices. While quantitative changes have undoubtedly occurred in terms of the physical stock, qualitatively, things remain very much the same. Government cuts, £46m in 1990–1 alone, will add to the difficulties of maintaining and improving the physical stock. Many in the construction industry will also lose their jobs. The reasons for doing little or nothing to overcome existing religious inequalities will continue to be presented as 'beyond our control'.

For over twenty years the British government and its various administrative agents have applied a wide variety of formulas in order to try to bring some form of stability and cohesion to a society which is fragmented by its very presence. As we prepare to enter the twenty-first century, the time for a more radical and as yet untried solution is at hand.

Notes

1 *Combat* 4, 9 (1980).
2 Harold McCusker MP, Letter to John Gorman, chief executive, NIHE (19 May 1981).
3 Hansard, cols 15, 16, 66 (10, 24 June 1981).
4 Judge Higgins, Belfast Recorders Court (29 April 1983).
5 Charles Brett, chairman, NIHE, Letter to Paul Shevlin (19 May 1983).
6 Charles Brett, Letter to Harold McCusker MP (22 May 1981).
7 Charles Brett, Letter to Harold McCusker MP (28 May 1981).
8 Harold McCusker MP, Letter to Charles Brett (29 June 1981).
9 *Investigation into the NIHE*, Fair Employment Agency, October 1985.
10 ibid.
11 Fair Employment Trust (December 1986).
12 *Equal Opportunities Monitoring, NIHE*, April 1989.
13 *Cameron Report – Disturbances in N. Ireland*.
14 The Campaign for Social Justice, *Northern Ireland: The Plain Truth*.
15 *Irish Times* (15 August 1964).
16 *1987 House Condition Survey*.
17 *Seventeenth NIHE Annual Report*.
18 NIHE press statements.
19 *Public Accounts Committee* (London: HMSO, 1989).
20 *Greater West Belfast Housing Study 1985–1990*, DOE (NI).
21 DUP *Newsletter* (23 January 1985).
22 *Irish News* (15 March 1982).
23 *Republican News An Phoblacht* (13 August 1987).
24 *Ulster* (September 1986).

BIBLIOGRAPHY

Campaign for Social Justice (1969), *Northern Ireland: The Plain Truth*, Dungannon.
Combat (Ulster Volunteers' Journal).
Gallagher, Frank (1957) *The Indivisible Island*, London: Victor Gollancz.
Graham, D. (1984) 'Opposition restricts, Poleglass Project', *Roof Shelter*, London.

Graham, D. (1985) *The Cutting Edge: The Impact of Housing Benefits on Northern Ireland*, Belfast.
Graham, D. (1985) *Unity Flats – Criminal Neglect*, Belfast.
Graham, D. (1986) 'Housing terror in Northern Ireland', *Roof*.
O'Dowd, L., Rolston, B. and Tomlinson, M. (1980) *Northern Ireland – Between Civil Rights and Civil War*, London: CSE Books.

NIHE publications

The Work of the Housing Executive, Belfast: NIHE, 1972.
1974 Northern Ireland House Condition Survey, Belfast: NIHE, 1974.
Preliminary Report, 1979 House Condition Survey, Belfast: NIHE, 1980.
1979 Northern Ireland House Condition Survey, Final Report, Belfast: NIHE, 1982.
Northern Ireland House Condition Survey 1984, Belfast: NIHE, 1985.
Fourteenth Annual Report: 1st April 1984 to 31st March 1985, Belfast: NIHE, 1985.
Greater Belfast Area Household Survey 1985, Belfast: NIHE, 1986.
Public Sector Survey, Belfast: NIHE, 1987.
Housing Selection Scheme Review, Belfast: NIHE, 1988.
Seventeenth NIHE Annual Report, Belfast: NIHE, 1988.
1987 House Condition Survey, Belfast: NIHE, 1988.
Housing in the 90's, Belfast: NIHE, 1988.
Equal Opportunities Monitoring in the NIHE, Belfast: NIHE, 1989.

Official publications

Belfast Regional Survey and Plan, Cmd 451, Belfast: HMSO, 1963. [Matthew Report]
Cameron Report: Disturbances in Northern Ireland: Report of the Commission appointed by the Governor of Northern Ireland, Cmnd 532, Belfast: HMSO, 1969.
Economic Development in Northern Ireland, Cmd 479, Belfast: HMSO, 1965. [Wilson Report]
Equality and Inequality in Northern Ireland, 4: Public Housing, London: PSI, 1989.
Greater West Belfast Housing Study 1985–1990, December 1984, DOE (NI), Belfast: HMSO, 1985.
Housing Order 1988, DOE (NI), Belfast: HMSO, 1988.
Interim Report of the Planning Advisory Board, Housing in Northern Ireland, Cmd 224, Belfast: HMSO, 1944.
Investigation into the NIHE, Belfast: FEA, 1985.
Northern Ireland Annual Abstract of Statistics no. 3 – 1984, Belfast: HMSO, 1985.
Northern Ireland Commissioner for Complaints, HC 2048 1970.
Northern Ireland Development Programme, 1970–75, Belfast: HMSO. [Matthew/Wilson Report]
Northern Ireland Housing Statistics – to December 1984, DOE (NI), Belfast: HMSO, 1985.
Notes on Northern Ireland, Belfast: NIO, Stormont Castle, 1978.
Public Accounts Committee, London: HMSO, 1989.

9 The women's movement in the north of Ireland

Twenty years on

Margaret Ward

Although this historical overview is primarily concerned with the fluctuating fortunes of Northern Irish feminists, the struggles and preoccupations of other groups of women – those in the nationalist community and the more recent grass-roots groups from Catholic and Protestant housing estates – cannot be ignored. The 'women's movement' has many constituent parts, each of which has had an effect upon the other, regardless of whether or not its members recognize any mutual interests. Much of the interlinking has been contentious; some of it has been fruitful. As a whole it has certainly added another dimension to the overall picture of women's lives in Ireland.

Irish society, north and south, is moving painfully slowly in shaking off the dead weight of puritanical morality imposed by all the dominant religions. As Maura Molloy has reminded us, referring to the struggle for contraceptive rights in the twenty-six counties

> In other countries a week may be a long time in politics; in Ireland a decade is but a moment. It took twelve years from the first efforts of a coalition government to legalise the sale of condoms, for another coalition to finally and traumatically complete a dreadful deed by making them legal for anyone over eighteen.[1]

The counter-offensive by the new right in the south, victorious in the anti-abortion referendum of 1983 and the divorce referendum of 1986, has been a serious setback to the struggle against state and Church insistence on the primacy of women's traditional domestic role. The demoralization experienced by southern feminists has had an impact in the north. There, women activists from differing political backgrounds had hoped that some limited form of cross-border unity could be created by mobilizing around issues which would appeal to all Irish women. In the changed political atmosphere of the mid-1980s, they soon realized that it was pointless to continue putting forward arguments to prove that a united Ireland would not necessarily be detrimental to women's interests. The reassertion of traditional Roman Catholic dogma in the south was enough to strengthen the determination of the mildest of Unionists. The link with Britain, some argued, was at least a guarantee of liberal social policies. Without doubt, the last few years have seen some depressing times, but not all the hard-won gains can be reversed. Women have been off their knees for too long to contemplate any return to the days when merely being married was enough for the majority to lose their jobs, or when contraception was confined to anxious calendar watching, unless one was fortunate enough to be able to arrange a trip to a chemist's shop in Belfast.

The first wave of feminist activity in Ireland occurred at the beginning of this century. That too was a period of political crisis. It was also a time of rising expectations and of great hope in the possibility of a new future: an independent Ireland free to decide its own laws and way of life. A suffrage movement campaigned for women to have the vote in Home Rule Ireland and during the war of independence of 1916–22 some suffragists joined forces with nationalist women, despite previous bitter disputes on whether feminist or nationalist aims should be given priority. However, as the partition of the country into six and twenty-six counties led to James Connolly's predicted 'carnival of reaction', demoralized women in the south fought a losing battle against the imposition of Catholic social and moral codes upon the entire population of the twenty-six counties of Ireland, and anti-Unionists in the north, outnumbered and defeated, withdrew as best they could from all the institutions of that unwanted, heavily Protestant, six county state.[2] Women were divided from each other: the traditions of the industrial north with its vibrant working-class culture were lost to the more rural south; northern nationalists were forced into a sullen silence; and what Irish women had done and what they had fought for was forgotten by everyone.

Such a level of political mobilization was not to be repeated until the civil-rights movement of 1968 onwards gave the nationalist population of the north some hope that Unionist rule would eventually come to an end. The late 1960s also saw the development of an international women's movement. Within a few years women in the south, followed by those in the north of Ireland, had also begun to organize.[3]

THE FIRST STAGE: 1973–7

'The personal is political' was one of the first declarations of this second wave of feminism. It was a realization prompted by the sexist treatment of women in anti-war movements and the American civil rights movement. To some extent it was a lesson endorsed by Irish women, as many of the earliest members of the new women's groups gained their first political experiences in the northern civil rights movement.

Northern Irish society has always been rigidly patriarchal, dominated by the influence of the Protestant and Catholic religions. Poverty and abominable housing conditions were unacknowledged scandals before the demands of the civil-rights marchers exposed the harsh realities of life in the province. What feminist campaigners tried to publicize was the extent of oppression suffered by the individual woman within her home: forced to bear sole responsibility for domestic labour, denied any childcare facilities until her children were of school age, denied equal access to education (a process only alleviated in 1988, when the differential, discriminatory treatment of girls in the eleven-plus exam was finally admitted by the authorities); many avenues to employment were blocked and equal pay was deliberately shelved by the British government until 1975, the last possible moment of implementation within European Economic Community (EEC) law. A married woman was unable to enter into hire purchase agreements without her husband's consent; she was treated as a dependant, not an individual, by social security, tax offices and other official bodies. If she was a victim of domestic violence she had no refuge; if she was raped, it was usually considered her fault, there was no one to help her to bring the attacker to court; if she did get to court she had no legal right to anonymity. Access to contraception was almost impossible for the unmarried or for Catholic women, whose religion prohibited the use of 'artificial' contraception. Abortion remained illegal, with life imprisonment the penalty.

While the tiny feminist groups began to analyse the cultural, social and economic causes of women's oppression, nationalist women, whose husbands were, after 1971, increasingly being taken off to internment camps, discovered some of those theoretical insights for themselves. They were suddenly on their own, forced to cope, to become social security claimants in their own right, organizing family care around prison visits and taking part in political protests on behalf of their imprisoned relatives. Those whose husbands served long periods inside also found themselves free of the burden of pregnancy and were often reluctant to go back to the old ways on their men's release. Some began their involvement in anti-internment protests only because they felt that otherwise their fathers and husbands would think they didn't care, rather than from any clearer motivation. But the self-confidence that developed and the ideological repercussions of seeing women out on the streets were deeply significant.

Women have left their homes and taken to the streets in increasing numbers over the years. Some may have returned to the home once family life resumed some normality, but as life in Northern Ireland has become increasingly abnormal, particularly for those in working-class ghettos, subject to the blunt edge of state repression and the worst effects of economic crisis, the wish for a more comfortable life is accompanied by the realization of its impossibility so long as the political situation remains unresolved.

In common with the women's liberation movement internationally, the first feminist groups were initially university-based, broadening out from those narrow confines as women gradually forged links with each other. A major concern was uncovering basic facts in order to enable the development of a fuller understanding of the reality of women's lives. No one knew the answer to the most basic of questions: what was the extent of childcare provision in the province; what percentage of women workers were members of trade unions; were contraceptives readily available to those who wanted them; were backstreet abortions being carried out? Women were almost completely obscured from official statistics. Sexual inequality was simply unrecognized and therefore not on anyone's agenda. Professional and academic women such as myself worked hard to change that and the small feminist groups undertook a great deal of research as they began to produce pamphlets, manifestos and newspapers to describe the pattern of women's lives in the six counties.

We tried to understand the political, social and economic factors that had shaped women's lives, and why we differed, for example, in legal rights, from women in Britain. The partition of the country had been so complete that most of us had very little awareness of how women across the border lived or how very different were the restrictions they faced. No one at that time was arguing for a united movement of women, so busy were we in simply trying to determine our own priorities and set our own agenda. In retrospect, one of the most important early events was a weekend of women's films, held in Belfast in April 1975, which indirectly led to the formation of the Northern Ireland Women's Rights Movement as the outcome of a resolution to form a women's organization which would campaign for the extension of the Sex Discrimination Act to Northern Ireland. At this stage Northern Irish women were only to get the Equal Pay Act, and that solely because of EEC stipulations on the rights of women workers within the Community. Since the abolition of Stormont and the introduction of Direct Rule in 1972, all changes of law had to be initiated by Westminster, and our British rulers, in their wisdom, had probably decided that legislation to counter any form of discrimination might result in unwelcome attention being paid to all the other blatant inequalities that were so evident throughout Northern Irish society. There was therefore to be no local Equal Opportunities Commission to monitor progress or to campaign for women's interests. So the formation of a campaigning body which was soon to be victorious in its aim of achieving the extension of the Sex Discrimination Act was one very positive result. Another, equally significant outcome of the film weekend was the presence of a small number of women students from the south, who brought along their feminist publications and who spoke of what they were doing, finally opening our eyes to the similarities and differences in our lives.

The year 1975 had been designated International Women's Year by the United Nations and that gesture enabled feminists to persuade many organizations at least to pay a little lip service to the UN declaration. It might have been fairly meaningless, but there was the small hope that things were going to be different; that once we had managed to document the reality of women's oppression, and organized groups to fight for change, we would then be able to go forward and achieve a radical reform of society. There was a flurry of activity as groups formed around the country. Women's Aid set up its first refuge in Belfast in September 1975. In October a Socialist Women's Group was formed by dissatisfied members of the NI Women's Rights Movement, who wanted an organization less concerned with seeking a parity of rights with Britain and more orientated towards the building of a women's movement which would be anti-imperialist as well as socialist. The university-based Coleraine Women's Group (soon to widen its scope) was to gather damning evidence of the levels of poverty in the province. A Socialist Women's Group was also formed in Derry and Women's Aid set up a refuge in that city too. This was the first stage: it was a period characterized by an overwhelming optimism that the energy and enthusiasm of this new movement could transform everyone's lives.

SECOND STAGE: 1977–80

Now, external political realities began to affect relationships between the groups – and the national question became overwhelmingly the most important issue. One part of the debate centred on whether or not feminists should declare their position on the British presence in Ireland, using that primary political stance to determine all other priorities. In other words, could it be possible to work for changes to women's status from within the existing constitutional framework (and implicitly accepting the legitimacy of the constitutional situation), or was the priority to be one of 'getting rid of the Brits'? The political differences were never that clear-cut: another part of the debate concerned those who did regard themselves as anti-imperialist but who, from within that perspective, saw no contradiction in working for short-term reforms.

An All-Ireland Women's Liberation Conference, held in Belfast in October 1977, was initiated by a previously unknown lesbian group, concerned about the divisions that were beginning to emerge. The conference provided invaluable space for meeting and discussion, but it also highlighted the extent to which those differences of opinion had begun to crystallize. Nevertheless, despite these sometimes bitter differences, all the feminist groups in the north came together in March 1978 to demand the release of Noreen Winchester. Women's Aid groups from Belfast, Derry and Coleraine, the NI Women's Rights Movement, Women Against Imperialism, Belfast Women's Collective, Women's Law and Research Group, Craigavon Women's Group and Twinbrook Women's Rights Group, were all represented at campaign meetings held in the Belfast Women's Aid refuge. Women from the peace movement which had recently emerged were also present, such was the solidarity, unprecedented and never to be repeated, expressed at the injustice of Noreen's seven-year jail sentence for killing her father, who had repeatedly raped her and her sister. Two weeks after the appeal judge had upheld the original sentence, imposed in March 1977, Noreen was granted a Royal Prerogative of Mercy.

Also in 1978 the Matrimonial Causes Act was extended to allow for easier divorce; this was the direct result of sustained lobbying by a small group of feminists calling themselves the Women's Law and Research Group. The English law reform of 1969 had not been introduced into Northern Ireland because the local parliament, dominated by Unionist men from the middle class and landed gentry had, since the inception of the state, steadfastly refused to implement any progressive reform. The welfare state came into existence despite their protests, and only because it was pointed out that to refuse it would create an uncomfortably wide gap between British life on the 'mainland' and the supposedly British way of life that existed in the north of Ireland. The deep-rooted conservatism of those in powerful positions in the province was made abundantly clear in the two and a half years of intense campaigning that eventually led to the divorce law being changed. Lord Justice MacDermott even took the unusually individualistic step of writing to the *Newsletter* to warn of the perils of destabilizing family life. The success of the campaign, like the winning of the Sex Discrimination Act in 1976, was undoubtedly the direct result of feminist effort.

Such issues were, of course, political minefields in a country whose national question remained unresolved. The obvious contradiction was that Direct Rule allowed for the possibility of progressive changes that were unheard of in the days of the old Stormont. So, raged one of the inevitable controversies, should demands for legal change be put to the British imperial state, or should women wait for an independent, united Ireland to legislate for women's needs? The division was not simply on whether nationalist concerns should be the major priority; these fundamental political differences also profoundly affected the strategies adopted by groups. A powerful example of this concerns the question of abortion law reform, which will be discussed shortly.

Another positive initiative during the period 1979–81, sometimes forgotten when the disagreements are recalled, were the monthly 'Unity' meetings where various groups and individuals met in an attempt to work out a common programme of action. An 'Action on Debt' campaign against the Payment for Debt Act (which had been imposed, after the rent and rates strike against internment had clocked up millions of pounds in payment arrears, so that social security payments could be deducted from claimants to cover unpaid bills) was launched as a direct result of discussion within the group. The Irish Congress of Trade Unions' May Day march finally agreed to allow a woman's banner to be carried, in response to a demand from the Unity meetings. This may seem a trivial point, but the *Women's Action* banner of the Socialist Women's Group had been forcibly taken away from them by the police, following a request by officials from the ICTU, when the group tried to join the May Day celebrations in 1977. The trade unionists' underlying fear was that politically active women must inevitably be connected with nationalism and, ostrich-like, they were still hoping that their movement could remain untainted by any contact with such forces. A still-quoted issue of the British socialist–feminist journal *Scarlet Woman* was also produced by a section of the Unity meeting participants (although by now the internal divisions amongst the Irish groups were becoming evident). A small group began to meet to organize a Rape Crisis Centre in Belfast, after a worker with the Dublin Rape Crisis Centre had given a talk on how they had set up their organization.

In 1980 the long simmering disagreements reached boiling point over the issue of support for the Republican women prisoners of Armagh Jail.[4] Armagh became a metaphor for everything that has kept Irish women divided from each other. The Socialist Women's Group and its successor, the less rigidly defined Belfast Women's Collective, which was formed in 1977, as well as Women Against Imperialism (a group that had in 1978 split from the Collective as a result of disagreement over the extent to which activities should be concentrated around the British military presence, to the exclusion of issues that might attract support from women outside nationalist areas), all came and went in this period: victims of intense anguish over the degree of support to give the prisoners' campaign. Two members of Women Against Imperialism served sentences in 1980, following incidents at an emotionally charged picket on Armagh Jail on International Women's Day 1979. They joined the other women prisoners in their no-wash protest, undertaken as part of the campaign for political status. Some burned up all their energies in working on this one issue, others felt it to be increasingly important to develop an analysis which would be anti-imperialist yet independent of Republicanism. The NI Women's Rights Movement, in attempting to develop a strategy that would unite working-class women, was vehemently opposed to the prisoners' demand to be given special-category status as recognition of their role in the fight against British imperialism. To concede that, they argued, was to accept the legitimacy of the armed struggle. For them, Armagh was a divisive issue that separated Protestant from Catholic; it had nothing to do with feminism. The small lesbian group also found that lesbians could be Unionist or nationalist, and it too dissolved, defeated by the wider political issue.

By 1980 there had been six years of finding out the problems and of developing analyses which could begin to explain the oppressed status of women in society. For many, they were also six years of increasing frustration with the fact that feminists were unable to develop a programme of action that could encompass all women's struggles without the danger of immediate sectarian schisms.

THIRD STAGE: 1980–4

For some women, the solution was to devote their energies to practical issues, to the provision of services. This third stage was characterized by the establishment of a wide range of organizations, all aimed at empowering women to fight back against the worst of the injustices they experienced. The work of Women's Aid had expanded across the province and it included intense lobbying to secure better legal protection for women forced to leave the matrimonial home because of battering, together with incessant publicity to increase public awareness of the level of abuse suffered by women and to encourage a more sympathetic and effective response by police, social services and housing authorities. The development of refuges was one visible sign of the impact feminists had upon the community; another was the setting up by the NI Women's Rights Movement of a women's centre in central Belfast in 1980, to be followed in 1982 by one on the Falls Road. The latter was initiated by ex-members of Women Against Imperialism, some of whom had gone on to join Sinn Féin after the breakup of their group.[5]

As a generation of women developed some understanding of the extent of their oppression, the new-found awareness found its way into the work place. Women's committees were formed in trade unions, women's sections in some political organizations, and social and community work practices subjected to an intense feminist scrutiny, resulting in a new awareness of the special needs of women. Political understanding that the role of the professional was not simply to enable women to become better wives and mothers, but to encourage them to develop their potential as people in their own right, regardless of domestic commitments, was slowly being inculcated, as feminist educators influenced their students.

In both Britain and Ireland, single-issue campaigns rather than broadly based organizations with detailed aims and demands have become the norm, and in the context of Northern Ireland, with its apparently intractable sectarian divisions, such a concentration of energies has undeniable attractions. Some measure of cross-community support can be obtained and feminists can co-operate with other like-minded groups without worrying about their more general political attitudes. Whether, in the long run, refusing to confront the reality of partition and its effects upon us all can be considered as a progressive option is another matter. In the short term, women can point to a substantial body of achievement, particularly in view of the lack of local government structures willing to contribute financial support, and the generally deeply conservative society that exists. Even the Equal Opportunities Commission for NI has a more visible presence, despite its very few staff, than its counterpart across the water. And that was due to a hard-fought battle on the part of those first appointed to its staff, who had the full backing of the trade union movement.

Law change remains contentious. From a nationalist perspective, it is acceptable to set up women's centres in various areas, to offer advice and information, but not to campaign for a change in the law. The most glaring discrepancy between Northern Ireland and Britain remains the lack of abortion rights. Pro-life platforms are one of the few issues on which nationalist and Unionist politicans agree. Homosexual law reform was only achieved in 1982 as a result of one gay man taking his case to Europe, but while Britain was forced, through EEC pressure, to bring about change in that area, no Irish woman has yet found herself able to perform the same function on behalf of the estimated 2,000 women who are forced each year to make the sad journey over to England.

The first feminist group to campaign for abortion was the Northern Ireland Abortion Campaign, set up in 1980 in response to the death of a young woman from a back-street abortion. NIAC publicized the issue through such imaginative actions as a lobby of Westminster MPs who were all presented with wire coathangers and facsimile airline tickets as symbolic representations of the choices open to Irish women. They succeeded in obtaining the backing of the *Belfast Telegraph*, an influential liberal Unionist newspaper. NIAC also undertook vital research on the attitudes of general practitioners, discovering that a significant number are in favour of the extension of the Abortion Act. The Northern Ireland Abortion Law Reform Association, composed of men as well as women, was formed in 1984 as a broader based body that courted the support of professionals, and which restricted itself to the obtaining of the 1967 Act rather than the feminist objective of the de-criminalization of abortion. As the Northern Ireland Office continues to maintain that law reform will not occur until a substantial body of opinion comes out in favour, NIALRA has extended the work of research and publicity in order to mobilize this elusive public opinion. In 1987 it held an impressive two-day tribunal in the prestigious Europa Hotel in Belfast, gathering overwhelming evidence of the desperate need for abortion law reform. Despite the high calibre of its panel and the fact that the event took place on the door-step of the world's press, media interest was minimal. Editorial censorship by those unwilling to offend the religious majority remains a crucial obstacle.[6]

The whole question of reproductive rights for women has been at the heart of the feminist struggle on both sides of the border and it has been the issue which has seen the most constructive unity between women north and south. There have been joint conferences and mutual support in the face of the most far-reaching right-wing backlash that has been experienced by women anywhere in Europe. The legalization of contraception in the Irish Republic in 1980 heralded the first significant breach between the laws of the state and the moral teachings of the Catholic Church, and the right quickly mobilized to claw back the initiative. The same year saw the formation of a tiny 'Right to Choose' group in Dublin, and it was rapidly countered by the Pro-Life Amendment Campaign, launched in 1981 with the backing of the American 'pro-life' movement, to try to ensure that abortion law reform could never come about. In the north, similar groups mobilized to lobby their politicians. Direct Rule from Westminster has meant that Northern Ireland no longer possesses any legislative body, but that fact has not deterred the powerless local councils from becoming the focus for a concerted campaign by the various 'Right to Life' groups. In a pre-emptive move, in the unlikely event of Northern Ireland ever regaining some form of local autonomy, these councillors have made it plain that they will never concede reform of the laws governing abortion.

And, at the moment, there the situation remains. The 1983 referendum in the south, conferring as it does an equal right to life for the foetus, has been followed by the Hamilton judgment of 1986, ensuring that Irish women with unplanned pregnancies can receive no information on the options open to them, as Justice Hamilton declared that the 'unborn child' – now protected by the Constitution – came into existence from the moment of conception.

FOURTH STAGE: 1984–

In the south, there has been a certain retreat from the body politic, as women concentrate on developing a specifically women-centred culture, enabling women's studies and women's education to make notable progress. It seems to be merely a tactical withdrawal. As Anne Speed has said, 'the women's movement is a creature of constant ebb and flow, a chameleon.'[7] It is also trying to maintain its existence in a period of desperate economic recession, when, as one activist has said, issues such as low pay, equality in the work force, part-time work and the right to unionize are seen as luxuries rather than fundamentals, because of the changed economic climate.[8]

Economic depression and war-weariness have been features of life in the north for so long that the mid-1980s have not been significantly different in that respect. However, the more recent Thatcherite dismantling of the welfare state – with its punitive attitude towards social security claimants, and its insistence on returning care back to the community, i.e. to women, as well as the more specific attack upon the National Health Service – is a substantial change from what has gone before: all that was a preliminary skirmish, compared to what we are witnessing now. And it is the work of women – at home, and in the community, through voluntary work and through the activities of the various women's groups, that is having to fill the vacuum created by the removal of financial and other forms of aid.

The organizational practices of feminism – the emphasis on the breaking down of hierarchical structures, the rotation of tasks, the validity of each woman's individual experience – is reflected within the practice of community based groups and community based activities that have sprung up. There are two women's centres in Unionist East Belfast, with regular contacts between women from there and women from the west of the city; there is a community based women's 'drop-in' centre in the nationalist Lower Ormeau Road area and a strong women's presence in the community centre in the loyalist estate of Rathcool. Outside Belfast, based primarily upon women's aid support groups, a network of small groups exists. Even the Belfast City Council (until the Unionist disruption of council business as a result of Anglo-Irish Agreement protests) has had a women's officer, one legacy of which has been the paper *Women's News* which continues to provide a forum for women and women's groups in the whole of the thirty-two counties.[9] The Women's Education Project has pioneered stimulating and relevant education classes for women throughout working-class Belfast, offering to women intellectual opportunities that have never before existed. Within the trade union movement, the women members of the National Union of Public Employees, composed mainly of the domestic and auxiliary staff of the hospitals, have initiated a vigorous and well supported campaign against the NHS run-down. The Women's Information Group, first set up in 1981 to protest against an increase in housing executive rents, has groups from across the sectarian divide at its monthly meetings. It is a positive example of the level of co-operation that can be achieved by women from the bleak housing estates of the north and it is also significant in that it has generated a genuine common interest between feminists and those who would not choose to describe themselves as such. However, the success of the Women's Information Group is achieved by a deliberate concentration on 'bread-and-butter issues' to the exclusion of more general political questions. While workshops will readily be organized to inform members on questions of social security, or topics on women's health, no one would contemplate discussing, for example, the Anglo-Irish Agreement and its significance for women, for fear that the underlying divisions would emerge and the group fragment. 'Networking' is the 'in' word nowadays: no detailed manifestos or analyses of society and the way forward. The emphasis is instead on a much more pragmatic approach: making alliances where it is possible to make them, ignoring differences if it is possible to ignore them. The desire to work constructively for some badly needed immediate changes has meant that fundamental differences over the 'national question' are still avoided as topics for debate.

In 1986, trade union activist Inez McCormick, chairing a symposium held to celebrate ten years of feminism, which ended in considerable division and acrimony, tried to give its participants a sense of the path that had to be taken – the 'difficult, dangerous honesty' that had to be articulated, so that those divisions could be talked about and faced up to. She did not believe in the concept of 'rising above our divisions' because that denied their reality; instead, she urged a greater discipline and maturity upon feminists, so that we would be able to face the national question with each other, just as the working-class women of NUPE, the union for which she worked, were attempting to do.[10]

Some took her words very much to heart. International Women's Day 1987 saw many more groups of women working together to deal honestly with those differences. A series of workshops entitled 'Dealing with our Differences' was organized and participated in by the Falls Women's Centre, Rape Crisis Centre, Lesbian Line, the Women's News Collective, Sinn Féin Women's Department and the Just Books Collective. That positive initiative has now been developed further as more groups have joined the International Women's Week planning meetings.

Lesbian feminists have rarely organized separately within Irish feminism, being, as one activist has said, 'concerned with the struggle of all women, we are, and have been, involved with a broad spectrum of the women's movement . . . we do not have a lesbian group as such in Northern Ireland – proof positive of the lesbian feminist's view of her place in the women's movement.'[11] But in recent years there has been an increasingly visible lesbian community in the forefront of the search for a woman-identified culture, and lesbian women have also been at the heart of the attempt to mobilize wider support for the International Women's Day celebrations. Republican women, who have found themselves increasingly marginalized within the women's movement, have been their unlikely allies in this regrouping of forces. But perhaps this alliance is not so unlikely; as Maggie Feeley has commented

> Both groups are directly threatening the status quo, refusing to comply with the established order. Both groups are obviously behaving in an unacceptable way for the coloniser, and those who would side with the coloniser – be it of their body or their country.[12]

Republican women have, in a sense, been drawn in from the cold by other feminist and community based women's groups, through the irony of a blatantly sectarian decision by the community services committee of the Belfast City Council refusing to renew its £2,000 grant to the Falls Women's Centre. Not all Unionist councillors agreed with the decision: the chair of the committee, Elizabeth Seawright, was prominent in her protests and she was joined by three other councillors, two of them male. Since then there has been a united campaign of support for the Falls women which includes the Shankill Women's Group and other groups from Unionist areas. International Women's Day 1990 was the occasion for a rally in Belfast city centre in which women from the Falls and women from the Shankill, as well as participants from all the other women's groups, in united voice condemned the attack upon the Falls Centre as an anti-woman action. They clearly realized that a threat to one part of the women's movement was a threat to all and they have been determined to stick together over the principle that all enterprises supporting women should be eligible for financial assistance.

Perhaps the time might come when women from the north and south will be able to discover some common identity and give each other meaningful support. In recent times the only cross-border activity has been an attempt to mobilize a 'save the clinics' campaign, after the Hamilton judgment led to the forcible closing of abortion referral agencies. But this was largely confined to those with nationalist sympathies. Any activity involving the border remains suspicious, tainted with nationalism, even though the reality is that women in the south have been struggling hard against the hegemonic rule of the Catholic Church, a struggle which will ultimately benefit all women.

The process of breaking down barriers must include women in the south. Partition has divided us and it has circumscribed our strategies for change. Until we can deal with that reality, the women's movement in Ireland will not develop as a strong and positive force. A movement exists, diffused though it is, and it has substantial achievements to its credit on both sides of the border, but in the changed conditions of the early 1990s, it no longer exists in a period of much optimism for the future. For that reason, the task is more difficult than some of us once thought. We have yet to advance a vision of the future that can convince women that we have reason to work together for a radical transformation of society.

Notes

1 Maura Molloy, *Out for Ourselves: The Lives of Irish Lesbians and Gay Men*, quoted by Ursula Barry, 'Women in Ireland', *Women's Studies International Forum* 2, 4 (1978) p. 317.
2 For further details on this period, see Margaret Ward, *Unmanageable Revolutionaries: Women and Irish Nationalism* (London: Pluto; Dingle: Brandon, 1983).
3 I am indebted to an article by Ailbhe Smyth, 'The contemporary women's movement in the republic of Ireland', *Women's Studies International Forum* 2, 4 (1978) pp. 331–41, for suggesting the various stages in the development of the Irish feminist movement.
4 For further discussion of the Armagh controversy, *see* Christina Loughran, 'Armagh and feminist strategy: campaigns around Republican women prisoners in Armagh Jail', *Feminist Review* 23 (Summer 1986) pp. 59–79.
5 A detailed description of events during the early years of the women's movement is given by members of the groups concerned in Margaret Ward, ed., *A Difficult, Dangerous Honesty: 10 Years of Feminism in N. Ireland* (Belfast: Women's News, 1987).
6 Northern Ireland Abortion Law Reform Association, *Abortion in Northern Ireland: The Report of an International Tribunal* (Belfast: Beyond the Pale Publications, 1989).
7 In Ailbhe Smyth, Pauline Jackson, Caroline McCamley and Anne Speed, 'Feminism in the south of Ireland – a discussion' [prefaced and edited by Ailbhe Smyth], *The Honest Ulsterman* 83 (Summer 1987) p. 49.
8 ibid., p. 44.
9 *Women's News* can be contacted at 185 Donegall Street, Belfast BT 1.
10 See Margaret Ward, ed., op.cit., pp. 58–9.
11 Maggie Feeley, 'Naming names, taking sides', in *Unfinished Revolution: Essays on the Women's Movement*, ed. Meadbh Collective (Belfast: Meadbh Publishing, 1989) p. 44.
12 ibid., p. 45.

10 The demolition squad

Bew, Gibbon and Patterson on the Northern Ireland state

Bob Purdie

Henry Patterson, together with Paul Bew and Peter Gibbon, is a partner in a team of demolition experts which has spent the last few years clearing the site left vacant by the successful take-over bid for the Irish left by Republicanism and . . . Loyalism.[1]

When the Irish question erupted again in 1968, it coincided with a period of unprecedented development in the scope, complexity and sophistication of socialist thought on an international scale. Beginning with the crisis within the world communist movement in 1956, there had been increased interest in the 'humanism' of the writings of the 'young Marx' and a turn to neglected Marxist theorists like Gramsci and Lukács. Marxist writers of the 1950s like Marcuse and Sartre achieved greater relevance and new theorists like Althusser, Colletti and Habermas appeared, all of whom provided a more complex and challenging interpretation of Marxism to replace the dogmatic certainties of the Stalin era.

This was one of the reasons why, before Bew, Gibbon and Patterson appeared on the scene, serious debate about Northern Ireland from a Marxist standpoint was rare. Most Marxist intervention took the form of activism; in so far as there was a theoretical basis, it tended to consist of quotations from Marx, Engels and Lenin torn out of context. This gave rise to a highly moralistic attitude of 'solidarity', in which Republicanism was seen as an expression of the oppressed Catholic minority and the vanguard of a national struggle which would 'complete' the unfinished work begun in 1916 and which was 'betrayed' by the Treaty of 1921. Since the prevailing Marxist interpretations had incorporated a great many Irish nationalist preconceptions, it was inevitable that revisionism should focus on challenging such influences, and restoring some balance to left-wing ideas about Unionism and the Ulster Protestant community. Bew,

Gibbon and Patterson have been the most successful exponents of this new Irish Marxism.[2]

Their analyses are more satisfactory than other revisionist Marxist interpretations; such as that of Anders Boserup in 1972. He saw a trend towards convergence of the economies of both parts of Ireland. Partition and its associated ideological systems, Irish nationalism and Orangeism, were, in his view, becoming obsolete. In the north the transition from family-based enterprises to public companies and foreign investment was weakening the old system. This normalization of relations between north and south was depriving Orangeism of its *raison d'être*, and in order to facilitate the process of convergence the south would have to be convinced that discrimination against the Catholics was on the wane. The strategy pursued in the mid-1960s by the Northern Ireland Prime Minister Terence O'Neill was an attempt to convince the northern Catholics and the south that change was on the way, while convincing the Protestants that the opposite was the case. At the same time welfarism and the breakdown of sectarian employment patterns were reducing the pressure on Catholics to emigrate. This had helped to produce a new Catholic middle class which was the social base for the civil rights movement. According to Boserup the crisis had been produced by the stresses and strains of the transition from the old system to the new. A similar analysis came from Belinda Probert in 1978. She saw increased state aid to industry in the post-war period creating a division between British and local capital, and weakening the old patronage system which operated in family-based enterprises. Like Boserup, she saw increased foreign investment and the development of new industries as having contributed to the numbers of Catholics employed and to the size of the Catholic middle class.[3]

These analyses fail to explain why the almost complete collapse of Northern Ireland's traditional industrial structures during the 1970s should have been accompanied by an unprecedented degree of polarization along traditional Orange/Green lines. Marxism can be illuminating when discussing broad spans of human history, but Marxists often seem to miss the significance of the intimacy of Northern Ireland politics and the role played by individuals and individual initiatives. They also tend to ignore the influence of contingency and plain misunderstanding: factors which cannot be ignored in a divided society where knowledge of the motives and activities of one community on the part of the other is limited, and filtered through many preconceptions and myths. The first wave of revisionist Marxist analyses failed to convince because they used concepts which were more appropriate for analysing larger-scale societies and they also lacked sufficient detailed knowledge of Northern Ireland, so that they made assumptions which simply did not meet the facts, such as the 'middle-class' basis of a civil rights movement which actually began as a tiny group of activists, and only became significant after the events in Derry on 5 October 1968 had mobilized almost the *entire* Catholic community.

Because Bew, Gibbon and Patterson do not agree with attempts to trace ideological conflicts to economic roots, and see ideology as part of society existing within specific social structures, they take much more seriously than the earlier revisionists what people in Northern Ireland have actually said about their beliefs. And since they also have a much more accurate historical and contemporary knowledge of the place, they do not make crass assumptions about what Marxism says ought to be, as opposed to what is. The three writers' analysis of Northern Ireland is part of a broader set of positions about Irish political history, and particularly about modern Irish Nationalism and Republicanism, but this article will focus on their analysis of Northern Ireland,[4] which is, undoubtedly the aspect of their work which is most controversial for the left in Britain, although less so for the Irish left. They have sought to offer a more substantial analysis than those offered previously of the special characteristics of Northern Ireland: sectarianism; discrimination; repression and violence. They root these explanations in an analysis of the Northern Ireland state and its relationship to Britain. Their contribution lies in four main areas: first, a critique of current Marxist theories; second, an analysis of Unionism as a multi-class political bloc, created over a period of time and in specific historical circumstances; third, the relationship of the working-class component of this bloc to the bourgeois component and the class-based tensions and conflicts arising from that relationship, and fourth, the role of the Northern Ireland state in keeping the bloc together and so maintaining the domination of the Unionist bourgeoisie over the other classes in the society.

The key questions they raise are: do these characteristics depend on the intervention in Northern Ireland of the British state, and, if that intervention were ended, would they disappear? They answer 'no' on both counts, and in giving this answer they raise a further controversial analysis when they examine the nature of working-class Unionism and its relationship to the bourgeois leadership of the Unionist coalition. But before examining these points further it is as well to deal with two common misrepresentations of their positions. First, they do not offer an apology for Protestant sectarianism, in fact they make a damning indictment of the Unionist party on this count. Second, they have no connection with the so-called 'two-nations theory', which the British and Irish Communist Organization (B&ICO) developed, in the mid-1970s, into a systematic justification of Unionism. Bew, Gibbon and Patterson must be counted with those theorists of the Northern Ireland problem who give priority to internal factors, as opposed to those who stress external intervention. Most partisans of the latter viewpoint sympathize with Republicanism, but the B&ICO can also be included in this camp, since they claim that it is the refusal of the British political parties to organize in Northern Ireland that is responsible for excluding the province from British 'normality'.

The central critique which the three writers offer of the prevailing Marxist analyses of Ireland is of the inheritance from James Connolly and Second International Marxism of a simplistic view of Unionism which sees it as an artificial entity held together by manipulation and deceit. This idea led to acceptance of a basically nationalist notion, namely, that once the artificial factors which sustain Unionism are withdrawn, Ireland would be united and the rift in the Irish working class, based on religion, overcome. Bew, Gibbon and Patterson also suggest that Marxist theories of imperialism have been misapplied. In so far as Britain has intervened in Ireland since 1922, it has been in favour of a united Ireland and, since the attempt to maintain a colonial relationship with the whole island was ended by the Treaty, the primary motive of British policy has been to avoid entanglement as much as possible. They further argue that the idea of 'incompletion' of the national revolution in Ireland is not consonant with Lenin's writings on the national question. They argue that for Lenin the national question was about the development of political democracy, not about the integrity of the national territory. While limitations on democracy in both Irish states are related to the activities of the Republicans, and thus are a consequence of the conflict over partition, a single Irish state would not necessarily be more democratic. In fact any attempt to coerce Northern Ireland Protestants into an all-Ireland state would result in a very much less democratic set-up.

On the side of incompletion stands democracy for three million in the south, albeit infringed by the 'sense of national grievance', accompanied by restrictions on democracy for a million and a half, in the north, the result of the forcible inclusion of a Catholic minority within the state's borders. On the side of completion stands the probability of restrictions on democracy for *four and a half million* as a consequence of the forcible inclusion of a Protestant minority within a thirty-two-county republic. The question of territorial completion, though it sounds revolutionary, is really Hobson's choice.[5]

This critique of popular Marxist analyses is surpassed in importance, however, by their writings on Unionism, the Protestant working class and the Northern Ireland state. The most impressive work produced by any of the three is Peter Gibbon's *The Origins of Ulster Unionism*. It is distinguished by clarity, economy of writing and breadth of analysis. Gibbon uses the Marxist, political–economic concept of mode of production, together with the sociological concepts of rural modernization, industrialization and urbanization, to explain the differentiation of the Ulster Protestants from the rest of Ireland.

> The most significant empirical characteristics of Ulster Unionism were its *regional* status, the uniformly *sectarian* character of its following, and its integration of all the major classes in Protestant Ulster. Each of these characteristics points to a comprehensive dualism in Irish society: a regional dualism (Ulster/the rest of Ireland), a religious dualism (Protestants/Catholics) and a political dualism (Unionism/Nationalism).[6]

Gibbon shows that Unionism, 'did not spring perfect and complete . . . from the home rule crises of 1886, 1892 and 1912'.[7] On the contrary, it was put together piece by piece over about a century, and was a new synthesis of elements which had existed within Ulster society for much longer. He examines the components of Orangeism, popular enthusiastic Protestantism, Conservatism and Liberalism and the fusing of these into a political party in the course of the struggle over the Home Rule Bills. His account of the foundation of the Orange Order is particularly impressive, showing as it does an awareness of the different political conditions existing in areas geographically very close, in Ulster at the end of the eighteenth century.

One of the best features of Bew, Gibbon and Patterson's work is their insistence on a precise reconstruction of the different phases through which politics in Ulster passed during the late nineteenth and twentieth centuries. However, this is sometimes presented in too skeletal a manner, so that a fair knowledge of Irish history is necessary in order to appreciate their points fully. This criticism is particularly relevant to Henry Patterson's *Class Conflict and Sectarianism*. The work develops Peter Gibbon's theme of Unionism as a political bloc incorporating different classes. Patterson examines the way in which the working class was incorporated into this bloc and the strains and ruptures within it. His central argument is that working-class loyalism provided the basis for a partial and limited articulation of class-based resentments and aspirations. Existing discussions of Protestant workers in Belfast, he argues, see,

> all political and ideological conflict over the various Home Rule bills . . . as little more than a diversion from the 'real struggle', that between capital and labour. . . .Orangeism is narrowed to an ideology which emphasises the common interest of employers and workers as Protestants threatened by Catholic power. . . .No attempt is made to investigate the relationship between Orangeism and classes in Belfast. Had this been done, it would have become evident that Orange ideology was not simply productive of class peace. It also provided the main categories by which certain limited forms of class struggle could be expressed.[8]

He insists, however, that working-class Unionism cannot be reduced to Orangeism. The Orange Order was a crucial component of the Unionist bloc, but its presence was a disincentive to many of the urban workers who were being wooed by the Unionist leadership. Many skilled workers, particularly trade unionists and supporters of Liberal and Labour politics, scorned the crude sectarianism of Orangeism, and would never have supported Unionism on the basis of how loudly it banged the Lambeg drum. What was much more crucial, he argues, was the rhetoric of the Unionist leadership about the 'progressive' nature of the industrial society of north-east Ulster, compared with the backward, rural and priest-ridden society of the south and west of Ireland. The Protestant workers united with the bourgeoisie to resist incorporation into that society, not out of simple bigotry, but to preserve a way of life which they perceived as being under threat. This was illustrated by the delegations of Ulster workers who lobbied the British labour and radical movements against Home Rule,

> This tactic . . . was a prominent feature of the Ulster Unionist campaign against all three Home Rule bills. . . .Its aim was to express tangibly one of the central themes of Unionist campaigns . . . . It stressed that the movement embraced all classes in the most progressive community in Ireland. It was not a reactionary attempt to thwart the Irish people's right to self-determination but represented the only path to economic and social development. Orangeism was treated as one part only of the political opposition

to nationalism in Ulster. But the influence of the Catholic Church in the political and social life of the rest of Ireland was held to justify Protestant fears for their 'civil and religious liberties'.[9]

Patterson does consider one significant component of Orangeism, the Independent Orange Order (IOO). He shows how, in the early years of the twentieth century, the IOO came to express the discontent of Belfast Protestant workers with the leadership of the Unionist party. The Independent Order began as a reaction against the insufficiency of vigour with which the leadership was pursuing Protestant interests, and against its alliance with the British Conservative administration which was perceived as being soft on 'Romanism', and influenced by the Anglo-Catholic wing of the Church of England. Patterson shows how these dissatisfactions were extended to complaints about the failure of Unionist MPs to support socially progressive legislation at Westminster, and this aspect came to be dominant for a period. This was when the IOO issued its 'Magheramorne Manifesto' of 1905, which was notable for its non-sectarian rhetoric. It also backed James Larkin and the strikers during the 1907 dockers' and carters' dispute in Belfast. However, when the Unionists broke with the Conservatives and then later, when the Liberal government became reliant on the Irish party for its majority at Westminster, the IOO returned to its sectarian roots. What he provides is a lucid explanation for a baffling phenomenon; by putting the IOO firmly into its historical/political context he shows how its seemingly contradictory evolution makes sense. He also shows how real was its articulation of working-class discontent, and explains its strictly limited ability to sustain opposition to the Unionist leadership.

Patterson's analysis of the Belfast Labour leader William Walker, however, can be questioned. He gives insufficient emphasis to the fact that Walker's strategy of supporting the Union of Ireland and Britain was one which he perceived as being for the Irish working class as a whole. It is essential to understand this in order to explain the evolution of Labour politics in Belfast and why so many Labour activists moved from opposition to Irish nationalism, to support for dominion Home Rule for the whole of Ireland. The threat of partition posed Walker with a problem for which he had no answer – the possibility that the northern workers would be severed not only from the British Labour movement, but also from their fellow workers in the south. Patterson also concentrates too narrowly on Walker's three election campaigns of 1905, 1906 and 1907. He suggests that Walker took from working-class loyalism his criticism of the voting record of the Unionists and the pledge to be rock solid on the Union, while voting with the Labour party on social issues. He does not sufficiently emphasize Walker's roots in British Labourism, and he presents what was probably an opportunist election strategy as something more central and more significant than it may have been.

In reviewing the book shortly after publication, this writer pointed out

> The problem is that this by-election and Walker's campaign become important for understanding Belfast Labourism in this period to no little extent because of the paucity of other sources. So much else of the day to day life of the labour movement and the evolution of the thinking of its rank and file has simply gone unrecorded. Elections are a rather artificial time in the life of a political movement. Walker's propaganda about the need for 'progressive' Unionists to offset the record of the Unionist Party can be seen as a response to the campaign of his opponents, which, as Patterson shows, was focused mainly on the Home Rule record of Walker's election agent, Ramsay MacDonald and that of the Labour Party at Westminster. The theme may have been borrowed from the IOO but the circumstances tend to diminish the long term ideological significance of the appropriation.[10]

This relates to a possible criticism of the joint work of the three, which tends to use somewhat narrow sources. (This is not so true of their individual historical work.) To some extent this arises from their method of approach; they are seeking to prove the validity of a few, highly important generalizations. Evidence is adduced to support these propositions, but the side roads are ignored and there is no attempt to reconstruct historical events in any degree of completeness. This narrow focus, however, is useful in producing genuinely creative work, as is evidenced by their most important collaborative effort, *The State in Northern Ireland*. The central argument of this book is that Northern Ireland can be understood in terms of a Marxist analysis of the state in which the state is seen as the mechanism through which the ruling class is united, while it simultaneously divides and dominates other classes.

> The state is the central Marxist–Leninist concept which makes it possible to elucidate class relations such as these. The state represents the 'condensation' of politics in bourgeois societies. Its content is both the necessary product of the general and specific antagonisms of such societies and the means by which

these are moderated to the advantage of the dominant class. The state provides a 'shell' for class rule, lending it a stable and more or less permanent institutional character. Above all the state is the means by which the dominant class subordinates and divides other classes.[11]

The result is innovative and original in terms of Marxist approaches to Northern Ireland, but their concentration on the state leads to a very great reliance on cabinet and government papers. The wheel has turned full circle and, ironically, the concentration of Marxist historiography on social and economic forces has been 'corrected' to the extent of getting back to something which looks very like traditional political history.

The authors argue that the central project of the Northern Ireland state was to unite the Protestant community behind the leadership of the bourgeoisie, while systematically excluding and discriminating against the Catholic community. They describe the dominant trend within the Unionist leadership as 'populist'. By this they mean that it consistently tried to hold the Unionist bloc together through concessions to its working-class component. The other main trend within Unionism stressed the importance of the link with Britain and was more responsive to pressures from that quarter. This explains the paradox that the most sectarian section of the Unionist leadership was the one which was most insistent on keeping in step with British social welfare legislation. The other fraction combined sensitivity to pressure from Westminster with support for an economic policy based on lower wages and a lower standard of welfare benefits than the rest of the United Kingdom; it also toyed with the idea of dominion status.

The above analysis is applied to the O'Neill premiership of the mid-1960s. O'Neill is presented as seeking to reintegrate the Protestant workers, sections of whom had gone over to the Northern Ireland Labour Party (NILP). The origins of the crisis which has racked Northern Ireland since 1969, therefore, are not to be sought in economic changes but in developments within the state. The authors do not agree with the interpretation put forward by some Marxists, that destabilization was a consequence of political changes brought about by the 'modernization' of the Northern Ireland economy following the decline of traditional industries. They state that it arose from a specific political problem: the loss of control by the Unionist party over key sectors of the Protestant working class, due to unemployment. In their view O'Neillism was a series of 'cosmetic' attempts to divide the opposition to the Unionist party by making a symbolic commitment to 'planning'. This was done to outflank the NILP and was, in a new form, simply the old Unionist strategy of seeking to maintain the unity of the coalition of social groups on which the Unionist party was based.

Bew, Gibbon and Patterson correctly argue that O'Neill did not fall because he had made too many concessions to Catholics; in fact, gestures such as the visits of the southern leaders Seán Lemass and Jack Lynch were designed to evade the necessity of eliminating discrimination, while at the same time disarming criticism from the Nationalist party and the Labour government at Westminster. This, they claim, led to a virtual collapse of opposition by the Nationalist party, when under Eddie McAteer's leadership it became, for the first time, the official opposition in the Stormont Parliament. They assert that this created a gap in oppositional politics which was filled by the civil rights movement. This in turn precipitated a crisis which led to the fall of O'Neill and eventually to the collapse of the state.

They are right to point out the way in which the concern of the Nationalists for better relations with the south was at odds with the concern of the growing opposition movement amongst Catholics, which focused on internal reform. They also argue effectively against the idea, which was current in the late 1960s and early 1970s, that the crisis in Northern Ireland was brought about by the stresses and strains created by modernization of the economy and the need to attract multinational investment. But their analysis, overall, tends to create a misleading sense of symmetry and of a remorseless process of unavoidable cause and inevitable effect. On a couple of points their analysis does not seem to meet all the facts. First, what was significant about the growth of the NILP vote in the early 1960s was that it was attracting a sizeable middle-class component, given to it as a non-sectarian party. The Ulster Liberal party too, was successfully competing for this sector. O'Neill's reformist rhetoric has to be seen as addressing the problem of an erosion of Unionist support amongst two different groups of voters who were dissatisfied with the sectarian emphases of Northern Ireland politics for different reasons. The adoption of planning and state investment stole the political clothes of the NILP and won back the Protestant workers, but the non-sectarian gestures were aimed, with equal success, at dissident middle-class voters and were not simply a tactical ploy against the Nationalists.

Second, they suggest that the two factors determining the timing of the civil rights movement were the expectations raised by the 1964

Labour government at Westminster and the fact that the Nationalist party, by becoming the official opposition at Stormont, had deserted its old role without finding a satisfactory new one. The general fluidity of Catholic politics gave an opportunity for new forces, including Marxist revolutionaries, to win influence. Once the civil-rights movement initiated street mobilizations it drew in the unskilled Catholic working class and the clashes with the police created militant areas and feelings of local solidarity. This later allowed leadership of the mobilized Catholic working class to pass to the Provisional Republican Movement. This is an interesting, if somewhat schematic analysis, but nowhere do the authors explain why the Northern Ireland conflict has to be traced back to one, exclusive, cause. And even if it is accepted that the adoption of the role of official opposition by the Nationalist party in 1965 created space for alternatives, why was it that these were most developed in Belfast, where the Nationalists had not had a foothold since before the Second World War? Furthermore, the civil rights movement did not become significant until 1968, two years after the Nationalists had jettisoned their illusions regarding O'Neill's commitment to reform and had returned to outright opposition. For most of those who helped to create the civil rights movement it was not the abandonment of opposition in 1965 which made them dissatisfied with the Nationalist party, but the negative, sectarian nature of its opposition until that point. The Nationalists' gesture in 1965 tended to recommend the party to them, rather than the reverse.[12]

In concentrating on the state, Bew, Gibbon and Patterson beg the question of how many of the characteristic problems of Northern Ireland actually arose at the level of civil society. Bigotry and discrimination were rife in Ulster before partition and they have survived the collapse of the apparatuses through which the Unionists exercised power. This lacuna calls into question the emphasis given by them in *The British State and the Ulster Crisis* to reform from the top by Westminster, as opposed to the attempt to achieve a political accommodation within Northern Ireland itself.

Publication of *The State in Northern Ireland* marked the end of the collaboration between Bew, Patterson and Peter Gibbon. Gibbon has moved on to other projects and has not returned to the Northern Ireland problem. The continued collaboration between Bew and Patterson reflects the way in which serious analysis of Northern Ireland during the 1980s became practically monopolized by writers living and working in Northern Ireland itself.[13] Bew and Patterson's subsequent work has reflected a much diminished emphasis on Marxist orthodoxy, and a greater concern for using concepts for their explanatory value, rather than their origins in the Marxist classics. The fact that they have continued to open up new ways of looking at Northern Ireland, and to challenge established analyses has been of great value. It is not necessary to agree entirely with them to gain much from their writings. Indeed, it is the possibility of using their work in constructing an alternative view which is the best proof of their serious socialist scholarship.

Notes

1 Bob Purdie, review of Henry Patterson, *Class Conflict and Sectarianism*, in James O'Connell and Tom Gallagher, eds, *Contemporary Irish Studies* (Manchester: Manchester University Press, 1983) p. 132.

2 Marxist supporters of the nationalist cause can be distinguished from plain nationalists by the fact that they explain events in Northern Ireland as a political crisis produced by economic factors. Michael Farrell, for example, in his *Northern Ireland: The Orange State* (London: Pluto, 1976, pp. 29–30) sees the change in the balance between the old and new industries in Northern Ireland as having produced a shift in the direction of a more modern 'technocratic' Unionism. This produced a grass-roots Protestant backlash and precipitated a crisis during which the underlying conflict burst out once more. Other Marxist writings which soldered an economist Marxism to an Irish nationalist historiography of this kind were Farrell's earlier pamphlet, *The Struggle in the North* (London: Pluto, 1969) and that of D. R. O'Connor Lysaght, *The Making of Northern Ireland* (Dublin: Citizens' Committee, 1970), which stressed the way in which the new departures of Unionism in the 1960s could be traced back to the weakening of Northern Ireland's traditional industries in the slump of the 1930s, from which the Second World War had given only a temporary respite.

3 A. Boserup, 'Contradictions and struggles in Northern Ireland', in R. Milliband, and J. Saville, eds, *The Socialist Register 1972* (London: Merlin, 1972). B. Probert, *Beyond Orange and Green. The Political Economy of the Northern Ireland Crisis* (London: Zed Press, 1978).

4 The works considered here are Peter Gibbon, *The Origins of Ulster Unionism* (Manchester: Manchester University Press, 1975); Paul Bew, Peter Gibbon and Henry Patterson, *The State in Northern Ireland 1921–72. Political Forces and Social Classes* (Manchester: Manchester University Press, 1979): Paul Bew, Peter Gibbon and Henry Patterson, 'Aspects of nationalism and socialism in Ireland', in Austen Morgan and Bob Purdie, eds, *Ireland: Divided Nation, Divided Class* (London: Ink Links, 1980); Henry Patterson, *Class Conflict and Sectarianism. The Protestant Working Class and the Belfast Labour Movement* (Belfast: The Blackstaff Press, 1980); Paul Bew and Henry Patterson, *The British State and the Ulster Crisis* (London: Verso, 1985).

5 Bew, Gibbon and Patterson, *The State in Northern Ireland*, p. 19.

6 Gibbon, op. cit., pp. 9–10.
7 ibid., p. 9.
8 Patterson, op. cit., pp. x–xi.
9 ibid., pp. 26–7.
10 Bob Purdie, 'Red hand or red flag? Loyalism and workers in Belfast', *Saothar* [Journal of the Irish Labour History Society] 8 (1982) p. 68.
11 Bew, Gibbon and Patterson, *The State in Northern Ireland*, p. 38.
12 For an account of Northern Ireland politics in the 1960s see Bob Purdie, *Politics in the Streets. The Origins of the Civil Rights Movement in Northern Ireland* (Belfast: The Blackstaff Press, 1990).
13 Paul Bew lectures at Queen's University, Belfast and Henry Patterson at the University of Ulster at Jordanstown.

11 The jerrybuilders

Bew, Gibbon and Patterson – the Protestant working class and the Northern Ireland state

Paul Stewart

INTRODUCTION

One does not need to go far these days to read that James Connolly's legacy has thankfully been returned whence it came – the rubbish bin of romantic Irish socialism. For too long, we are told, his simplistic, historicist, Second International Marxism stifled the development of more subtle and appropriate socialist explanations of the nature of capitalist domination in Ireland, north and south. It seems that a new pragmatism in socialist approaches has replaced the old historicist views of the Protestants of Ulster. The problem, however, is that whatever else Connolly may have messed up, he did emphasize correctly, if perhaps too crudely, that capitalist states are regimes of domination. But of course, it was not Marxists alone who argued this; Weberians have been ready to point out that even though one of the main characteristics of the capitalist state is that it depends upon legitimacy, it is still engaged in a process of domination. However, unlike the Weberians, what the new breed of post-Connolly socialists fail to recognize is the extent to which the conditions for class domination depend upon institutions and structures of subordination which labour itself facilitates. These structures and institutions of subordination (for example, the long-standing exclusionary employment practices in which Protestant workers have colluded and for which their trade unions bear some measure of responsibility) facilitate class domination and they also equally depend on other social relations and identities, which may be stunted in the process of ensuring this class exploitation. These other social relations include relations of ethnicity and gender. In Northern Ireland, these help(ed) to sustain class rule. In the process this has ensured that gender and ethno-religious identities have also been subordinated.

Although this was mostly implicit in Connolly's writings, much of his work can allow the space for this approach to the nature of class rule to be extended. Indeed without properly recognizing this, it seems so easy to say that he failed merely because he did not take the Protestant working class seriously. Yet this view of Connolly is surely simplistic. His failure was due to an imperative against working-class unity on Protestant trade unionism's terms. This was to prove a costly principle to stand by. It should be said that this is a problem not just of Connolly's making. The problem for the left is that in spite of the cogency and perspicacity of some recent critiques of his writing, he did get the crux of the problem right.

This is not the place to elaborate on what few virtues one is still permitted to allow Connolly (see for example, Austen Morgan's attempt to deny him any useful legacy), but it is important to make the point that in addition to his perception that class rule involves some degree of self-subordination, he was also addressing the problem of the relation between socialism and democracy, or what Meiksins-Wood has termed class and non-class issues respectively.[1] Although this relationship has only recently been revived in mainstream socialist writing,[2] Connolly recognized that if class and non-class politics are indissolubly linked because the contradictions of everyday life contain, but do not presume, class, then the resolution of class and non-class contradictions depends upon politics founded in a recognition of their unity. They are not synonymous, but the question is, how does one articulate the other?

The blind spot about Connolly also allows some on the left to regard as progressive, and by extension, potentially socialist, only those politics which tend towards an economic class unity. There are problems here, for what politics espoused by many different kinds of workers have remained unsullied by the temptations of other ideological–political concerns; even trade union politics pure and simple? Yet it is often assumed that the 'pure' class politics of economic struggle remain the uncompromised vision, or the light at the end of the tunnel. This was certainly something that Connolly, with his commitment to Irish national autonomy, would have found problematic.

I want to challenge the theoretical and political myopia on which this economism rests. I want to try to reclaim something implicit in Connolly's writing, namely, the recognition of the necessary ties between class and non-class phenomena and the certainty that not all working-class politics are unproblematically (or even at root) progressive.

Besides Morgan's thesis, the most significant attempt to end Connolly's claims to socialist legitimacy derives from the assumption that 'pure' working-class politics (or, trade unionism and a parliamentary party) are the antidote to reactionary Irish nationalist discourse, whether from left or right. This assumption comes in many forms, but I want to concentrate on the most sophisticated.

The three writers Paul Bew, Peter Gibbon and Henry Patterson (hereafter, Bew *et al.*) have done most to develop and sustain the post-Connolly socialist tradition in Ireland. However, as yet there has been no sustained appreciation and consideration of their contribution to redefining the nature of the Protestant working class and the legacy of Stormont. Apart from veiled side-swipes from the Labour party left and Sinn Féin, there has been no real attempt to meet Bew *et al.* on their own terrain. The arguments they seek to sustain about the relationship between the bourgeois state and civil society in general and in particular in the context of Northern Ireland since 1920, have long awaited a thorough and measured appraisal.

Since most of their critics have confined themselves to an elaboration of the pitfalls of the strategic implications of their analysis, it is high time to address the foundations of Bew *et al.*'s arguments. I have made reference elsewhere to what I think are the political implications of their arguments and any strategic prognosis deriving from them. However, in this chapter, my main intention is to consider in more detail the theoretical underpinnings of their work and the arguments and assumptions which sustain these.

The underpinnings are sometimes difficult to locate and when found they can be quite complex, but the time has come to consider them fully. Other work, though not specifically seen as a confrontation with Bew *et al.*, has more adequately addressed the problems which their strategies for reform throw up at an empirical level (see for example, O'Dowd *et al.*, 1980; Gaffikin and Morrissey, 1990; and Rowthorn and Wayne, 1988). Although Purdie's contribution here addresses some of the issues I raise, his interest is directed in a more pragmatic fashion to establishing the level of adequacy of their work as a series of explanatory tools: I largely concur with his closing observations but I have taken a different route. While I seek to assess this level of adequacy, I am concerned to do so on their own terms. I am interested in what their analysis might lack. At times, their problems stem from an inability to recognize some progressive elements within the minority politics of the marginalized nationalist community. At others, it flows from a mishandling of their historical data (their blindness to nationalist marginalization for example).

More frequently it stems from an incomplete appreciation of those post-Connolly socialist concepts that they are seeking to use.

THE NEW POST-CONNOLLYITES

The clearest and most vociferous rebuttal of Connolly from the left is also the most interesting because it derives not only from a tradition of Irish socialist writing reaching back to William Walker, Connolly's great opponent in Belfast, but is formed out of a consideration of a number of strands of contemporary European Marxism inspired by Althusser, Balibar and Poulantzas. The central 'discovery', as Bew *et al*. see it, is the recognition of the relative independence of the realm of the superstructures.[3] What is important for socialist and democratic thinking on Ireland is that the relationship between the economic and the political is seen as problematic. What is important about the writing of Bew *et al*. is that they are the first to do this in relation to the problems of Irish labour, from the left and in an environment where, hitherto, democratic discourse (or what is taken for such) has been the preserve of liberal democratic Irish nationalists and/or the forces of Ulster Unionism in its many guises. The possibilities that Bew *et al*. have opened up cannot be overestimated, and the space they have created makes possible new theorizations of the problematical realm of the superstructures in a way never before considered on the Irish left. With this emphasis upon the import of superstructures (political and ideological) the significance of non-class and class relations can be registered.

Notwithstanding Bew *et al*.'s innovativeness in opening up a new discourse in a hostile climate, many problems remain with their theorizations of the nature of Protestant Labour and the Protestant class alliance. It is important to retain the idea, as they do, that not all nationalist ideologies are progressive. Neither, likewise, are all working-class discourses, just because they are working class. A recognition of the necessary combination of class and non-class phenomena as a starting point for analysis can help us question much of what Bew *et al*. take for granted.

I shall consider the following aspects of Bew *et al*.'s arguments, which present difficulties for any attempt to view their work as having presented a much more acceptable analysis than the Connolly tradition they reject.

i)   The Protestant alliance and its social basis: the Protestant class alliance is presumed to be more progressive than its antithesis, the Catholic class alliance.

ii) The nature of the Northern Ireland state and its relation to the alliance: Bew *et al*. end up with an analysis of the state which places it outside the contradictions of civil society even though these are the basis of its conditions of existence. This occurs where they seek to view sectarianism as a motive of particular Unionist regimes rather than the more sustainable view in which sectarianism is understood as being inscribed in the very practices of the state. (See O'Dowd *et al*. 1980.)

iii) Ideology and the nature of the Protestant working class: *a priori*, the ideology of the latter is taken to be more progressive than the ideology of the Catholic working class.

As a consequence of these difficulties, it can be argued that,

iv) Bew *et al*. place the Protestant working class and Protestant class society 'above' sectarianism.

v) In so doing they underestimate the extent to which Protestant working-class politics were not, and are not now, above sectarianism and reaction. This is a central paradox in Protestant trade unionism and secular trade unionism in the six counties. It leads to a politics of economism.[4]

vi) In following these concerns they inadequately conceptualize the central problem for all socialists – the foundation and dimensions of class rule, particularly where they fail to incorporate the nature of Catholic subordination within their analysis of class rule in the Stormont state.

Thus, class and ethnicity are not independent aspects of state and social subordination. Rather are they inextricably linked in the way that the state and civil society subordinates individuals and social groups on the basis of their class, gender and ethno-religious characteristics. Obviously, the extent to which one of these will take precedence over the others in characterizing the terms of subordination will depend upon the nature and the history of a particular state–civil society complex. Indeed, there may not necessarily be one characteristic which is more important in the process of social subordination. Usually, the problem is to define the nature of the combination of all or some of these characteristics.

BEW *ET AL.*'S GENERAL ARGUMENT

Bew *et al.* represent the most developed revision and critique of

Connolly's rejection of the democratic claims of the Protestant working class. They are clearly situated in the post-1968 Marxist writing which argues for the recognition of the relative autonomy of superstructures. My analysis here focuses upon their arguments in *The State in Northern Ireland, 1921–1972* and 'Some aspects of nationalism and socialism in Ireland: 1968–78' (hereafter 'Some aspects').[5] I shall concentrate for the most part on *The State in Northern Ireland, 1921–1972*.

Bew *et al.* claim that Ulster Protestants constitute an alliance of capital and labour, wrought out of mutual dependence. Protestant capital, concerned about the need to keep support in the new state, ensured, through a populist trade-off, Protestant working-class support in the form of sectarian advantage in the operation of the state. The social basis of the 'alliance' and of the state was an economic one. Bew *et al.* argue that Protestant working-class support was maintained through a kind of early Keynesian state interventionism that benefited Protestant labour.

Bew *et al.* want to argue that Northern Ireland was an ordinary bourgeois state. The thing to note, they say, is that in class society one must understand the relation of the state to the class struggle. In Northern Ireland, whatever the state was like, different regimes which controlled it used ideological and economic means to ensure that they ruled over labour. This involved intra-bourgeois competition too, between populist and anti-populist wings. To the extent that the state represents the condensation of class power in society, according to Bew *et al.*, Northern Ireland can be seen in this way. Thus, the alliances we perceive it to have been based upon were Protestant. But this, following their argument that we are talking about capitalism, is secondary to the fact that the focus of analysis is bourgeois rule. The response by the state, therefore, is to seek to disrupt the unity of labour.

Bew *et al.* concentrate upon the 'Protestant alliance', arguing that a class struggle raged within it between Protestant capital and labour. The rise of the Northern Ireland Labour Party (NILP) is indicative of the development of class politics within the Protestant working class.

I think that whilst the analysis of the intra-Protestant bloc (containing the Protestant working class and bourgeoisie) is long overdue, there must be problems with the argument that an analysis of the relation of the state to bourgeois rule and the class struggle is adequate if Catholic labour fails to appear in the discussion. It is understandable that one should consider intra-Protestant differences.

Whether one could call these historic conflicts of a class character is another matter.

Bew *et al.* argue that the Protestant all-class alliance was more 'progressive' in that it derived from a more industrially advanced part of Ireland and its class struggle was more developed. The result of this is an undue optimism about the potential class character of Protestant working-class politics. The rise of the NILP is problematical for anyone who assumes that its politics were untainted by sectarianism. Bew *et al.* argue that the NILP was a class-struggle organization whose fortunes served as a barometer by which the rise and fall of a socialist consciousness within the working class in general and Belfast Protestant workers in particular could be judged. However, what Bew *et al.* fail to address is the extent to which the NILP's labourism served to reinforce ethno-religious subordination as a result of its ethno-religious blindness.

This is always so where the importance of sociological differences within the working class and other subordinate social groups are seen as secondary, rather than integral, to economic corporate identities constituted at the point of production. This subordination finds support in, and is in its turn reconstituted by, the state and its structures and apparatuses, in the context of its subordination of, and dependence upon, a sectarian civil society. This is a classic blindness of labourism and it was this failure which haunted the NILP. As a consequence of this, the NILP failed to recognize that Catholic subordination in the field of housing provision and local government was directly linked to exclusionary state practices founded in the irreformability of the sectarian state and its institutions. Therefore it was insufficient that the NILP picked up on Catholic exclusion from full participation in civil and political society, for the party failed to link this to the indelibly sectarian character of the state and civil society.

This has important consequences for the relative autonomy of the state, as perceived by Bew *et al.* We can say that what guided the principle of the relative autonomy of the Stormont state was its ability to continue to recast its *raison d'être* – the exclusion of Irish nationalism and the majority of the Catholic community from unfettered participation in civil society and the state. In this sense, the scope of the concept of relative autonomy is rather limited in Bew *et al.*, where they seek to normalize Northern Ireland as an 'ordinary' class society because they perceive social subordination as external to the capital–labour relation. However, as I have pointed out, there is nothing normal about this economistic view, rather the contrary. 'Normality' is that state of social subordination within capitalism where struggle occurs within and between economistic-corporate class, gender and ethno-religious identities.

In the case of Northern Ireland, the class struggle was structured around the relative autonomy of the state, where it could make and remake the conditions for social peace between and within Protestant social forces and, on occasion, Catholic social forces and the state. One of the conditions for this was that Protestant labour should be incorporated and at the same time subordinated. The main condition for this was that Catholic labour and Irish nationalist demands should be excluded. This had the effect of refracting Catholic labour and Irish nationalist demands through the prism of McAteer's Nationalist party. In the end, Bew *et al.* are distancing Protestant working-class politics from any 'essential' corruption by sectarianism.

PROTESTANT LABOUR AND SECTARIANISM

It is the consequences of this myopia for Bew *et al.*'s understanding of the nature of class rule and its relation to the character of Protestant working-class politics and Catholic subordination that I wish to investigate.

Bew *et al.* concentrate on a class struggle between Protestants by excluding the nature of Protestant labour politics from the process of Catholic subordination. Sectarianism is important because of the extent to which it was used by Protestant workers against Protestant capital, to achieve their own aims. It is assumed that if Protestant labour had fought for the NILP its sectarianism would have somehow been reduced, but this tends to view sectarianism as a voluntary rather than a structural effect of the state–civil society complex in which the Protestant working class is constituted. Nevertheless, the assumption continues to be made that concentration on economic issues alone can guarantee an economic class unity. It will be worth developing this point in the context of what has just been said about the multiplicity of identities (class, gender and ethnicity, etc.) which sustain social subordination in class society in general and in Northern Ireland in particular.

In Northern Ireland, the economic was politicized from the beginning. Any progressive strategy which denied or ignored this was simply going against the way economic divisions between Catholic and Protestant subordinate social groups found their origins in political and ideological structures of subordination. To put it another way, economic disunity within the working class was founded upon the domination of Catholic workers as economic agents within society (sometimes through the exclusionary practices of Protestant workers in, for example, the shipbuilding, aircraft and engineering industries). It was also founded upon the domination of Catholic workers and subordinate social groups as citizens within the state, on the basis of political and ideological exclusion, for example, in relation to local government and housing, as has already been mentioned.

It was not enough to take up 'basic' trade union issues to achieve a corporate class unity, for this focus denied the root cause of the grievances of Catholic workers. These were consummated at the level of civil society and were in turn consecrated at the level of the state. The state was supportive of Protestant labour's superordinate position in relation to jobs and housing. Clearly then, if trade unionists and the NILP raised as a central element in their strategy the problem of Catholic subordination, they would come up against Protestant society. Of course, this could not be sustained. This is why commitment to 'basic' class issues merely serves to reinforce the problem of working-class division. It derives from an attempt to view Northern Ireland as somehow an ordinary class society where sectarianism is merely one option amongst many which the state might employ. However, if we see it as central to the state, we can view the state not as normal (for 'normal' read as other late capitalist states). The point is that 'normal' is not a helpful term here as there is no such thing as a 'normal' bourgeois state.

This flaw in Bew *et al.*'s notion of 'normality' inevitably leads to the view that the onus must be upon Catholic workers to link up with their Protestant counterparts on economic class issues. This, rather than a sectarian Irish nationalism, which excludes Protestants, is seen to be the way to bring about socialism. For Bew *et al.*, the proof is that Protestant labour, through trade unionism and the NILP from time to time shows signs of some interest in basic class-struggle issues. Even the 'success' in ensuring a 'Keynesian' style set-up after 1920 is some indication of this, they argue.

BEW *ET AL.* ON CLASS RULE AND SECTARIANISM IN THE IRISH LABOUR MOVEMENT

Bew *et al.* have responded to the theoretical lacuna surrounding the question of the character of class rule by a proposed break from all approaches on the Irish left.[6] Such a claim in itself is important and from it we might reasonably assume that a definitive critique of the left would follow.[7] I am not always convinced by their argument, that a definite break exists on some issues: for example, the way in which Bew *et al.* promote the idea of the democratic resolution of struggles deriving predominantly from intervention into a parliamentary arena.[8] This always assumes a downgrading of extra-parliamentary activity, their valid criticism of Connolly's closing gambit in Easter 1916 notwithstanding. However, Connolly was eternally suspicious of the nature of parliamentary institutions, if only because his blinkered opinion dismissed all bourgeois democratic institutions in Ireland as essentially British inspired (though he often changed his mind on this).[9] Some of their arguments about the need for democratic parliamentary forms of struggle for labour are hardly even innovative, let alone contentious.

Bew *et al.* deny the importance of Irish nationalism in the place of an authentic socialist politics. They underplay the role of external forces as an integral part of the new state's creation in 1920. They ignore the penetration of imperialism as a world system, which structures the social class and political trajectory of the Irish milieu. It is to these lacunae and silences that I now turn, while acknowledging the following commitments to non-economism

> It requires a considerable effort to make the point against this prevailing orthodoxy that the problem cannot be understood at the level of the 'Protestant community' on the one hand and the 'Catholic community' on the other. It must be insisted that the problem of 'the two communities' is the problem of the reproduction of two class alliances.[10]

> The state represents . . . the necessary product of the general and specific antagonism . . . moderated to the advantage of the dominant class.[11]

and

> Above all, the state is the means by which the dominant class subordinates and divides other classes.[12]

These are apparently laudable assertions. The point to be stressed here is that they appear to be contradicted by the later substantive claims where the role of Catholic and possibly, therefore, class subordination is overlooked.

THE STATE AND CLASS STRATEGIES

Both in *The State in Northern Ireland 1921–1972* and 'Some aspects', competing analyses of the nature of the state and its relation to the working class are at times discernible. *The State in Northern Ireland*

1921–1972 is concerned to elaborate the nature of class struggle in the six counties and the relation of the state to it

> Understanding Northern Ireland's politics is in this sense understanding the class struggle in Northern Ireland and the relation of the local state to it.[13]

This involves an analysis of how particular classes fought over the reproduction of class power, achieving, where possible, the best outcome available. Bew *et al.* want to examine particular class strategies in this fight, whose outcome was Northern Ireland

> It is understanding the specific class strategies which arose in relation to the class struggle and how these reproduced specific forms of class power.[14]

The Stormont state grew out of these struggles which it mediated benignly. The role of the state, in other words, was to maintain a social and political *homoeostasis*.

Bew *et al.* point out that the outcome of these strategies was determined by particular struggles. But they nevertheless make it clear that these struggles occur within a capitalist society and that this gives the bourgeoisie a clear advantage. To repeat

> The state represents the 'condensation' of politics in bourgeois societies. Its content is both the necessary product of the general and specific antagonisms of such societies and the means by which these are moderated to the advantage of the dominant class.[15]

and again

> Above all, the state is the means by which the dominant class subordinates and divides other classes.[16]

So the bourgeois character and the capitalist nature of the state has been established in theory. Bew *et al.* intend to apply these categories in this way to the passage of the Northern Ireland state so they can

> understand . . . the process by which these strategies (of class) were built up, and the effects on the state of the form they took. It should not need saying that it also means understanding the contradictions and crises which became embodied in the dispositions of the bourgeoisie's class power, and how these were affected by certain social changes.[17]

But they conclude with the following intention

> The emphasis in the analysis that follows will, in other words, be on the internal relation within the Protestant bloc.[18]

An analysis of the Northern Ireland class struggle should surely not be so restrictive in focus. Their reason for this will, I think, become clear later.

BOURGEOIS STRATEGIES: POPULISM AND ANTI-POPULISM

Bew *et al.*'s view of the nature of the class struggle and its relation to the state tells us something about the peculiar character of 'Northern Ireland class society'. It still does suggest an ordinary bourgeois state as they refer to it in 'Some aspects'.[19] Their answer to the problem of the nature of intra-bourgeois contradictions, proletarian domination and state formation is the following.

> The clue to the nature of the [Northern Ireland] class struggle is the historically exaggerated dependence of the bourgeoisie upon the Protestant masses. Its object was the unity/disunity of the working class, Protestant and Catholic, *at any level*, even the most economistic, reformist, 'educated'. Disunity between the Protestant and Catholic working classes was Unionism's *sine qua non*. Populism was a strategy which made sense only in this context.[20]

Following Balibar's view on the nature of the state they say that

> the conflict of and dominance by particular bourgeois fractions, etc. arises not only from organic internal divisions of that class but from the state's relationship to the proletariat and *its* divisions.[21]

Bew *et al.* devote their efforts to an account of the differences within the Unionist bourgeoisie, to counter the idea prevalent on the left, of an undifferentiated Unionist state. This account delineates the different class-struggle tendencies and their strategic lines. Bew *et al.* suggest that these differences were represented, on the one hand, by a populist strategy and, on the other, by an anti-populist opportunism which sought to capitalize on populism's success in achieving working-class disunity. As Bew *et al.* put it, the anti-populist line served to 'save the [former] from its own excesses'.[22]

The 'populists' led by James Craig and Edward Carson founded cross-class Protestant organizations like the Ulster Unionist Labour Association (UULA). This organization, with the remnants of the old Ulster Volunteer Force, constituted an auxiliary police group which, with the blessing of British Prime Minister Lloyd George, became the B. Special Constabulary, in November 1920. The B. Specials were a paramilitary force created specifically to defend the state against the assumed threat of IRA subversion. The 'Specials' policed the Catholic community for fifty years.

Bew *et al.*'s point is that the populist wing constituted itself as the dominant faction in the Ulster Unionist bourgeoisie by virtue of its ability to sell to the Protestant labour aristocracy its former class exclusivism, reconstituted within the orbit of the state proper. The populists filled a gap in vociferous Ulster Protestant working-class ideology, vacated when the Independent Orange Order lost rhetorical and political weight to Ulster Unionism after 1905. It was the ability of what Bew *et al.* call the populist wing of Unionism to base itself upon the 'mass line' as they call it, that provided the basis for its ascendancy within the Protestant bourgeoisie. Ultimately this strategy was able to create the Northern Ireland state. The use of orthodox Orangeism undermined what Bew *et al.* refer to as the 'distinct ideology combining militant anti-Catholicism with democratic anti-landlord and anti-capitalism sentiment'[23] of the Protestant labour aristocracy, urban petty-bourgeoisie and rural employers. To the extent that traditional, 'progressive' proletarianism survived, it did so 'in the form of a militant lack of deference to bourgeois authority'.[24]

Politically, the populist military apparatus of the Ulster Volunteer Force (UVF) provided the anti-institutional focus for this 'anti-authority' residue. The populists, as Bew *et al.* argue, ensured that the social basis of the alliance they built between worker and employer was sound. The social basis of the new state was an economic one, which was '"productivist", protectionist and, in a purely practical way, Keynesian'.[25] This ensured the survival of a situation unknown in the rest of Britain: 'the exaggerated dependence of the bourgeoisie upon the Protestant masses'.[26]

The peculiar nature of Ulster Unionist capitalism demanded for its existence the perpetuation of labour disunity – at any level. Populism ensured that

> Its 'solution' to the danger of a united working class was to weld even more tightly the links between the Protestant bourgeoisie and the Protestant masses, to the visible exclusion of the Catholic masses. Like any such political strategy it had economic conse-quences, among which was the perpetuation of a certain 'social basis'.[27]

WORKING-CLASS CONTAINMENT AND CLASS RULE: PROTESTANT WORKING CLASS IDENTITY AND PROTESTANT PROGRESSIVENESS

Bew *et al.* thus give an interesting answer to the question of the social basis of Protestant working-class commitment to Unionism, highlighting in the process some aspects of bourgeois strategy. Unlike Connolly, they suggest a connection between the *real needs* of Protestant workers and their fulfilment in a containment strategy which began with the rise of the Ulster Unionist Council, the usurpation of workers' radicalism/anti-authoritarianism in the UVF in 1913, the UULA after the First World War, and the B. Specials, in 1920. The consummation of this is the Stormont state.

The other side is, of course, that the anti-capitalist sentiment, as Bew *et al.* refer to it, was transformed into a new kind of anti-Catholic sentiment which was against pan-working-class unity, for it could not countenance class unity in terms other than Protestant brokerage and patronage. This was a social nexus which could hardly have been expected to generate pan-working-class ideology and politics! (Patterson, who addresses this point in the conclusion to *Class Conflict and Sectarianism*, does not venture this far.) The earlier Protestant labour aristocracy's anti-capitalist sentiments which were transformed into pro-capitalist rhetoric in the form of Orangeism and Stormont (and the UULA, one of its nascent apparatuses) became the defender of labour 'gains': even if only part of labour gained and the nature of the gain was virulently against labour unity and avowedly anti-Catholic.

Thereafter, Bew *et al.* consider that, with one or two riders about unwanted state sectarianism, one is referring to a 'normal' bourgeois state. However, I think that the idea of normality may obscure a number of features of Ulster Protestant-bourgeois class rule. It is important to keep in mind that one is referring to Protestant society and that this implies something which Bew *et al.* underplay – the defeat of Irish nationalism and the consequences of this for the nascent socialist discourse. I think they put together a notion of 'correct' trade unionism and working-class politics by closing their minds to the rest of Northern Ireland's class society. And they can only do this if they exclude other possibilities such as Catholic Irish nationalism. In so doing they exclude a radical socialist tradition in 'northern' labour. The result is that only one tradition is accepted as radical and progressive. This is a tradition in labour movement politics that closely resembles British social democratic trade unionism.

Is it only a convenience then, that despite their careful distinctions between the Northern Ireland populist 'Keynesian', and British bourgeois class strategies for labour disunity, they are really talking about the same thing using different terms – an 'historic *quid pro quo*'? Their argument that the bourgeoisie in the north was unusually dependent upon labour suggests that some of this may be so. Their approach suggests that any 'class mobilization', even on economic grounds, was a danger to Unionist rule: disunity of labour at any level was essential. To reiterate, any kind of working-class unity was anathema to the Unionists, 'even the most economistic, reformist, "educated"'.[28]

The rub is this: Bew *et al*. assume that basic expressions of *class* (indeed, we can read this as 'bread-and-butter'-issue politics, which in Ireland meant Protestant skilled trade unionism) association constituted a potential danger of historic proportions for Unionist capital. This explains their emphasis on the extraordinary character of the Unionist bourgeoisie's dependence upon labour. It was hardly peculiar to the north of Ireland and in any situation unity of the oppressed can *potentially* threaten capital(ism). But it is difficult to see how Protestant working-class mobilization could threaten capital in the north since it could only go so far while the Protestant alliance had to be maintained. Bew *et al*. cannot have it both ways. On the one hand, Protestant ideology is seen to be relatively independent of working-class Protestants, which allows for the view that economic struggles can undermine the Protestant state. On the other hand, Protestant ideology is central to their identity. In fact, the reality was that Protestant workers saw themselves as precisely that – workers who depended on the Unionist alliance and state for their identity. Catholic workers could be supported in so far as they played class-struggle games on this terrain. But this raises the question – what of their interests? It might look like class unity but it would really be class subordination.

Following on from this is the problem of how exactly Bew *et al*. account for the political character of Protestant labour politics. Despite what they claim was the progressiveness of Ulster Unionist politics compared with Catholic Irish nationalism, Bew *et al*. do not say what are the implications of workplace exclusion of the latter for the character of a socialist politics founded on Protestant labour. By denying any progressive content to Irish nationalism, they assume that, in itself, this makes Protestant labour progressive because it indicates class defensiveness against the Protestant bourgeoisie. The problem here is that it is not only Irish nationalist ideas that were negated, but Irish nationalist labour also. Unfortunately, when Bew *et al.* minimize the importance of the latter, they also pass over the many radical socialist and progressive elements in the history of Irish nationalist politics. (Their dismissal of Connolly is the most obvious.) Their commitment to the idea of some haven of normality (the Protestant class struggle) in a sea of abnormality (Catholic Irish nationalist struggles) emphasizes trade unionism, 'bread and butter', 'basic issues' politics above other possibilities. It effectively counterposes Irish nationalist to Protestant Ulster universes by favouring the latter, and it isolates their mutual experiences – two separate alliances, Irish Catholic and Ulster Protestant: why not then, logically, two separate nations?

SECTARIANISM: IN THE STATE OR OUTSIDE THE STATE? NORMAL STATE OR EXCEPTIONAL STATE?

The conceptualization of sectarianism raises a further problem here. Bew *et al.*, rather than seeing it in the same way as every other aspect in society, as a feature in the condensation of class politics, commit it to the realm of arbitrary actions of state procedure. The problem is that all the strategies of the state were – as they say – designed not just blandly to preserve class peace, but actively to disrupt working-class unity. They themselves emphasize the extraordinary character of this bourgeois class 'obsession'. It was a motive of the state to be sure, but as a feature in the 'condensation of class politics', all motives of *this* state were accordingly geared towards ensuring class peace. However, the discourses of the state and its institutional practices were sectarian.[29] If the state was an exceptional state, this was the reason for it. Following O'Dowd *et al.*, I think sectarianism might better be understood as a structural concept defining a particular type of society. One could talk of Northern Ireland as a sectarian society, using sectarian in the way one uses racist to refer to South African society. It could be used to describe the pivotal form of class rule within the capital–labour relation.[30]

Bourgeois class strategies did not combine only positive action for Protestant labour, they negated bourgeois democratic rights at a local level for the other part of labour, the Catholic working class. In fact, by accounting for Protestant labour support for the traditional 'historic *quid pro quo*', Bew *et al.* are only telling part of the history of working-class commitment to Britain/Ulster Unionism. It is important that notions of bourgeois class rule contain concepts of internal working-class subjugation. 'Bread-and-butter-issue' politics or, to call it by another name, the social-democratic ideology of labourism, was not simply defensive (indeed, Bew *et al.* see it as a class-aggressive strategy); it was also a corporatist ideology.

Is sectarianism, as part of labour's traditions a form of working-class exclusionism, sometimes taken advantage of by the bourgeoisie? Or is it actually part and parcel of the character of the state proper: an 'essential' structure of bourgeois rule in the six counties? Perhaps it is both. This is not always clear in Bew *et al.*: they do, after all, say that

> The dominant strategy involved continuing the sectarian caste of the state apparatus . . . and continuing to endorse extra apparatus forms of sectarianism. Of these, work-place discrimination was the most important.[31]

This suggests that internal labour sectarianism is crucial to the state proper and not just a conjunctural strategy to create labour disunity. Yet they see the possibility for bourgeois class discrimination in the north, without it necessarily being a sectarian state, just what they call a 'normal' bourgeois state.[32] Sectarianism was not endemic to state practices, but just to 'populist' and 'anti-populist' regimes. They are making a clear statement about the relative autonomy of the state: 'the pre-1972 state in Northern Ireland was in many respects an ordinary bourgeois one.'[33]

State sectarianism and sectarianism in labour

It is worth pursuing the argument about the supposed ordinariness of the state. It is difficult to see how the state could have been reformed without dismantling the fundamental social alliances on which it was founded and that it sought to perpetuate. Any challenge to this would have rendered labourist politics obsolete. The point is that if sectarianism was an 'impulse within the state', surely it was central to the state's domination. And again, if it was part of working-class Protestantism, it was part of labour's terms of 'self-subjugation': by denying Catholic workers, they also denied themselves.

At the end of 'Some aspects', Bew *et al.* distinguish between the 'Orange State' (Northern Ireland), Stormont governmental regimes and capitalist state rule. They conclude that the sectarian character of the Northern Ireland state apart, it was the attempt by the last Unionist regime of Terence O'Neill to control this sectarianism, that is, to do away with the relative autonomy of the state, that proved to be the undoing of the state. Bew *et al.*'s point is that this illustrates the way the bourgeois state must maintain relative autonomy for its survival: the bourgeoisie try to ensure that this relative autonomy will prevail. In *The State in Northern Ireland 1921–1972*, they write the Unionist bourgeoisie had historically been obliged to especially extend the relative autonomy of the state from central bourgeois control in order to maintain its dominance.[34]

Sectarian apparatuses, like the B. Specials which were 'independently' organized,[35] were important to the smooth running of the state, yet it was important to ensure a 'unity in diversity' of the different apparatuses, enabling bourgeois class rule to continue. This avoids Bew *et al.* adopting an instrumentalist view of the state, one of which they are particularly critical.[36] Thus, the Stormont state did not use these 'apparatuses' and sectarian ideologies simply to delude the Protestant workers, but in order to reassert their control over the 'alliance'

> Harbinson argues that Unionists banged the big drum because they wanted to delude the workers; Buckland that they did so because they had to. In fact they banged the big drum when the class struggle dictated greater bourgeois forbearance of independently generated popular Protestant activity.[37]

Yet again, this commits sectarianism to 'populist' bourgeois strategies as well as to certain moments of state policy. It confines sectarianism to a specific layer within labour – the labour aristocracy. And this labour aristocracy, it should be remembered, following Bew *et al.*, was a short-lived social layer, the result of a particular moment of state policy. State policy, one should remember, was instigated by a particular bourgeois fraction, through the outcome of a particular alliance of Protestant masses/bourgeoisie, what they call a 'condensation of politics' in class society.

For Bew *et al.*, sectarianism is not a structural component of the state, reflecting all the institutions of domination, even those of labour itself. It is rather the outcome of particular moments of class struggle at any time. It is also not seen as endemic to the bourgeois state. Bew *et al.* see it as central only to the various Stormont regimes and their particular sets of alliances. But it was not part of Protestant labour's armour in their class struggle against the Unionist bourgeoisie. To advance their own interests, according to Bew *et al.*, Protestant labour shed its 'Orangeism' by entrusting 'sectarianism' to the bourgeois state. This was, in a peculiar way, the basis of the state's weakness because the trust could be (and was) withdrawn at any time. The rise of the Northern Ireland Labour Party (NILP) signified the ascent of 'authentic working-class politics'.

The conclusion appears to be that the Protestant working class, and engineering workers in particular, have been unproblematically Orange supporters of the Unionist bourgeoisie. Yet the Protestant working class has by no means supported its bourgeoisie through thick and thin. Through the medium of the NILP it frequently opposed it in secular class terms. . . . Moreover, the backbone of the NILP was the engineering workers, that is, the body here identified as the most unrelentingly Orange.[38]

This still poses the question: how far is sectarianism a 'moment' of the state and how far is it integral to class hegemony? Bew *et al.* themselves suggest, in 'Some aspects', that sectarianism has an important 'institutional' role in the state, *qua* bourgeois state. This poses another question about where the state ends and civil society begins. I am not sure that state rule, founded upon 'compromises both between sections of the power bloc and crucially between this bloc as a whole and the masses'[39] did not also depend upon those institutions of the masses, the NILP and the trade unions.

THE 'PROTESTANT' WORKING CLASS, DEMOCRACY AND SOCIALISM IN IRELAND TODAY

The problems associated with the survival of the Protestant all-class alliance make one doubt the possibility of any democratic initiative deriving from it. If the Protestant class alliance has contained, as a *sine qua non*, working-class subordination, it is difficult to imagine any emancipatory impulse issuing from it. This is an important aspect of the substance of Protestant class politics in Ireland, conjoined with the British military presence. When one talks of the Protestant working class breaking from the Protestant bourgeoisie, it is important to question what this would mean. What exactly are the democratic features of nation and class within the Protestant community with which a progressive Protestant working class might engage?

In suggesting a split in this 'old alliance', two questions are revealed. First, would the working class remain Protestant in the secular sense of defending trade union issues? Secondly, would it remain Protestant in the political–historical sense of remaining avowedly exclusivist? There are a number of possible answers. One suggests that Protestant labour would fight for trade union concerns pure and simple. A second suggests a commitment to exclusivism and sectarianism. What is rarely considered is that both are not only reconcilable but also mutually indispensable conditions for an anti-Irish and anti-socialist discourse and practice. How is this? Are not trade unionism and Protestant exclusivism mutually irreconcilable world views? A brief survey of the history of craft-trade unionism in Belfast since at least the formation of the Irish Congress of Trade Unions (ICTU) in the 1880s suggests that rather than trade unionism acting as a bulwark against Protestant exclusivism, these have often been mutually sustainable. Indeed, as Patterson has demonstrated, Protestant labour played 'fast-and-loose' with Orangeism when the need arose to protect employment. Patterson illustrates how Orangeism and trade unionism were bound very closely together.[40]

The difficulty here lies with how one sustains the argument that Protestant labour could be anything other than determinedly *Protestant*, where Catholic labour is absent, and this brings us to the heart of the issue. For it is clear that for Bew *et al.*, a decision has been taken that it was (and is) the practice of *Protestant labour* as Protestant *labour* that counts and that the atavistic interests of Catholic *labour* are both Irish, *Catholic*, and by association historically less realistic and desirable.[41] This means that trade unionism as expressed by Protestant labour was against nationalism and other 'non-socialist' diversions because, of course, Protestant needs were fulfilled and nationalism was no longer an issue. This is so because the nation of Protestant labour was Britain – Britain had resolved its national dilemmas. For Belfast labour, economic success and socialism lay in and with the empire. The response to this, of course, depends upon the starting point. Bew and Patterson have recently argued that a series of reforms at the institutional level of the state would suffice and although they recently admitted to underestimating the difficulties of the implementation of reform (*The British State and the Ulster Crisis*), the crux of their analysis remains that this is an ordinary bourgeois state with sometimes exceptional apparatuses and practices. I would suggest the idea of reform of the institutional structures and practices of the state in Northern Ireland is unsustainable.

This is not the same as arguing that the support for democratic reforms is unwisely given. But as many have shown (in particular the well argued account of the history of reform and sectarianism by O'Dowd *et al.*), structural reform within the present context as defined by Britain and the Protestant alliance is inconceivable.[42] Not only does Protestant labour show no signs of denying its Protestantism and heralding the secular labour politics sought by Bew *et al.*, it is quite valid to argue that Protestant labour's politics and trade unionism keeps 'winning'[?] *because* of its Protestantism – its alliance of subordination to capital ensures this. One could go further, making the point that the trade unionism defended by Bew *et al.*, as the basis of secular and later socialist advance, is actually part of the problem to be resolved, for it is a trade unionism with little relevance to combating anti-Catholic sectarianism in Northern Ireland. The political abstinence of trade union leaders has demonstrated a lack of immediate concern with the social problems confronting Catholic labour in a sectarian labour market.

The Fair Employment Agency supports the view that sectarianism and anti-Catholic discrimination are alive and well. Trade unions have been silent in these matters, being more concerned with issues of pay bargaining (which on their own tend to reinforce sectarianism). Their 'democratic' issues have been settled. Where these Protestant 'democratic issues' are questioned by Britain it is the Protestant working class *through its trade union organizations* which consistently supports (and often leads) calls for more repression. Where Britain is seen to let 'our people down', the old Protestant working class–bourgeois/petit bourgeois axis asserts itself. Socialists sometimes pass over the discomfort caused by the massive support Peter Robinson of Ian Paisley's Democratic Unionist Party (DUP) obtains from the shipyard and aircraft workers of East Belfast.

Protestant labour's politics deny anything that raises democratic possibilities to challenge the ascendancy at its roots (which is what the relative dominance of Protestants of all social classes is, even if the term is not fashionable these days). Protestant labour's *labour* politics are labourism in an Irish context. They reinforce labour's subordination in the capital–labour relation by denying any politics which open the possibility of democratic progress in terms that might engage the nationalist population in the north. The only politics that concern them are a Protestant definition of trade unionism which is seen as synonymous with secularism, and a Protestant definition of nation which is taken as democratic.

PROTESTANT LABOUR AND ITS INDEPENDENCE

A working-class Protestant Ulster, were labour finally to triumph and assert its line, would be a peculiar entity. The question is not whether this would be successful; whether, that is, Protestant labour's triumph within the Protestant alliance would work. The question is, what would happen if it attempts this and 'refuses' its traditional location as historically subordinate to capital, where the latter depends upon its consent for class and social domination. The answer is that a situation of greater instability would be achieved, where Protestant labour could assert its claims independently. This has never happened before. The projects to claim Protestant ascendancy have always been instigated and prosecuted with capital in command. An Ulster Protestant working-class democracy would be bound physically to confront its opposition because its Protestantism would for the first time (because it was hegemonic) have wholly superseded its 'labourism'. It would be mobilized wholly on the basis, and for the purpose, of demonstrating the validity of the 1910–14 revolution against Home Rule – the creation of the Ulster national–popular will against the long line of successes by Irish nationalism since 1968, as the UDA and its supporters see it.

In the present period, where Irish nationalism continues to set the main agenda, behind whatever constitutional arrangements appear from time to time, a new Protestant loyalism would emphasize again the extent to which some ideologies inhibit progress, or even articulate modes of social closure. The struggle within the ideology of nation and class should privilege neither Protestant labour's Protestantism nor its labourism. It is within this context therefore that the struggle within some ideologies can be seen to be rather inappropriate, especially where they are founded upon social and class domination.

If the rule of capital is founded upon a necessary domination of distinct, but related, social identities, the alliances of the oppressed which could be born out of this rule will need to be aware of the few democratic openings that arise. The alliances must avail themselves of strategic options that advance the interests of those whose exclusion from full participation in civil society is still as much a feature of the post-Stormont regime as it was before 1972. The enduring reality of discrimination in employment continues to remind us that this economic exclusion is only the tip of a very persistent and solid iceberg of social exclusion and domination. If a labourist or an 'ordinary' Protestant labourist politics will not suffice, it is because such politics cannot accommodate a view which locates this exclusion both in their own practices and in the structure of the state and civil society which gave them sustenance.

Therefore, the problem which an analysis of the Protestant working class must resolve is the issue of class rule. This involves recognition of the place of domination, as well as consent (or commitment) where individuals and social groups take on their rights and obligations of citizenship. What Bew *et al.*'s analysis makes clear is the unwillingness to accept the problem of the role which the Protestant working class plays in processes of class domination. The reason this raises difficult questions is because it is supposed to be labour that acts as the repository for our most cherished hopes.

CONCLUSION

We must define the limits and horizons of both commitment and subordination which are inspired by the working class itself. For without doubt, capital is no more 'aware' of these processes. The point is, where and with what ideological conglomerations are different classes faced, in the process of their mutual reproduction? Because labour ideologies articulate a world of class defined by nation, they are themselves in the process of producing just such amalgams.

What I have argued here is that some parts of labour, with different experiences and material at the point of production and in civil society in general, put together ideologies more suited to extend the possibility of social progress. Not all do. This derives from a recognition that the structure of class rule depends upon class self-subordination. If one considers what the Protestant working class achieved in the Stormont state in terms of the material *quid pro quo*, it is still true to say that a regime of instability after 1920 was created, for one part of the 'nation' was excluded from the processes of nation building and citizenship – the Catholic working class. Unless one recognizes that the process of class rule depended upon (amongst other crucial variables) Catholic subordination, the notions of 'ordinariness' and 'normality' merely serve to reinforce the 'Alice in Wonderland' optic which was the prevailing way of viewing Northern Ireland from Westminster between 1920 and 1968. In fact, what really made Northern Ireland 'ordinary' was the fact that, like other capitalist states, its rule depended on its ability to sustain the subordination of individuals and social groups within the oppressive civil society over which it prevailed.

In this sense then, we can see how it is that some ideological combinations of class and nation might foreclose social progress – loyalism, a form of Ulster social democracy is one such view. This is because it articulates ideologies of class and nation which render democratic imperatives impossible. These ideologies consistently turn a blind eye to the gerrymandered origins of the state and the internal settlement founded on it. Protestant labour has had every reason to be complacent about its province, for it was a steady commitment to British Empire ideologies which helped sustain the belief that Protestant Ulster's 'national' question was resolved – even if today there are fewer signs that this commitment is paying the dividends it once did.

It is worth repeating, too, that in no sense could one urge unambiguous support for what is sometimes a no less restricted and inadequate set of extant Irish nationalist ideologies (*see* Claire O'Halloran's very interesting thesis).[43] That these are subordinate to Protestant views of nation and class does not necessarily make all that they have to offer more attractive. An analysis of these alternative views of nation and class is undoubtedly essential but unfortunately it lies beyond the compass of this chapter. However, it is possible to say that despite many of the inadequacies of Irish nationalist and class discourses, in no sense can they be equated with those of Protestant labourism and its attendant historical blindness.

That the mass mobilizations of the Ulster Clubs after 1986 failed to get off the ground gives little indication that the institutional politics of the Protestant working class will be any less vociferous. This is because at heart they are exclusionary, rather than all-encompassing politics, and labourism at the level of economic class has always sustained this. Such is clearly the case, whatever openings labourism might have appeared to offer; the NILP and labourist ideologies always turned a Nelson's eye to the foundation of Catholic subjugation which was at the centre of the state and civil society, Bew *et al.*'s prodigious efforts notwithstanding.

Notes

1   For recent writing on the dimensions of this relation *see* Laclau and Mouffe (1980) and Meiksins-Wood (1986).
2   For an early and perceptive critique of the separation of these *see* the late Neil Williamson. He illustrates how class and nation are inseparable characteristics in socialist struggle in *Red Weekly*, 1977.
3   I elaborate the implications of this more fully in my unpublished Ph.D. thesis, University of Leeds (1986).
4   O'Dowd *et al.* have suggested that economism is a political position and that a denial of, for example, Irish nationalism can lead to and reinforce sectarianism. Economism and ordinary trade unionism are undoubtedly part of the nexus of reactionary working-class politics in Ireland.
5   In Morgan, A. and Purdie, B., eds (1980).
6   Introduction to *The State in Northern Ireland*, pp. 1–10.
7   In general they are referring to Irish nationalist writing since Connolly and in particular to the socialist contributions of Michael Farrell and Geoff Bell.
8   Bew, Gibbon and Patterson (1980), pp. 169–70.
9   For example, Connolly (1973a). On the import of parliament, cf. Connolly

(1973b).
10 Bew, Gibbon and Patterson (1979), p. 212.
11 ibid., p. 38.
12 ibid.
13 ibid., p 39.
14 ibid.
15 ibid., p. 38.
16 ibid.
17 ibid., p. 39.
18 ibid.
19 Bew, Gibbon and Patterson (1980), p. 155.
20 Bew, Gibbon and Patterson (1979), p. 89.
21 ibid., p. 86.
22 ibid., p. 89.
23 ibid., p. 46.
24 ibid., p. 47.
25 ibid., p. 90.
26 ibid., p. 89.
27 ibid.
28 ibid., p. 89.
29 After 1945, as Bew *et al.* point out, the isolation of Northern Ireland from Great Britain was ended as post-war British social democracy intervened in Stormont's quiet life, with a vengeance.
30 Cf. O'Dowd *et al.* (1980).
31 Bew, Gibbon and Patterson (1980), p. 156.
32 ibid., pp. 168–70.
33 ibid., pp. 154–5.
34 Bew, Gibbon and Patterson (1979), p. 195.
35 ibid., p. 50.
36 ibid., introduction and conclusion.
37 ibid., p. 216.
38 ibid., p. 218.
39 Bew, Gibbon and Patterson (1980), p. 164.
40 Patterson (1981), cf. introduction.
41 I consider the analytic and empirical vagaries of Patterson's argument in my unpublished Ph.D. thesis.
42 O'Dowd *et al.* (1980) and Rolston (1983).
43 Cf. Claire O'Halloran (1987). It seems to me O'Halloran's thesis about the overly Catholic dynamic in much Irish nationalist discourse is pretty uncontentious. Nevertheless, I cannot see how one can sustain this without recognition of how partition, in all kinds of ways, both culturally and politically, continues to marginalize those more assuredly secular traditions of independence that, for example, the Field Day theatre company amongst others, are attempting to recover or construct.

BIBLIOGRAPHY

Bell, G. (1976) *The Protestants of Ulster*, London: Pluto.
——(1984) *The British in Ireland, A Suitable Case for Withdrawal*, London: Pluto.

Bew, P., Gibbon, P. and Patterson, H. (1979) *The State in Northern Ireland, 1921–1972: Political Forces and Social Classes*, Manchester: Manchester University Press.

——(1980) 'Some aspects of nationalism and socialism in Ireland 1968–1978', in Morgan and Purdie, *Ireland: Divided Nation, Divided Class*, London: Ink Links.

Bew, P. and Patterson, H. (1985) *The British State and the Ulster Crisis*, London: Verso.

Connolly, J. (1973a) *Labour in Irish History*, Dublin: New Books Publications.

Connolly, J. (1973b) 'Socialism and Irish Nationalism', in P. Beresford Ellis, ed., *James Connolly: Selected Writings*, London: Penguin.

Farrell, M. (1970) *Northern Ireland: The Orange State*, London: Pluto.

Gaffikin, F. and Morrissey, M. (1990) *Northern Ireland: The Thatcher Years*, London: Zed Books.

Laclau, E. and Mouffe, C. (1980) *Hegemony and Socialist Strategy: Towards a Radical Democratic Politics*, London: Verso.

Meiksins-Wood, E. (1986) *The Retreat from Class. A New True Socialism*, London: Verso.

Morgan, A. (1988) *James Connolly: A Political Biography*, Manchester: Manchester University Press.

Morgan, A. and Purdie, B., eds (1980) *Ireland: Divided Nation, Divided Class*, London: Ink Links.

O'Dowd, L., Rolston, B. and Tomlinson, M. (1980) *Northern Ireland Between Civil Rights and Civil War*, London: C.S.E. Books.

O'Halloran, C. (1987) *Partition and the Limits of Irish Nationalism*, Dublin: Gill & MacMillan.

Patterson, H. (1981) *Class Conflict and Sectarianism*, Belfast: Blackstaff.

The Ripening of Time, A Journal of Sociology and Politics, Dublin: Trinity College. [various issues]

Rolston, B. (1983) 'Reformism and sectarianism: the state of the union after civil rights', in Darby, J. ed., *Northern Ireland: The Background to the Conflict*, Belfast: Appletree Press.

Rowthorn, B. and Wayne, N. (1988) *The Political Economy of Northern Ireland*, London: Polity Press.

Stewart, R.P. (1986) *An Analysis of Ulster Loyalism: the 'Protestant Working Class' and the Emergence of the Northern Ireland State in an Age of Passive Revolution*. Unpublished Ph.D. thesis, University of Leeds.

Williamson, N. (1977) *Red Weekly, Battle of Ideas*.

12 Patrick MacGill
The making of a writer

Patrick O'Sullivan

The early works of Patrick MacGill, most famously his book *Children of the Dead End*, have, from the moment of their production, found themselves serving two linked functions.[1] To the middle classes they opened a window onto the intriguing, hidden lives of the poor: MacGill is quoted in letters to *The Times*. The wandering Irish poor themselves discover MacGill, as Patrick MacGeown did, and rediscover him, to find validation of their own experiences, and a troubling continuity.[2]

In recent decades social historians have also found MacGill: I met him in the works of James Handley and Terry Coleman.[3] A much needed paper by Owen Dudley Edwards, tidying up the bibliographic questions about MacGill, is subtitled 'the making of a historical source'.[4] And it is as a historical source, significantly for 'The modernisation of the Irish female', that the 'Donegal novelist' appears in a recent work of social history.[5]

Approaches to MacGill the writer are elusive and contradictory. John Wilson Foster tries to place MacGill in 'Ulster fiction'. He appreciates MacGill's Irish anti-clericalism and his 'sympathy for that British industrial phenomenon, the Irish navvy', but 'MacGill's novels labour under many literary shortcomings. His social criticism is ideologically simplistic, his poetry bad, his characters too often caricatures, his endings sentimental.'[6]

Studies of working-class writing in Britain have considered the 'novel that made a reputation', *Children of the Dead End*. Ruth Sherry talks of MacGill's 'political convictions': MacGill's hero 'becomes a convinced socialist'. In contrast, Jack Mitchell speaks of the 'ominous' relapse into kneeling prayer at the end of *Children of the Dead End*: 'the book entirely lacks a practical revolutionary perspective.'[7]

According to Mitchell, 1914 is the *annus mirabilis* in the history of the British proletarian novel. In that year appeared Robert Tressell's

The Ragged Trousered Philanthropists, MacGill's *Children of the Dead End*, and John Macdougall Hay's *Gillespie*. (This British *annus mirabilis* thus depends on the work of a Scotsman and two migrant Irishmen.) For Mitchell, after Tressell and Hay, MacGill is, politically, a poor third. 'His success was used against him and his class. He was turned into a kind of "official" working-class writer to put across the propaganda of the ruling class in the language and idiom of the workers themselves.'[8] But Mitchell is not contrasting like with like. 'Robert Tressell', Robert Noonan, had died, of tuberculosis, in 1911, and never saw his book in print. John Macdougall Hay died, of tuberculosis, in 1919. Neither was a professional writer.

MacGill lived until 1963. The appearance of *Children of the Dead End* in 1914 was part of the process whereby he turned himself from a navvy into a novelist, a worker by hand to a worker by brain. MacGill made the choice, one not available to Tressell or Hay, to earn his living by his writing. Or should MacGill too have died, unpublished, of tuberculosis? In popular sociological terms, it is true that MacGill changed his social class. But he did not thereby cease to be a worker.[9] His new kind of work substantially increased his chance of living into old age: there are a lot of dead navvies in MacGill.

This chapter looks at the conditions under which MacGill's works were made, precisely the factors missing from Mitchell's strictures. It is thus more of a contribution to the sociology of literature than a piece of social history or literary criticism. It is not a reading of MacGill, but prepares the ground for a reading, whether MacGill is seen as a literary figure or as a historical source. The chapter looks at the notion of the artist as producer, the writer as workman. A key concept, then, is MacGill's relationship with the mode of production. This is often analysed as simply a relationship between person and machine (the factory worker, for example). But it is also a relationship between person and person. We have by now a considerable, if repetitive, theoretical literature on these themes: we lack studies of individual artist's works that are not reductionist or belittling.[10]

Here are some of the questions that arose, for me, after my first reading of MacGill. The address of the author is given as '8, Jamaica Street, Greenock' in MacGill's first little samizdat verse collection, *Gleanings from a Navvy's Scrap Book*. In his second book of verse, *Songs of a Navvy*, his address is '4, Cloisters, Windsor'. Is this an appropriate address for 'the navvy poet'?

MacGill's best known book, *Children of the Dead End* is subtitled 'The autobiography of a navvy'. But the 'I', the narrator of *Children of the Dead End*, is not called 'Patrick MacGill': his name is 'Dermod Flynn'.[11] The book is written in the form of a novel, using all the devices of a novel. Does this affect the detail of our reading? What, in the end, was MacGill's project, in his verse, in his novels, in his life? In what follows I shall take seriously MacGill the writer, and his project.

THE EARLY VERSE

The details of MacGill's early life, as given in his own *Children of the Dead End* and that introduction to *Songs of the Dead End* by 'J. N. D.', are now well known. The twelve-year-old boy was sent to the hiring fair, 'the slave market'. The fourteen-year-old boy, by now making his own decisions, went to Scotland, to work first as a potato picker, then as a navvy.[12]

The navvy began to read, and to write. In 1910, at the age of nineteen, he published, from that address in Greenock, *Gleanings from a Navvy's Scrap Book*. But *Gleanings* was printed in Ireland, in Derry, by the Derry Journal Limited, Shipquay Street. This press produced a number of such privately published books of verse, by writers, usually middle class, from the surrounding area.[13] It is an interesting choice of press. Did MacGill already have some contact with the Derry Journal? Was he aware of the work of these other self-published poets? What financial costs were involved?

Comment on MacGill's verse can be patronizing or dismissive. But is his poetry simply 'bad'? Brian Maidment's analysis of the lives and works of the 'artizan poets' of the nineteenth century can be applied to Patrick MacGill.[14] There is this difference: MacGill's life reads like that of a 'working-class poet' who has read Maidment. There seems to be a self-awareness within MacGill, and an awareness of the road ahead.

Maidment identifies three types of endeavour within working-class verse:

1) radical writing linked with other forms of political activity, notably, in Maidment's writers, Chartism.
2) what Maidment calls 'the Parnassian strand', whose aim was to demonstrate cultural achievement within the working classes. This is a conscious cultural attempt to join in literary discourse at the highest possible level, to have a voice, on equal terms with all others, in the cultural and philosophical debates of the time. This endeavour denies middle-class claims to sole ownership of literary

tradition. It is 'both culturally necessary and often personally heroic'.

Middle-class readers find it hard to give this kind of verse a considered reading: to them it can seem derivative and pretentious. But the best 'Parnassian' working-class verse is like nothing else in English literature. The poems are quite different from those of middle-class sympathizers protesting on behalf of the working class.[15]

3) 'homely rhyming', articulating shared feelings or experiences, often using dialect or the vernacular.[16]

In Maidment's terms, we find very little 'radical writing' in MacGill, and it is difficult to link what there is to a specific political activity. But, as we shall see, this is not to deny awareness in MacGill. We find much 'Parnassian' writing in MacGill's early verse, and much 'homely rhyming'. Again as we shall see, in MacGill's best 'Parnassian' verse there is a tension between method and subject matter. As his titles suggest, some of his work links with the living song tradition. In the later, more formally published collections of verse, *Soldier Songs* and *Songs of Donegal*, we are almost entirely in the world of 'homely rhyming', but homely rhyming produced for a very specific market.[17]

Of the middle-class interest in working-class writers Maidment says, 'this middle-class interest was primarily *biographical* rather than literary, though the two were, to middle-class thinking, interdependent.' The lives of the self-taught poets were far more interesting than the poetry, and the poetry was often silent on the very subjects that most interested the middle classes.[18] Maidment's working-class poets are often victims of this middle-class interest. MacGill exploited the interest. The 'navvy poet' sent copies of *Gleanings* to journals and influential people.[19]

Gleanings is a pamphlet of some fifty-six pages. It gives us forty-four poems or songs. The 'Contents' list forty-seven items, plus the prose introduction. But the forty-seven include some prose fragments. For example, 'What do You Think?': 'If some men rose from the dead and read their epitaphs they would think they had got into the wrong graves.' MacGill, like many writers, was a great re-cycler: these prose fragments are not wasted. In *Songs of the Dead End* this one is given an exclamation mark, printed as an epigraph to a new poem, 'The Gravedigger', and ascribed to 'Moleskin Joe'. 'Moleskin Joe', the great success of *Children of the Dead End*, is an aspect of his creator.[20]

Another prose fragment in *Gleanings* reads: 'Two Rules of Life. (1) To Know what you want and (2) to see you get it.' At this stage in his writing career MacGill plays with the idea of a book, and with his role in life. In the prose introduction he jokes: '"En passant" may I remark that a labourer has one consolation no other mortal has, though he has remote (very remote) possibilities of rising, he can never sink to a lower level of society than the one he occupies.'

As well as straightforward 'navvy' poems and songs, *Gleanings* contains versions of Fables by La Fontaine: '(Happy thought! What were fables without foxes?)', and poems from the German of Ruckert and Goethe. A long hymn to 'My Book-Case' becomes at times a directory of Parnassus: 'For me has Homer sang of wars.'[21]

In 1911 the navvy was called to London, to work on the *Daily Express*. He began to make use of the contacts made through that distribution of *Gleanings*. An undated letter in MacGill's hand survives.

c/o The Daily Express
8 Shoe Lane
E. C.

Dear Sir,
    Some time ago, I sent you a little book and in reply you told me to inform you if I ever came to London.
    I have come – I suppose the inevitable must happen. I am on the Daily Express, so I thought I would let you know.
    Yours very Sincerely
    Patrick MacGill[22]

The letter is brief, but revealing. MacGill's intention with his little book was not simply to sell it on the streets of Glasgow, a bard to the working class. He wanted 'to rise'. The broadcast posting of *Gleanings* provided contacts. In London ('the inevitable') MacGill built on those contacts.

MacGill knuckled down in a workmanlike way to produce what was wanted in his new workplace. At this point MacGill was by no means an 'Irish' writer. For example, he wrote a poem (which appears in none of his collections) called 'The Men of the Thames'. This was recited 'by Mr. Charles Knowles, the famous English baritone, at the great "Express" Meeting held at Greenwich to demand a warship for the Thames'. In the poem, MacGill speaks for English workers:

We are the men who labour, and little we understand
Why right to live is denied us, here in our native land . . .
Bravely our fathers laboured, back in the early years,
In the spring of England's glory, for this – a harvest of tears;
Theirs were the hands that fashioned, when England's weal was at
stake,
The ships for the daring sailors of Frobisher and of Drake.[23]

This singing of Drake is not what we are taught to expect of Irish bards.

By 1912 MacGill had met Canon Dalton, the King's Chaplin at Windsor. It has been suggested that MacGill may have sent Dalton a copy of *Gleanings*. As we have seen, MacGill might well have written to Dalton on arriving in London.[24] It has further been suggested that Dalton had a homo-erotic interest in handsome young men of working-class origin, and MacGill was a handsome young man, judging by the photograph on the title page of *Gleanings*. The migrant young must negotiate such ambiguities and Dalton was certainly capable of acts of great kindness to the struggling young: he was not rich, yet he paid for one young man to go to Oxford. Without there necessarily being any overt sexual interest, Dalton, it is clear, enjoyed the company of young, working-class men. His aim may in part have been to shock the more staid members of his own class. He certainly shocked his own son, the future Labour minister, who, at the old man's death, burned the letters young men had sent to Dalton.[25]

The relationship between Dalton and MacGill seems not to have followed precisely the pattern described by Maidment, where members of the middle class patronize (in every sense) the working-class writer. Dalton, the 'J. N. D.' of the introduction to *Songs of the Dead End*, did, to some extent, take on the role of intermediary between the poet and the public. Edwards suggests that he may have supported financially the publication of MacGill's verse. But the impression we have of the relationship between the young and the older man is of comradely friendship. Edwards has amusingly demonstrated, on the basis of rhythm and rhyme, that the Latin tags in MacGill's poem 'Logic' owe much to Dalton's high-church English 'ladidah'.[26] Dalton gave MacGill a sinecure: space, without toil of hand or brain, to develop as a writer.

In 1912, from Dalton's address in Windsor, MacGill published his second little book of poetry, *Songs of a Navvy*: again he turned to the distant Derry Journal Limited for the printing. *Songs of a Navvy* gives us sixty poems. It is a less playful production than *Gleanings*. But

MacGill is confidently in control of his own production. The rhymed 'Foreword' says

> These, the songs of a navvy, bearing the taint of the brute,
> Unasked,* uncouth, unworthy, out to the world I put.

The asterisk by the word 'unasked' directs us to a note: 'These verses were not published at the earnest request of several friends.' The word 'not' does read oddly here: I take it that the friends had objected to the inclusion of these particular verses in the earlier publication, *Gleanings*. Had MacGill already met the pressures, described by Maidment, to package and prettify? It is in *Songs of a Navvy* that we first meet that resonant MacGill phrase 'Dead End'. 'Down on the Dead End' is a mournful little song with a jaunty rhythm.[27]

In 1913 appeared MacGill's first 'proper' book from a known publishing house: *Songs of the Dead End*. The book begins with a note, outlining MacGill's life so far, and signed 'J. N. D. Windsor, July, 1912'.[28] *Gleanings* and *Songs of a Navvy* were put together. *Songs of the Dead End* is designed, a handsome book, especially when (no insult to the Derry Journal Limited intended) put alongside the earlier volumes. Each poem begins on a new page. If its length takes it one stanza on to the next page, so be it: let there be white paper. The MacGill of *Gleanings* would have filled the space with epigrams from 'Moleskin Joe'. A pick and a shovel, crossed, are embossed on the cover.

Songs of the Dead End gives seventy-two poems (seventy-one listed in the 'Contents', plus the unlisted 'I do not sing'). Only ten of these poems were selected from the forty-four in *Gleanings*. Fifty-three poems came from the sixty poems in *Songs of a Navvy*. The pattern is confused because MacGill gave some poems new titles in the new collection. There are nine new poems. So, despite the strictures of 'several friends', the bulk of the poems from the self-published *Songs of a Navvy* made it into the more formally produced volume.

The pattern of what is left in and taken out is worth pondering: for example, the La Fontaine translations have gone. The nine new poems, meditations by MacGill from his new position in his new existence, deserve a detailed reading. 'The Navvy' looks at the navvy, from the outside. 'Heroes' gives MacGill's manly reflections on the loss of the *Titanic*: so it was certainly written after 2.20 a.m., 15 April 1912. 'The Old Lure', subtitled 'Fleet Street, 1912', looks romantically back to life on the road.[29] But it is the dense texture of the new poems, not their subject matter, that makes them significant. They are like nothing MacGill offered again.

THE MAKING OF THE PROSE

Middle-class patronage of the working-class poet, with its stress on the moral worth of poetry, conceals, in a very confusing way, the market value of literature. It suggests that this work has no market value at all. Maidment develops formal distinctions between the work of poets acting as 'working-class bards', other work produced under patronage and the work of professionals. His account of the patronage system implicity opposes it to the idea of professionalism. However, 'professionalism was on the whole a totally unrealistic aim for most self-taught writers, however talented.'[30] But professionalism was MacGill's aim.

On 15 December 1913 MacGill signed his first 'Memorandum of Agreement' with Herbert Jenkins Limited, of 12 Arundel Place, Haymarket, London. MacGill is to provide a book called *Children of the Dead End*. Jenkins will print not less than 1000 copies, at six shillings each. The author's royalty will be 10 per cent on the first 1000 copies, 15 per cent on the next 2000, 20 per cent on all subsequent copies. The author is to offer the publisher first refusal of his next three books. Next to this paragraph is written, in MacGill's own hand, 'not poems'. At this point MacGill still had hopes of further, independent, development as a poet.

This 'Memorandum of Agreement' is one of a handful of documents and letters which have survived from the archives of Herbert Jenkins Limited.[31] We now need to say something about Herbert Jenkins, the man and the limited company. Jenkins the man, a minor littérateur (he wrote a respectable *Life of George Borrow*), became a successful popular publisher. He had a knack for picking authors and for nurturing them. He rescued P. G. Wodehouse from poor sales: Wodehouse became a successful comic novelist only when his books appeared in the distinctive Jenkins format, with the winged centaur on the spine. Jenkins also published A. S. Neill, the apostle of kindly education; W. Riley, the Yorkshire novelist; and Francis Ledwidge, an Irish 'self-taught poet', whose literary life bears comparison with MacGill's.

Jenkins was particularly good at publicity and marketing. When he had found or created a successful book he pursued every possible sale with cheap and cheaper editions. Herbert Jenkins Limited was thus 'market-led': and this meant that there gradually developed a less adventurous house style, as Jenkins discovered what would and would not sell. Whilst the house format remained the same, the content of the books more and more approached what we now associate with Mills & Boon: light romantic fiction.

This tendency is illustrated in Jenkins's own writing. For the littérateur, the temptation to play with the genres proved irresistible: in 1916 Jenkins published the first of his Bindle series. Bindle is a Cockney cabman: Jenkins writes about the section of the working class with which he had most contact. This is the working class as comic relief, with laborious comic dialect. The 1918 *Adventures of Bindle* is dedicated 'To the children of the dead end'. Herbert Jenkins Limited went on to publish *Patricia Brent, Spinster*, with no author's name on the title page: a romantic comedy, it could have been written by almost anybody.[32] It was written by Jenkins himself. After Jenkins's death in 1923 the key figure in the company was his partner, John Grimsdick, and in turn, after Grimsdick's death, Grimsdick's son. After *Children of the Dead End*, all MacGill's books, including the poetry, were published by Herbert Jenkins Limited. MacGill's further development as a writer was shaped by his involvement with this market-driven company.

In the archives are letters from Jenkins to MacGill and MacGill to Jenkins: respectful and friendly, they call each other, in the manner of the time, 'Dear MacGill' and 'Dear Jenkins' or 'My Dear Jenkins'. To a letter, dated 9 October 1917, about royalties on *The Brown Brethren*, Jenkins adds: 'I much enjoyed our dinner and chat last night. These have been very strenuous days with me, and such a break was very welcome.'

MacGill, the confident, best-selling author, negotiates with his publisher. On 18 May 1920: 'Dear Jenkins, Yes, you can have my permission to publish "The Rat-Pit" at 3/6 net, provided that no books other than my wife's and mine are advertised within or on wrapper. To awaken demand for our other books such an advertisement would be of use. On "C of D. E." wrapper I notice other books are advertised and not mine.'[33]

MacGill was still writing verse, but it is verse in the service of his novels. In a letter, dated 30 July 1919, dealing with the royalties on *Maureen*, he writes: 'Each chapter which has not yet got a poem will have one when the muse permits. There are four chapters without poems I believe. It will take two pages for each poem, no more.' The *Maureen* poems were recycled, some a little revised, to appear in MacGill's last book of verse, *Songs of Donegal*.

In a letter written on 5 November 1920 MacGill is 'Glad you're bringing out SONGS OF DONEGAL on Armistice Anniversary'. A long PS deals with copies for reviewers: 'Also one to Dr. Crone of Irish Book Lover. The Derry Journal would be worth bearing in mind, for it's the paper read by all the priests in Donegal, Tyrone and Derry. These clergy hate me so much that they buy my books for the pleasure of burning them.'

Throughout this period, from 1917 to at least 1926, MacGill's address is 'St. Margaret's, Queen's Road, Hendon, N. W.'; one letter, dated 10 May 1918, gives the address as '16 Queen's Road'. It would seem that MacGill had given the house a name to honour his wife. Large family houses survive from that period in Queen's Road, Hendon, and it looks as if the MacGills settled there soon after their marriage.

Contracts or options for some fourteen of MacGill's books survive. Of these, the most poignant are the first and the last. As we have seen, the original contract for *Children of the Dead End* survives. It is impossible not to imagine his emotion as, with strong and confident hand, he signed it.

The last document was typed by Herbert Jenkins Limited in London and sent to MacGill at 1320–4 South Figueroa Street, Los Angeles, for signing. It is signed, shakily, and dated '23.1.36' by MacGill. In consideration of the payment of £150 MacGill cedes his rights in two novels, *Helen Spenser* and *The Diary of an Unwanted Girl*. Further: 'I undertake to deliver to Herbert Jenkins, Ltd., by the 30th June 1936 a carefully revised and rewritten version of THE DIARY OF AN UNWANTED GIRL, and I also agree to read the proofs of both books and make the necessary corrections.'

In 1937, *Helen Spenser* was MacGill's last published novel. The paragraph about *The Diary of an Unwanted Girl* tells us that there was a further unpublished manuscript which failed to satisfy the regime at Herbert Jenkins Limited. It is not known what happened to that manuscript. The title suggests that MacGill may have returned to the themes, and the techniques, of *The Rat-Pit*.[34]

There has long been debate about the precise genre to which MacGill's first full-length prose work, *Children of the Dead End*, should be assigned.[35] It would seem to belong to the genre that the sociologists of literature have called 'the literature of fact', or 'the non-fiction novel'. What has brought the existence of the genre to attention is the emergence, in recent years, of powerful examples:

works by Truman Capote and Norman Mailer spring to mind. Recognition of the power of such efforts has encouraged attempts to find other examples of the genre in the past: Defoe's *Journal of the Plague Year* is often seen as the progenitor.

We can no longer picture MacGill writing *Children of the Dead End* in a garret in Glasgow: it was written in very comfortable circumstances in Windsor. And at MacGill's shoulder were Dalton and Jenkins, later to be joined by MacGill's fiancée, the lovely Margaret Gibbons. How far MacGill was actually guided in his approach to his material, for example by Herbert Jenkins himself, is not clear. But what is clear is that the novelistic approach to his own autobiography solved many problems, for the writer. The question of the point of view, which is a technical problem in autobiography, is overcome. The approach exploits but transcends the middle-class interest in the biography of the 'navvy poet'. In one leap it changes MacGill from literary oddity to popular professional novelist.

The genre allows the writer to weld together observations of reality, giving an assurance that this is reality, with the descriptions of internal psychological life that we are used to from the novel. Our culture now expects and values such accounts of internal psychological life: Freud's case histories, marvellous pieces of 'novelistic' writing, attempt to marry that mode of understanding to the scientific method. MacGill's *tour de force*, in this respect, is in chapter 2 of *The Rat-Pit*, where Farley McKeown, the gombeen man, savours his power and decides to do . . . nothing.[36]

In the non-fiction novel, polemic points can be made through narrative devices. 'Dermod Flynn', in *Children of the Dead End*, struggles with socialists, socialism and socialist texts. 'Hours upon hours did I spend wading through Marx's *Capital*, and Henry George's *Progress and Poverty*. The former, the more logical, appealed to me least.' It may be that a man from Ireland, where political discussion focused on issues around land rather than class, would find Henry George more appealing. There is nevertheless, in *Children of the Dead End*, a strong awareness of class difference and class conflict. But in MacGill's second novel, *The Rat-Pit*, all 'progressive' and 'advanced' ideas are given to the despicable people: Alec Morrison the seducer; and the sailor, Norah Ryan's drunk client who turns out to be her brother.[37]

Now we can explore internal contradictions in MacGill's works. Look at 'Dermod Flynn's' rage at his mother, her demands, her stupidity, her fecundity:

'Why was I not sending home some money?' she asked. Another child had come into the family and there were many mouths to fill . . . just as if man and woman had nothing to do with the affair. . . .Bringing me into the world and then living on my labour – such an absurd and unjust state of things!

Compare that with MacGill's reverential poems about Irish motherhood, 'An Irish Mother's Lament', in *Songs of a Navvy*, and 'Mater Dolorosa' in *Songs of the Dead End*

I weep through all the lonely night,
An' pray an' pray upon my knees,
That maybe with the morrow's light
He'll come back.

This is 'Irishness' as a version of pastoral.[38]

THREE DECISIONS

In 1915 MacGill made three decisions which shaped the rest of his life and work. Like every would-be professional writer he had to decide: what should be the theme of his second novel? He fell in love, and decided on marriage and a family, comforts not available, as he tells us in *Children of the Dead End*, to the navvy. The third decision faced every man within the British Empire: what should be his attitude to the war with Germany?

The second novel must build on the success of the first. MacGill chose to retell, in *The Rat-Pit*, the story of the *Children of the Dead End*, but to tell it from the woman's point of view. The woman's tale of migration is as worth telling as the man's. In narrative terms, therefore, *The Rat-Pit* is shaped by *Children of the Dead End*.[39] This partly accounts for that brooding sense of remorseless fate that hangs over *The Rat-Pit*: the writer has no freedom and the characters have no freedom. But there is another reason as well.

The theme of sexual misunderstanding is a common one in the 'romantic' novels of Herbert Jenkins Limited; it is a common theme in the plays of Shakespeare. A woman is suspected, unjustly, of sexual misbehaviour; she is suspected of prostitution. To choose at random a novel published by Herbert Jenkins: in *Hidden Fires* by 'Mrs. Patrick MacGill', the name under which Margaret Gibbons wrote after her marriage, Lola, 'girl-wife and mother', pretends to her war-wounded husband that she works in an antique shop in Blackheath. In fact, she is in the chorus line of 'Wedding Belles'. The plot is about the working out of misunderstanding.[40]

In *The Rat-Pit* there is no possibility of misunderstanding. Prostitution is deliberately chosen as the only realistic alternative to starvation for mother and child. The narrator makes it clear that the processes that led Norah Ryan to prostitution are logical and progressive, and began in rural Ireland. In *Songs of a Navvy*, MacGill's second little pamphlet, there is a poem which begins

> I do not sing
>> Of angel fair or damozel
>>> That leans athwart a painted sky . . .
> I do not sing
>> Of plaster saints or jealous gods,
>>> But of the little ones I know
> Who paint their cheeks or bear their hods
>> Because they live in doing so
>> Their hapless life on earth below.[41]

Parnassian, Tennysonian words, like 'athwart', place MacGill's discourse in tension. This is a path, little trod by English verse, well explored by some of MacGill's French contemporaries: traditional technique and diction allied to 'sordid' or realistic subject matter.

The structure of the line puts hod and painted cheek side by side, and gives them equal weight. What is the difference between those who live by the hod and those who live by the painted cheek?: gender. MacGill's terrible perception is that the very same forces that propel young Irish men into navvyhood propel young Irish women into prostitution. What could the male-centred socialism of MacGill's time have done with that perception?

The theme is developed in 'The Song of the Lost', one of the poems in which MacGill speaks with the woman's voice

> What will be left when the siren city
> Ceases to lure and ceases to pay . . .
> The kisses I've had were born of passion,
> And the love was the lust of brutal men
> Wild from the bar or gambling den,
> My jewels were bought in a soul's eclipse,
> For I was gay in an evil fashion –
> Queen of the sodden alley, when
> They paid for kissing my painted lips.[42]

Painted cheeks and painted lips: these poems prepare us for the writing of *The Rat-Pit*, where Norah Ryan arms herself, like a

Homeric hero, for her new profession.[43] And MacGill recycles his own experiences: in *Children of the Dead End* 'Dermod Flynn' peers through the window of a large house to sneer at the diners; in *The Rat-Pit* Norah looks through the window into the warm home of her seducer.[44]

'The Rat-Pit' itself is a lodging house for women: '"a good decent place it is – threepence a night for a bunk"'. But in calling his novel *The Rat-Pit* MacGill summarizes his vision of the world Norah Ryan must inhabit. The resonant phrase, 'dead end', from the sombre little poem in *Songs of a Navvy*, is used in two of MacGill's titles. MacGill's feeling is that the road that led him out of Ireland into navvyhood leads nowhere. It is a dead end: it ends in death. As mentioned above, there are a lot of dead navvies in MacGill: even 'Moleskin Joe' dies, not in the poem called 'The Death of Moleskin' (there he is dead drunk), but in 'Hic Jacet', one of the poems that did not make it from *Songs of a Navvy* into *Songs of the Dead End*.[45]

If MacGill's beliefs, as he worked them out, can be seen as a coherent whole and given a name, that name would be Christian socialist: there is the Christian wish for values that transcend the contingent. The shared ending of the first two novels, with its appeal to prayer, foreshadows the detailed working out of the Christ story that MacGill gives in *The Carpenter of Orra*.[46]

MacGill had by now written about migrants at length and importantly. Being an Irish migrant is not the same thing as being Irish. And his handling of migrant themes, notably the story of Norah Ryan in *The Rat-Pit* was not such as would endear him to the Irish in Ireland.[47] But Britain, despite being a considerable receiver of migration, did not see itself as a migrant-receiving country. Britain saw itself as happily welcoming refugees and political exiles, but that perception, almost by definition, excluded the migrant Irish. In Australia and the United States the arrival of the migrant has its place in literature. But his British readership read MacGill as if he were an 'Irish' writer, and MacGill and his market-driven publisher accepted this. My copy of *Children of the Dead End* has an advertisement for a later MacGill book: 'a typical MacGill story – a tale of Ireland and Irish folk.'[48]

MacGill had left Ireland at the age of fourteen; his feelings about Ireland are, at the very least, ambivalent. His visits to Ireland as a tourist or journalist do little to bridge the gap, a gap that widened further as MacGill's other life decisions took him even further away from the course of Irish history in the twentieth century.

The first two novels meant that MacGill was associated with 'low life' themes: a window onto the hidden world. But MacGill himself now lived on the other side of the window: where 'Dermod Flynn' and Norah Ryan peered in, MacGill peered out. In his rendering of dialect and accent, MacGill increasingly follows the strange convention that standard written English expresses phonetically the accent of the English middle and upper classes, while other kinds of people must be shown to talk oddly.[49]

By 1917 MacGill had become a professional writer, with a new life, soon to have new responsibilities in Queen's Road, Hendon. In 1912, when MacGill's first proper book, *Songs of the Dead End*, was in preparation for The Year Book Press, that same press had published *The 'Good-Night' Stories* by Margaret Gibbons. Margaret, in her photographs, is a beautiful young woman; and 'well-connected'. We must imagine the two young people meeting and falling in love. We must imagine it for (and here I betray an interest in the biography, rather than the works) there is very little about this experience in MacGill's writings: a dedication, and a poem, 'To Margaret'.[50]

When MacGill married Margaret Gibbons in the Catholic Church in Hampstead in November 1915, the bride was given away by the son of F. D. Maurice, the Christian socialist. The best man was Herbert Jenkins, who also paid for the reception. As we have seen, Margaret Gibbons continued to write popular romances, published by Herbert Jenkins Limited, under the name 'Mrs. Patrick MacGill'. So much, we might say, for the writer's relationship with the mode of production.[51]

MacGill's third decision had to do with the war against Germany: where did his duty lie? There seems to have been no debate, given the milieu within which he now lived. Like many thousands of young Irishmen, in Ireland, England and throughout the empire, he enlisted. MacGill joined the London Irish Rifles, served in France as a medical orderly, and was wounded at Loos.

MacGill wrote a series of books about the war in France. The earlier books in the series are workmanlike developments of his journalism. *The Great Push*, in particular, is a hypnotic account of the surreal world behind the front line. As we have seen, Herbert Jenkins was, throughout this time, supportive, publishing MacGill's *Soldier Songs*: it was seen as part of the war effort. The later books in the war series are Herbert Jenkins Limited pot-boilers, squeezing every possible sale out of public interest in the war: *The Dough-Boys; The Diggers: The Australians in France*. 'Mrs. Patrick MacGill' wrote *The Anzac's Bride*.[52]

Meanwhile, the novel-buying public lost interest in the war, a fact sourly noted by another popular novelist at the time.[53] The war, and the books he wrote about it for Herbert Jenkins Limited, proved an expensive detour for Patrick MacGill the writer. After the war he struggled to find, or re-find, his themes. He continued to write for Herbert Jenkins Limited, but soon Jenkins himself was no longer there. He wrote about Ireland: his public assumed him to be an insider, but, to an Ireland afflicted with 'collective amnesia' about Irish involvement in the war, he was an outsider. MacGill's last published novel, *Helen Spenser*, plays out a Herbert Jenkins Limited romance against the background of another war, the Irish war of independence. There is some suggestion, in *Glenmornan*, of the migrant writer dealing with MacGill's experiences of being de-cultured (not uncultured) and unclassed. But these are not major issues for his public, and his publisher.[54]

In his later years Patrick MacGill suffered from ill-health, neglect, and estrangement. His hobby of 'mowing Irish meadows', listed in an old *Who's Who*, is more a matter of public persona than private reality. In 1953 in Donegal, Patrick MacGeown found only bitterness and inaccurate memory.[55] Attempts to recapture MacGill for 'Irishness' amount to a misreading of a man who, in his life and in his work, remained an unforgiven migrant. It is as a migrant writer, with all those contradictions and compromises, that we should read him. It is right that, to understand Patrick MacGill, his work and his project, we should, like Patrick MacGeown, make pilgrimage to Donegal. But we should go on, to walk down Jamaica Street, Greenock, and the Cloisters, Windsor. And we should go to Queen's Road, Hendon, where so many of MacGill's books were written, and stand there, looking south towards the hills of Hampstead.

Notes

1　The following abbreviations for the early works of Patrick MacGill are used:
　G = Patrick MacGill, *Gleanings from a Navvy's Scrap Book* (Greenock: P. MacGill, 1910).
　SON = Patrick MacGill, *Songs of a Navvy* (Windsor: Patrick MacGill, 1912).
　SDE = Patrick MacGill, *Songs of the Dead End* (London: Year Book Press, 1913).
　CDE = Patrick MacGill, *Children of the Dead End: The Autobiography of a Navvy* (London: Herbert Jenkins, 1914).
　R–P = Patrick MacGill, *The Rat-Pit* (London: Herbert Jenkins, 1915).

My thanks to those who commented on early versions of this paper, in the Department of Theology, University of Durham, 1986 and at History Workshop 20, Leeds, 1986. My especial thanks to Bernard Aspinwall, Bernard Canavan, Owen Dudley Edwards, Sheridan Gilley,

Brian Maidment, Alison Pearce and Century Hutchinson Limited.

2 'The novel that made a reputation. The little known and wonderful life of a navvy': the advertisement at the back of my copy of the third printing of Patrick MacGill, *The Great Push: An Episode of the Great War* (London: Herbert Jenkins, 1916). Douglas Woodruff, ed., *Dear Sir: A Selection of Letters to the Editor of The Times* (London: Methuen, 1936) p. 420; Patrick MacGeown, *Heat the Furnace Seven Times More* (London: Hutchinson, 1967) p. 34.

3 James E. Handley, *The Navvy in Scotland* (Cork: Cork University Press, 1970) pp. 349–62. Terry Coleman, *The Railway Navvies*, revised edition (Harmondsworth: Penguin, 1968) pp. 161–2.

4 Owen Dudley Edwards, 'Patrick MacGill and the making of a historical source: with a handlist of his works', *The Innes Review* (Scottish Catholic Historical Association) 37, 2 (1986) pp. 73–99. This paper by Edwards is now the indispensable starting point for serious study of MacGill: some earlier, informal papers by other hands are inaccurate on bibliographic detail.

5 David Fitzpatrick, 'The modernisation of the Irish female', in O'Flanagan, Ferguson and Whelan, eds, *Rural Ireland: Modernisation and Change 1600–1900* (Cork: Cork University Press, 1987) p. 170.

6 John Wilson Foster, *Forces and Themes in Ulster Fiction* (Dublin: Gill & MacMillan, 1974) p. 89.

7 Ruth Sherry, 'The Irish working class in fiction', in Jeremy Hawthorn, ed., *The British Working Class Novel in the Twentieth Century* (London: Edward Arnold, 1984) p. 114. Jack Mitchell, 'Early harvest: three anti-capitalist novels published in 1914', in H. Gustav Klaus, ed., *The Socialist Novel in Britain* (Brighton: Harvester, 1982) p. 79.

8 ibid., pp. 67, 75.

9 See Gavin Kitchen, *Rethinking Socialism: A Theory for a Better Practice* (London: Methuen, 1983) pp. 8–9, for the distinction between the popular sociologist's 'working class' and the Marxist use of the term to mean all those who live by selling their labour power and do not control the means of production.

10 'Valéry is a petit bourgois intellectual, no doubt about it. But not every petit bourgeois intellectual is Valéry': Jean-Paul Sartre, *Search for a Method*, trans. Hazel E. Barnes (New York: Vintage, 1968) p. 56. Macherey and Wolff are useful: Pierre Macherey, *A Theory of Literary Production*, trans. Wall (London: Routledge & Kegan Paul, 1978); Janet Wolff, *The Social Production of Art* (London: Macmillan, 1981). A. Stewart Crehan, 'The artist as producer', in [Ann Thompson and Anthony Beck, eds,] *Social Roles for the Artist* (Liverpool: The Arts, Politics and Society Group, 1979) is a good, brief outline of the issues.

11 *G*, p. 6; *SON*, title page; *CDE*, p. 16.

12 *SDE*, p. ii. Edwards, op. cit., p. 97, gives the arguments for 1913 as the year of the British publication of *Songs of the Dead End*.

13 As an example I offer 'The Women of Ireland' from L. Mullen, BA, *Miscellaneous Poems* (Donegal: L. Mullen, 1912) p. 34

    Their deep virtue and sense
    Are their beauty's defence,

> Wherever they are, at home or afar;
>   They're faithful in love,
>   They're pure as the dove –
> The fair ones who smile on our own green isle.

14 Brian Maidment, 'Essayists and artizans – the making of nineteenth-century self-taught poets', *Literature and History* 9, 1 (1983) pp. 74–91, and *The Poorhouse Fugitives: Self-Taught Poets and Poetry in Victorian Britain* (Manchester: Carcanet, 1987). As Maidment acknowledges, there is a problem of terminology: even 'self-taught poets' seems wrong, implying as it does that other, more acceptable poets went to some sort of bardic school.

15 Maidment, *Poorhouse Fugitives*, pp. 14–15. See 'Just Instinct and Brute Reason' by 'A Manchester Operative', ibid., p. 47.

16 ibid., p. 15.

17 Patrick MacGill, *Soldier Songs* (London: Herbert Jenkins, 1916) and *Songs of Donegal* (London: Herbert Jenkins, 1921).

18 Maidment, *Poorhouse Fugitives*, p. 17.

19 Edwards, op cit., p. 96.

20 *G*, p. 47; *SDE*, p. 75. Of 'Moleskin Joe', Mitchell, op. cit., p. 81 says: 'It is as if some character out of Shakespeare had turned proletarian and shouldered his way back into English literature.'

21 *G*, pp. 10, 5, 8.

22 The letter survives in the Brotherton Library, Leeds University; all of it, including the address, is in MacGill's hand. It is not clear who was the recipient of the letter: it seems to be associated with the T. Edmund Harvey bequest. A. E. Day, 'From Irish navvy to royal librarian', *Library World* 71, 831 (1969), notes the existence of the letter.

23 'The Men of the Thames' was printed as a leaflet, a copy of which survives in the Brotherton Library, Leeds University. The leaflet gives its source as, 'the London "Daily Express", November 29th, 1911' and tells us, 'This Poem, by Mr. Patrick McGill [sic], was recited last night by Mr. Charles Knowles, the famous English baritone, at the great "Express" Meeting held at Greenwich to demand a warship for the Thames.'

24 Day, op. cit., p. 70.

25 Ben Pimlott, *Hugh Dalton*, revised edition (London: Macmillan, 1986) pp. 20, 66, 198.

26 Edwards, op. cit., p. 91.

27 *SON*, pp. 11, 67. Both these poems reappear in *Songs of the Dead End*, the 'Foreword' without its asterisked footnote and retitled 'By-the-way', p. 18; and 'Down on the Dead End' with a note in brackets 'On tramp, 1909', p. 130. A number of the poems that first appeared in *Songs of a Navvy* have these bracketed notes in *Songs of the Dead End*: their purpose seems to be to link MacGill's poems with his biography, and to vouch for the authenticity of his experience.

28 *SDE*, p. ii.

29 ibid., pp. iii, 158, 161. If 'Heroes' invites comparison with Hardy's 'The Convergence of the Twain', 'The Old Lure' reminds us of Yeats's 'The Lake Isle of Innisfree'.

30 *See* Maidment, *Poorhouse Fugitives*, pp. 326–9, for this important discussion, ending with the moving account of John Clare's attempt to market his own works. MacGill moved very quickly through the phase that brought Clare to despair.

31 The 'Memorandum of Agreement' survives amongst the Herbert Jenkins Limited papers, in Century Hutchinson Limited's archives. The train of take-overs in the publishing world means that, at the time of writing, Century Hutchinson owns what remains of Herbert Jenkins Limited's interests. Further quotations in this paper from the MacGill/Jenkins correspondence and from MacGill's contracts with Herbert Jenkins Limited come from documents in those archives. I would stress that very little survives: documents only survive if they have straightforward contractual implications. I understand that many of Herbert Jenkins Limited's documents were destroyed during the London Blitz.

32 Herbert Jenkins, *Bindle* (London: Herbert Jenkins Limited, 1916); *Adventures of Bindle* (London: Herbert Jenkins Limited, 1919); *Patricia Brent, Spinster by the author of?* [by Herbert Jenkins] (London: Herbert Jenkins Limited, 1920).

33 This letter suggests that MacGill had an interest in, and to some extent control over, the advertisements that appeared in his books. Such advertisements are a striking feature of many of the books published by Herbert Jenkins Limited.

34 Patrick MacGill, *Helen Spencer* (London, Herbert Jenkins Limited, 1937); Edwards, op. cit., p. 79, mentions a rejected novel, quoting Patrick MacGill's daughter, Chris: now we know its title.

35 ibid., p. 74. There is a brief outline of the genre in Ken Plummer, *Documents of Life* (London: Allen & Unwin, 1983) pp. 26–7.

36 *R-P*, p. 26.

37 *CDE*, p. 140; *R-P*, pp. 159, 265.

38 *CDE*, pp. 116–17; *SON*, p. 26; *SDE*, p. 141. 'An Irish Mother's Lament' is one of the poems in *Songs of a Navvy* that did not make it into *Songs of the Dead End*. 'Mater Dolorosa' is entitled 'Waiting' in *Songs of a Navvy*.

'Version of pastoral' refers to William Empson's title, *Some Versions of Pastoral* (London: Hogarth, 1935). For a discussion of pastoral see Bryan Loughrey, ed., *The Pastoral Mode* (London: Macmillan, 1984). 'Irishness' as 'pastoral' would link Empson's comment that good proletarian art is usually 'Covert Pastoral' (Loughrey, op. cit., p. 83) with Lerner's curious mix of Pope and Freud: pastoral as an illusion in which 'wish-fulfilment is a prominent factor in its motivation' (Loughrey, op. cit., p. 154).

39 Foster, op. cit., p. 89.

40 Mrs. Patrick MacGill, [Margaret Gibbons], *Hidden Fires* (London: Herbert Jenkins Limited, 1921).

41 *SON*, p. 10. This poem is reprinted in *Songs of the Dead End*, p. ix, where it is untitled, not listed in the 'Contents', and with the date 1911 added at the end.

42 *SON*, p. 62, and reprinted in *SDE*, p. 30. This poem links with another of MacGill's themes in his early works: the fear of a childless, poverty-stricken, neglected old age. See *CDE*, p. 4; *R-P*, p. 213.

43 *R-P*, p. 251.

44 *CDE*, p. 121; *R-P*, p. 193.

45 *R-P*, p. 212; *SON*, pp. 67, 44, 68.

46 Patrick MacGill, *The Carpenter of Orra* (London: Herbert Jenkins Limited, 1924): this novel is not set in Ireland.

47 Edwards, op. cit., pp. 83, 97. MacGeown, op. cit., p. 176, tried to collect memories of MacGill in Donegal in 1953: '"He went away", said one old man, "when he was fourteen years old and he never came back. It was just as well, for his books were not good and there would be no welcome for him here." In that very Catholic part of Ireland I knew what he meant.'

48 The novel so described is Patrick MacGill, *The House at the World's End* (London: Herbert Jenkins Limited, 1935). My copy of Patrick MacGill, *Sid Puddiefoot* (London: Herbert Jenkins, 1926), has two pages of advertisements for 'Patrick MacGill's Famous Novels of Irish Life'.

49 MacGill's practice is complex. *See*, for example, MacGill, *Sid Puddiefoot*, p. 31, where Sid himself is given eye-aching Cockney and 'the Irishman' speaks standard English.

50 Margaret Gibbons, *The 'Good-Night' Stories* (London: The Year Book Press, 1912) is a collection of Barriesque fairy stories told to her children by an upper-middle-class London mother. MacGill's dedication is in *The Great Push*; his poem, in *Soldier Songs*, p. 88, begins, 'If we forget the fairies. . .'

51 Edwards, op. cit., p. 98.

52 Patrick MacGill, *The Great Push: An Episode of the Great War* (London: Herbert Jenkins Limited, 1916); *The Dough-boys* (London: Herbert Jenkins Limited, 1918); *The Diggers: The Australians in France* (London: Herbert Jenkins Limited, 1918) [see Edwards, op. cit., p. 78 for these datings]. Mrs Patrick MacGill, [Margaret Gibbons], *The Anzac's Bride* (London: Herbert Jenkins Limited, 1918).

53 Ian Hay, *The Willing Horse* (London: Hodder & Stoughton, 1921) p. 7: 'One is informed that novels touching upon the war are no longer read.' This reduces the novelist to the following alternatives: writing a novel set in some period before 1914, writing a novel which pretends that the war never happened, or writing a novel about people who took no part in the war: 'Certified Lunatics, Convicts in residence, and Conscientious Objectors.' That he might have added 'Irish Nationalists' underlines the very different paths that the two countries have followed during this century.

54 Patrick MacGill, op. cit. (1937) and *Glenmornan* (London: Herbert Jenkins Limited, 1918).

55 MacGeown, op. cit., pp. 175–6.

13 Bringing the margins into the centre

A review of aspects of Irish women's emigration

Ann Rossiter

In consigning the Irish and their contribution to the success of the British Industrial Revolution to the end of his book, *Industry and Empire*, in a chapter headed, 'The other Britain', the economic historian E. J. Hobsbawm[1] was merely reflecting the level of importance ascribed to the Irish in Britain, up to the late 1960s when the book was published, and indeed, until quite recently. Hobsbawm was probably the first writer to use the term 'the invisible Irish' which is now widely used to describe the low profile of Irish immigrants. Though increased academic interest in the USA, Britain, Australia and elsewhere over the past decade or so means that the notion of invisibility is now less apt where males are concerned, sadly, it remains an accurate description of the treatment of female migrants. As Brownwen Walter,[2] in her paper, *Gender and Irish Migration to Britain*, points out, 'Irish women have been hidden behind Irish men in academic studies . . . accounts of emigration from Ireland ignore gender but deal implicitly with men's moves'. This should come as something of a surprise, since as early as 1973, Robert Kennedy in his path-breaking work, *The Irish: Emigration, Marriage and Fertility*,[3] stressed the fact that women have dominated the outflow of Irish migration in most periods of the nineteenth and twentieth centuries and that their reasons for emigrating did not mirror those of their male counterparts. However, the importance of these distinguishing features seems to have had little impact, for in more recent works such as *The Irish in the Victorian City*[4] and *The Irish in Britain, 1815–1939*[5] women, if they appear at all, do so merely on the margins.

The marginalization of women in history has been a major preoccupation of the current wave of British feminism and Anna Davin[6] spoke for many when, in 1972, she wrote 'Women's history – and therefore people's history – has yet to be written, and to write it is part of our present struggle. We are formed by the past, and yet we know nothing about it.' Almost twenty years on, and a great deal of feminist research later, we have learned much about women's lives in past generations. We are now more knowledgeable about British women in the family and work place, and about the political and ideological forces that have shaped their destiny. However, British feminist scholarship has tended to concentrate on gender and class to the exclusion of all other factors, such as nationality and race. This means that the presence in Britain of Afro-Caribbean, Asian, Chinese, Irish and other ethnic minority women, as well as their contribution to the building of the land, has been ignored, as have women generally in male scholarship.

Acutely conscious of their 'invisibility', Irish women immigrants have begun to record their presence and their achievements. In 1988, *Across the Water: Irish Women's Lives in Britain*[7] – an oral history and the first book dealing exclusively with Irish women's emigration to Britain – appeared (this has recently been joined by an oral history of Irish women in the USA by Ide O'Carroll[8]). Together with a novel by Maude Casey,[9] charting the painful journey of a young second-generation Irish girl in coming to terms with her Irish identity, and a collection of short stories by Moy McCrory[10] about growing up Irish and female in Liverpool, these works have sparked a great deal of interest and opened the way for future research and writing. A number of articles have also been published in British feminist journals such as *Spare Rib* and *Trouble and Strife*, as well as reports of the London Irish Women's Conferences,[11] published by the London Irish Women's Centre, which have appeared at intervals throughout the 1980s. A further report, *Irish Women in London, the Ealing Dimension*, by the British geographer Bronwen Walter,[12] provides valuable insights into the numbers of Irish women in London in the contemporary period, their geographical distribution, demographic characteristics, employment and housing. Two scholarly works, *Erin's Daughters in America: Irish Immigrant Women in the Nineteenth Century* by Hasia Diner[13] and *Ourselves Alone: Women's Emigration from Ireland 1885–1920* by Janet Nolan,[14] both concerning the exodus to the USA, have appeared in the 1980s. Lynn Hollen Lees's *Exiles of Erin, Irish Migrants in Victorian London*,[15] while not exclusively a study of women, is the only academic work on the Irish in nineteenth-century Britain to give serious treatment to women as a separate category.

IRISH WOMEN'S EMIGRATION IN THE NINETEENTH CENTURY

As a result of British colonial intervention, economic distress and religious persecution, emigration had become a fact of Irish life long before the nineteenth century. In the thirty years between the end of the Napoleonic wars and the eve of the Great Famine of 1845–9, an estimated 800,000–1,000,000 had crossed the Atlantic to North America.[16] In 1841 there were 419,256 Irish-born residents in Britain; a decade later the figure had climbed to 727,326 as a result of the Famine influx.[17] Between 1845 and and 1870 at least three million people left Ireland as a whole and 1.1 million emigrated between 1871 and 1891.[18] Added to these were large numbers of seasonal migrants, both male and female, who travelled to England, Scotland and Wales on a yearly basis.[19] During the Famine period and immediately after it, whole families emigrated, but subsequently the migrations were largely made up of young, single people. Precise figures for the sex ratios of emigrants first became available in the late 1800s, and consequently we know that of the 1,357,831 who left between 1885 and 1920, 684,159 were female; of these, 89 per cent were single and most were under the age of twenty-four.[20] Diner remarks that this constituted a mass female movement without parallel in the history of European emigration and a 'defeminization' of the Irish countryside. Both Diner and Nolan inform us, as did the work of Maxine Seller[21] and Kristian Hvidt[22] almost a decade earlier, that the extent of this emigration of single Irish women, travelling alone and independently of parents or husbands, was an anomaly in the history of overall European emigration to the United States. It stood in marked contrast to the custom among other European groups, such as Danes, Italians or Jews, where women's emigration was generally led and financed by male relatives. In the case of Ireland annual remittances from America amounted on average to five million dollars between 1848 and 1900 and financed the emigration of at least three-quarters of all those who went to the United States in that period.[23] Much of the passage money came from women anxious to secure an independent livelihood for their female siblings and relatives and to help them regain the respect and status that wages brought.

While work on women migrants is still in its infancy, the social processes which propelled this unique exodus of women out of Ireland in the nineteenth century are now better understood. Although there were significant differences in the economic roles of women according to class, research on the role of rural women in the eighteenth and early nineteenth centuries shows that they played a significant part in the type of mixed agriculture prevalent at the time. Lynn Hollen Lees,[24] in her essay on the Irish family economy of the mid-nineteenth century, quotes contemporary reports, such as Edward Wakefield's of 1812: 'They [women] are subjected to all the drudgery generally performed by men: setting potatoes, digging turf, and the performance of the most laborious occupations.'[25] Other observers reported that women were engaged in binding corn, digging potatoes, saving hay and looking after fowls. The dependence of the family economy on women's labour was crucial, especially on those activities which could be converted into cash. Arthur Young in the 1770s had found that: 'They make their rents by a little butter, a little wool, a little corn, and a few young cattle and lambs.'[26] Women's role in this process was crucial, says Hollen Lees, 'for they made the butter, spun the wool, cared for the pigs and poultry, and sold the eggs, diverting food away from the family'.[27] It was reckoned that men fed the family by their labour in the fields and women paid the rent by spinning. On the western seaboard, knitting was an important cottage industry, and in the towns the wives of craftsmen shared some of the tasks of the workshop and supervised the welfare of apprentices and servants. Widows continued to manage businesses until children were sufficiently grown to take over responsibility.[28] This is not to suggest that women enjoyed equality with men in the patriarchal society that Ireland was in the eighteenth and nineteenth centuries, but their status was undoubtedly enhanced by their ability to contribute to the family economy, and this was reflected in their freedom to marry more or less at will and at a relatively early age.

By the mid-nineteenth century this situation had dramatically altered. The market for homespun thread virtually disappeared as the British Industrial Revolution began to make itself felt in Ireland with the dumping of factory-made goods. The Act of Union of 1800 had created a free-trade zone between the two countries, and, given Britain's position as the world's leading industrial nation, especially in textiles, it is not surprising that Ireland's more primitive wool, linen and cotton industries were quickly undermined. It was only in the Belfast area that any significant native industry developed and provided women with paid work. Mary E. Daly[29] points out that manufacturing industry employed a mere 17 per cent of the Irish work force in 1891 compared with 27 per cent in 1841, the brunt of the decline being borne by women workers. The proportion of women recorded in the census as occupied fell steadily from 29 per cent in 1861 to 19.5 per cent in 1911, the 1861 level never being regained. Women's employment was further affected by the shift away from tillage caused by falling prices and the repeal of the Corn Laws in Britain in 1846. The flooding of the British market with cheap foreign grain was a devastating blow for Irish producers, not least for women, whose role was even further marginalized, with the switch to less labour-intensive and male-dominated activities, such as the keeping of livestock. The lack of any significant industrial infrastructure outside the Belfast area meant that few opportunities for paid employment occurred for women over the next century, the only significant exception being domestic service. The pattern was repeated in the farmyard. Joseph Lee[30] draws our attention to the mechanization of dairying, previously a female domain, but one which had become exclusively male by the end of the nineteenth century as creameries took over from domestic production.

In 1884, Frederick Engels[31] had noted that as the household economy dwindled in importance, so did the role of women. Having been pushed out of participation in social production, their oppression then became fixed through confinement in the household, and although there were variations according to class and to financial need, the domesticated wife became the ideal to which all classes aspired. In the case of Irish women, this development is striking and the link between economic status and social position seems inescapable. Large numbers of women who could no longer find independent employment or supplement family income, now became vulnerable as the dependants of fathers and husbands. Marriage and motherhood increasingly came to be the only occupation available to them, but this avenue was reserved for those who could secure a dowry. The custom of dowering daughters had previously been confined to the larger farmers and gentry. Amongst the lesser peasantry, land was continually sub-divided to provide for children once they married. This arrangement found favour amongst absentee British landlords who were primarily concerned with the high income such an arrangement brought. The system of subdivision came to an end by the mid-nineteenth century for a number of reasons, not least the successive failure of the potato crop, the staple food of those who tilled the dwindling, dwarf-sized plots. The post-Famine restructuring of the economy favoured larger farms for cattle grazing and, although there was a significant drop in the population, land became scarce and the earlier, more spontaneous attitude to marriage was soon a thing of the past. Only one son now inherited the farm and his bride was required to provide a substantial dowry. Marriage in this context, writes Hugh Brody, 'was fundamentally unromantic: arranged by a matchmaker, attended by endless negotiations and wranglings over dowry and worth, the wedding eventually paired a girl of twenty with a man often well over forty'.[32] Although there is a certain amount of controversy over when precisely the new social order took root, writers are in agreement that the Great Famine was a watershed in Irish life. In the post-Famine period people were subordinated to the land in a manner that was unique in Europe. Between 1845 and 1914 the age of the average male at marriage rose from about twenty-five to thirty-three and the age of the average female from about twenty-one to twenty-eight. Husbands were generally older than the wives as a result of the reluctance of the man's parents to relinquish the farm and allow a new family to be formed. Large numbers did not marry at all and celibacy became increasingly common. By the turn of the century 88 per cent of women between the ages of twenty and twenty-four were unmarried as were 53 per cent of those between the ages of twenty-five and thirty-four.[33] By postponement and reducing the rate of marriage, the Irish peasantry attempted to curb population and ensure that the trauma of famine would not be repeated. They were aided in this enterprise by a restructured and revitalized Catholic Church in the latter half of the nineteenth century. A huge church building programme was put in motion, the number of clergy increased dramatically and the population underwent what has been described as a 'devotional revolution'. A strongly puritanical attitude to all matters concerning sex became widespread, and a rigid moral code was enforced, which heavily punished all those who deviated. Opinion has differed on how instrumental religion was in the forging of this new morality, but there now appears to be general agreement with Eugene Hynes's assessment

> They [the Irish peasantry] accepted puritanical teaching because, from their own experience, they knew that illegitimacy would threaten the foundations of the stem-family system and increase the number of mouths dependent on a given farm. But, and this is the important point, the people were discriminating in regard to what teaching they accepted from the church, and the church was a follower of the people, not vice versa. Officially, Catholicism favoured early marriage, but the people did not marry early. The priests were 'ineffectual champions of marriage' . . . because, for very good reasons, people did not believe in early marriage. Early

marriage would virtually have made impossible what they wanted – a higher standard of living.[34]

This uncompromising order was accepted by successive generations of men and women who remained in Ireland, although Pauline Jackson[35] found that folk poetry of the time reflected a certain rebelliousness concerning the arranged marriage and dowry system. Those who chafed at the idea of loveless marriages determined by matchmakers, and the many who failed to secure a dowry, emigrated to find a freer and more independent existence. For those women who left Ireland, suggests David Fitzpatrick,[36] the nineteenth century was often a period of triumph rather than subjection.

THE SEARCH FOR WORK

The large numbers of single women, surplus to the needs of nineteenth-century Irish society, who crossed the Atlantic, and the smaller number who made their way to Britain, Australia and New Zealand, were primarily employed as domestic servants. They entered the labour force at the very bottom of the hierarchy and in the USA occupied a position possibly as low as that of black women. However, such work was favoured, as it not only solved accommodation problems, but made saving money and the sending of remittances to Ireland much easier. Many women were also occupied as seamstresses, milliners, factory and mill workers. Although the vast majority were unskilled workers, there is ample evidence to show that some became successful. Diner refers to community histories and parish and charity records in various parts of the USA which testify to the impressive sums of money accrued by numbers of unmarried Irish women, which they sent back to Ireland, gave to their parish church or invested in property.[37] She also considers that the tradition of late marriage or non-marriage, which had sprung up in post-Famine Ireland, remained strong among Irish immigrant women, even when marriage opportunities existed. The importance attached to family and the farm in Ireland may have accounted for this, since marriage would have signalled a drying up of vital financial aid.[38] Rita M. Rhodes,[39] researching letters from Irish women in America, concludes that female emigrants were a more reliable and constant source of remittances, since sons would be more tempted to spend the money on themselves. Two of the letters she quotes are especially poignant.

I am sending you two pounds Annie is sending you one pound and Liz is sending you ten shillings so you see you are not forgotten here although Liz is a great many years here I don't think I would forget you either if I was away so long Indeed I never could forget my darling mother.[40]

I sent home every dollar and cent I could scrape and after seven years I came home myself. They were very comfortable at home, taking it quiet and easy, and then I began to see that there was never any need for me to go to America at all.[41]

Unlike the tendency in America for Irish women to remain unmarried, their sisters in Britain seem to have returned to the pre-Famine practice of universal and early marriage.[42]

The pattern of work for single women migrants in Britain was broadly similar. Domestic service headed the list, but Irish women faced considerable competition from their English counterparts in this line of work. Catholic priests frequently issued warnings of the dangers facing girls in London, seeing that it was not uncommon for them to quit work or be fired, their only recourse then being begging or prostitution.[43] In Britain, as in the USA, there was a strong tendency for Irish women to retire from work outside the home once married. To supplement family income, many took in piecework of different types – sewing, embroidery, artificial flowers, lint scraping, fur pulling and, of course, laundry. The practice of taking in lodgers was also widespread. Among the poorest, women with their small children hawking in the streets and markets were a common sight.[44] We know little or nothing of those Irish women who found employment in the textile areas of Britain. For instance, in 1851, the census figures show that 13.1 per cent of the population of Manchester and Salford was Irish-born (this figure does not include their descendants). We learn from a feminist study of Lancashire women textile workers, *One Hand Tied Behind Us*,[45] that not only had the industry a predominantly female work force, but a tradition of women continuing to work after marriage. Because the study makes no mention of ethnic origins, we do not know if this tradition existed among Irish women.

As the nineteenth century closed, Irish women in the USA moved into nursing, clerical, secretarial and sales work and teaching. Upward mobility was probably more delayed in the case of Irish women in Britain, but in both countries women climbed the social ladder more quickly than men. The reasons for the disparity between men and women have been examined by David Fitzpatrick,[46] and he argues that this was due in no small measure to the higher literacy and numeracy rates amongst women. These he ascribes to declining work opportunities for women and children as domestic industry collapsed, the greater diligence of girls in the schoolroom, and the culture of emigration, built into the life-cycle of women, which recognized the merits of education.

WOMEN EMIGRANTS IN THE TWENTIETH CENTURY

Between 1901 and 1921, a total of 510,400 men and women left the thirty-two counties of Ireland and from 1926 to 1961, the net figure for those leaving the twenty-six-county independent state was 882,149.[47] The Free State (later to become the Republic of Ireland) was bequeathed the legacy of a backward rural economy, with a minute, unsophisticated industrial sector still vulnerable to the dumping of British goods despite independence. Between 1949 and 1956, a period when many European countries were experiencing a major economic boom, national income in the independent state rose by a mere 8 per cent and emigration averaged about 40,000 a year.[48] The severe depopulation of the Irish countryside evoked memories of the Great Famine diaspora, and the consequences of this new outflow again permeated national life to a major degree. Demographically, it produced an unbalanced population structure and a high dependency rate. Socially, by draining the country of its youth, energy and discontent, it removed an important source of change. Unlike nineteenth-century emigration, the destination of most emigrants was Britain, as a result of the quota system operated by the authorities in the USA and the contraction of the labour market there. The composition of the emigrant flow was broadly similar to that of the latter part of the nineteenth century, as far as age structure and sex balance were concerned. The majority of emigrants were under the age of twenty-five, but women tended to be younger than men. The rate of male to female emigration varied, with women outnumbering men at various stages.

Although valuable insights into the lives of Irish women in contemporary Britain and the USA have been provided by the two oral history works recently published, the lacunae in our knowledge of Irish female emigrants in the twentieth century are vast. From existing information we know that, as in the nineteenth century, women's reasons for emigrating were primarily economic, and that there was also a strong desire to improve status. Clearly, the long struggle for an independent Ireland, in which women had participated, failed to deliver them from their marginalized position, both economically and legally. Female suffrage was achieved, it is true, but Irish women paid the price of a partitioned Ireland, where two mutually antagonistic states adopted ideologies which were religiously orthodox and patriarchal. Protectionist measures to help the ailing southern economy were introduced in 1924 and lasted until the end of the Second World War. In this period women's share of the industrial work force increased from 20 per cent to 22.4 per cent, but by 1961 this share had only risen to 23 per cent.

The majority of those employed were unmarried women under the age of twenty-five.[49] In 1935, the Conditions of Employment Act provided powers to bar or restrict the numbers of women working in a host of industrial occupations. In keeping with the tenets of orthodox Catholicism and right-wing ideology prevalent in Europe at the time, marriage bars were introduced in the civil service, local authorities and health boards, obliging women to leave work as soon as they married. This misogynist attitude received its fullest expression in Article 41 of the southern state's 1937 Constitution, which defined the role of mothers as properly belonging in the home. The same constitutional article introduced for the first time a prohibition on divorce. Given this combination of economic and social factors, it is hardly surprising that so many young women repeated the nineteenth-century pattern of seeking economic opportunities, independence and social status elsewhere.

EMPLOYMENT OPPORTUNITIES FOR IRISH WOMEN IN BRITAIN

The outbreak of the Second World War provided Irish women immigrants in Britain with their first significant opportunity to break out of the traditional mould of domestic service. Ireland had declared its neutrality at the outset of the war and severe restrictions were imposed on travel between the Republic and Britain. However, the demands of war created labour shortages in the public services and certain sections of British industry, which resulted in an agreement being reached early in 1941 between the British Ministry of Labour and the Irish Ministry of Industry and Commerce. In all, approximately 100,000 Irish workers arrived in Britain during the war years and a substantial number of them stayed. Female recruits were employed as teachers, nurses, midwives and domestics in hospitals and hotels, while others were directed into the munitions factories, the cotton mills and transportation, particularly bus-conducting.[50] After the war, when travel restrictions between the two countries were lifted, the Irish contribution to the reconstruction of the British economy was highly significant. In 1947 alone, 1,176 Irish women travelled on assisted passage and went into nursing.[51] With the creation of the National Health Service, the demand for health personnel was high and British hospitals regularly advertised for staff in the Irish national and local press. By 1951, 22.4 per cent of Irish-born women were engaged in professional occupations, mainly nursing and midwifery. The rest were to be found in domestic, clerical and general manufacturing.[52] Interestingly, the occupational patterns of Irish female immigrants, as revealed by the 1966 census, continued to show a generally higher socio-economic status than their male counterparts in Britain. E. J. B. Rose's study categorizes 48 per cent of Irish women as middle class, compared with 19.7 per cent of Irish men.[53] The *Limerick Rural Survey*, published in 1964, confirmed the continuation of the nineteenth-century practice of girls receiving some post-primary education where non-agricultural jobs were limited, thus enabling a greater proportion of them to take up more attractive and socially desirable jobs after leaving school.

The 1970s saw a reversal of the emigration trend, with the numbers returning being greater than those leaving. Of the 104,000 who returned between 1971 and 1981, there were almost equal numbers of married men and women, but only half as many single women as men.[54] In the 1980s, however, economic recession in the Irish Republic resulted in another huge outflow. It is estimated that at least 200,000 people left in the 1980s, and of those remaining behind, one-third live below the poverty line. Census figures indicate that more men than women have left, but the *School Leavers Report*, recently issued by the Irish Department of Labour, shows that more girls than boys have emigrated at school-leaving age. A large proportion of the new exodus make Britain, and especially London, their destination, but a minimum of 150,000 Irish people have emigrated illegally to the USA since 1981. In both of these countries there is disturbing evidence to show that although young Irish women are frequently well educated, they find employment only in those sectors traditionally open to the Irish, namely, domestic work and service industries, such as nursing and catering. Young Irish men also tend to be confined to their traditional area of employment – the construction industry. A survey conducted by *Irish Voice*, the New York newspaper for the Irish community, found that in 1987 54 per cent of Irish women were employed as home helps or *au pairs*, 28 per cent were waitresses and only 18 per cent were engaged in office or other types of work.[55] While their illegal status may be cited as a major cause of Irish women's low occupational status in the USA, a report by the London *Guardian* on Irish women in 1987 stated, 'In fact young Irish women are among the best educated in London, though this is not often reflected in their employment status. Many are apparently unable to find jobs reflecting their educational skills.'[56]

PUTTING DOWN ROOTS

Although there was a wide and varied geographical distribution of Irish-born migrants in nineteenth-century Britain, closely-knit communities in areas of heavy concentration, known as the 'Irish rookeries', probably sustained a sense of an Irish identity. There were also high levels of inter-marriage which maintained the social cohesion of the community. Gradually, as class differences made themselves apparent and a certain degree of upward mobility took place, the Irish became more dispersed, but a notion of 'Irishness' was retained through the many immigrant organizations which sprang up, ranging from the political to the social, though all but a minority of these were closed to women. Southwark Irish Literary Club (later Irish Literary Society), set up in 1883, and the Gaelic League, for example, admitted members of both sexes. Above all other institutions, it was the Catholic Church, formally restored in Britain in 1850, which occupied a pivotal position in the lives of Irish women immigrants. Some writers, such as Sheridan Gilley, assert that the Irish community in Britain was essentially constructed by the Church and that the survival of an Irish identity was crucially bound up with the survival of Catholicism in Britain.[57] Through fund-raising for vast church building programmes, parish devotional associations, sodalities, guilds, confraternities, welfare organizations and, not least, Catholic schools, the Church established strong links with the immigrants. While men dominated virtually all the secular organizations, women formed the backbone of church-based activities, but their work is, as yet, entirely hidden from history.

The extent to which women, and mothers in particular, are involved in the processes of integration (or possibly assimilation) of the Irish, especially of the second and subsequent generations, is rarely discussed, most commentators regarding the Catholic Church and the Labour movement as the significant agencies of assimilation of the Irish in Britain. Looking generally at the link between women, the state and national or ethnic processes, Nira Yuval-Davis and Floya Anthias[58] suggest that the female role extends far beyond the biological reproduction of an ethnic or national grouping. Women also act as 'cultural carriers' of the group, since they are the main socializers of children. Reading through the case studies of Irish women immigrants presented in *Across the Water, Irish Women's Lives in Britain*,[59] it is difficult not to be struck by the extent to which this takes place. Noreen Hill recounts

> When I was bringing up my children it was very important to me to try and pass on a sense of Irishness to them. I told them about Irish history, read Irish story books to them, tried to teach them a little bit of the Irish language, tried to teach them their prayers in Irish. I tried to tell them about the Famine, and things like that. But they were very young and I was the only one that could tell them, there was nobody else. . . . They were fine while they were in the catholic school. After that, the Irishness dwindled away, apart from what I was trying to inject into them.[60]

While the authors of *Across the Water* found that none of their interviewees considered herself to have assimilated, all identifying themselves very much as Irish, and many clearly making strong efforts to transmit an Irish culture to their children, it is difficult to reconcile this evidence with Liam Ryan's[61] argument that Irish assimilation into British society is among the fastest that occurs among immigrant groups anywhere in the world, assimilation being practically complete in a single generation.

WOMEN AND THE CATHOLIC CHURCH

The role of the Catholic Church in the lives of Irish women immigrants has yet to be researched and analysed. Traditionally, the Church has been a source of strength and solace for many women, as well as an outlet for their organizational abilities, most particularly in the nineteenth century, when many political and social organizations barred them. The strength of women's allegiance demonstrates itself in a number of ways. Bronwen Walter's work on Irish women in Ealing[62] shows that Irish-born women – predominantly southern, married women – tend to drop out of employment in the child-bearing years at a greater rate than in other groups analysed in her report – 'white UK', 'Afro-Caribbean' and 'Asian'. From this we can probably conclude that the exclusively familial role ascribed to mothers by Church and state in Ireland can survive in a different economic and social environment. At certain times, however, women are forced to confront the central paradox that their religion is, on the one hand, the embodiment of ideological and institutional sexism, and on the other, a consolation and an inspiration. This contradication perhaps becomes most apparent to those who step outside accepted norms, when, for instance, they become unmarried mothers or have abortions. Consequently, there is a strong tendency for women to remain silent, to depend on their own individual resources to resolve their predicament, and not to challenge the status quo.

There is also a long tradition of pregnant, single women leaving Ireland to give birth in Britain, and of others fleeing from broken marriages or domestic violence. Rarely do such immigrants appear in the annals of Irish migration, and if they do, it is as deviants. For example, Father McSweeney, Director of the Irish Centre in Camden Town, London, reported that the 1950s surge of emigrants contained an increasing number of what he termed 'social casualties', which included alcoholics, unmarried mothers, prostitutes and petty criminals who, he said, were a source of concern to the Church authorities.[63] The emigrant section of the Catholic Social Welfare Bureau, set up in Ireland in 1942, has produced annual reports based on its operations in Britain. A 1956 report stated 'As in other recent years registry office marriages, laxity in attendance of religious duties and, in the case of young girls, irresponsible conduct and moral delinquency continue to provide the main case problems.'[64] No comment was made on the morals of young Irish male immigrants.

Some of the traditional silence surrounding the taboo area of sexuality has been broken in recent years, with the official publication in Britain of yearly abortion figures indicating the numbers of Irish residents who have had abortions in private British clinics since the passage of the 1967 Abortion Act. In 1972, it was reported that 261 women normally resident in the Republic of Ireland obtained legal abortions in England and Wales during 1970. By 1986 the figure was 5,642 and it is widely believed that the real figure could be 10,000, given that most women give fictitious British addresses and are therefore included in the figures for England and Wales. In 1981, the Irish Women's Abortion Support Group (IWASC) was set up in London to give emotional and material support to Irish women who travel over from Ireland. IWASC members have stressed the importance of working in an organization which has active political links with Ireland

Women choose to get involved in IWASC for different reasons. For some it provides the opportunity to continue their involvement in issues that they'd previously worked on in Ireland. For others of us it is a practical way of taking some action around an important issue. We are conditioned as women to be helpful, to look after other people, but there seems to be a contradiction in providing support for women having an abortion, as it would never be seen to be a good cause by either our families or the Irish State. It is a subversive activity – enabling women to have terminations undermines the dominant values of both the Church and State in Ireland.[65]

The link between Britain and Ireland which IWASC provides is probably more crucial now than ever before. In 1983, following a referendum in the Irish Republic, an amendment was inserted in the Constitution which granted an absolute right to life to the foetus from the moment of conception, thus placing the status of the unborn on a par with the born. The Republic made legal history with this constitutional development, which now places a serious legal impediment in the way of any future reform of abortion law. This means that pregnant women who are HIV positive, mentally handicapped, minors, the victims of rape or incest, or who are seriously ill, will continue to be denied a termination, even though all other Western European countries have liberalized their abortion law to allow for such cases. Given this development it is unlikely that there will be a decrease in Irish abortion figures or that the importance of IWASC's work will diminish.

Furthermore, what could previously be described as a domestic problem with an unfortunate tendency to spill over into another country, has now assumed a new dimension. Following the successful prosecution by the Society for the Protection of the Unborn Child (SPUC) of the Dublin-based Well Woman Centre and Open Line Counselling in 1986, and the Irish University Students' Union in 1989, for providing Irish women with the names and addresses of abortion clinics in Britain, the Republic's Censorship Board recently requested the British women's magazines *Cosmopolitan* and *Company* either to drop articles and advertisements about abortion or to face being banned in Ireland. The 5,000 copies of *Cosmopolitan* distributed there now have their abortion advertisements lifted, leaving blank spaces in their place. IWASC, together with Women Against Fundamentalism, a British feminist group with Irish members, and students' unions throughout Britain, have begun a campaign against this form of censorship.[66]

IRISH WOMEN IMMIGRANTS AND THE NATIONAL QUESTION

Political links with Ireland have also been sustained through activities related to the national question. The extent to which historians have excluded women from Irish political history has been explored by Margaret Ward in her study of women in Irish nationalism,[67] but women's involvement in Irish politics in Britain has yet to be excavated. Possibly one of the earliest all-women secular organizations to be formed in Britain was the Ladies' Land League. In response to the outlawing of the Land League in Ireland and the imprisonment of the leaders, Parnell and Davitt under Gladstone's Coercion Act, Anna and Fanny Parnell set up the Ladies' Land League in Ireland in 1881. Being without the franchise, and in certain respects regarded as minors, it was assumed that the women would not be subjected to the full rigours of the Coercion Act and thus could keep the organization on ice until the men were released from jail. But Margaret Ward's work demonstrates that the Ladies' Land League did a great deal more than just that. An Anti-Coercion Association containing a number of feminists was set up in Southwark, an area of south London where the Irish accounted for at least 10 per cent of the local population. In February 1881, the English radical feminist, Helen Taylor, organized a London branch of the Ladies' Land League and set about fund-raising for the sister organization in Ireland. Further branches were opened in Southwark and Poplar in east London. By the summer of that year, the Ladies' Land League was reported to be making great headway and a group of English feminists went to Ireland at the invitation of Anna Parnell. By the end of the year the League had developed in Britain to such an extent that it could challenge the police without male support. By December it had caused sufficient disaffection to warrant its suppression by the British government.[68] No information exists on any other Irish women's political organizations until the 1970s. It is likely that Irish women became involved in British movements such as that for women's suffrage, and records of a few individuals like Frances Power Cobbe, an Irish feminist and reformer in Victorian London, have been published. Although a considerable amount of information is available on US labour leaders, such as Elizabeth Gurley Flynn and Mother Mary Harris Jones, records of Irish women Labour leaders in Britain have still to be uncovered.

The current wave of British feminism coincided with the second major upsurge of Irish nationalism this century, and Irish feminists in Britain, together with British and other women, formed feminist groups and campaigned on Irish issues. A Women and Ireland Group was set up in London in 1972 to discuss and publicize the war in Northern Ireland and to highlight the crucial role being played by women, especially in the nationalist community. By the early 1980s a network of Women and Ireland groups existed in twelve British cities, from Bristol to Dundee, campaigning on a number of fronts, but particularly on the issue of political prisoners.[69] In 1980, the London Armagh Group was formed to work specifically on women prisoners, and after a long campaign the group was instrumental in securing the release of Pauline McLaughlin, a young prisoner in Armagh Jail who was seriously ill. An International Women's Day demonstration has been organized outside Armagh Jail each year, and the group has brought demonstrators from Britain and many other countries. A 'stop the strip searches' campaign, initiated by the group, became active in Britain in 1983 and it succeeded in gaining widespread opposition to the practice from a number of trades unions, and political and human rights organizations.[70]

In the aftermath of the deaths of ten hunger strikers in Long Kesh Prison in 1981, a dramatic change took place in the politics of the Irish in Britain. The level of anti-Irish racism, amplified to hysterical proportions by the media, and echoed in many sections of British society, caused a mushrooming of organizations with an exclusively Irish membership. Given that British feminism at best provided only a marginalized space, struggles against the Prevention of Terrorism Act, the wrongful convictions of the Guildford Four, Maguire Seven, Birmingham Six and Judith Ward, and, indeed, anti-Irish racism, Irish women-only groups were formed. A London Irish Women's Centre came into being in 1983 which, among many other activities, hosts the annual Irish Women's Conference. Conference reports give some indication of the range of groups active in the London area alone, e.g. the Irish Lesbian Network, Irish Women's Housing Action Group, Irish Women with Children Group, Video na mBan and a wide range of cultural groups. The effect of these groups has been to raise the profile of Irish women, and especially feminists, in community activities and in the local Irish press, although the latter is still extremely hesitant over the issues of abortion and lesbianism. The lack of an Irish immigrant women's journal is keenly felt, but as Marian Larragy, in a recent review article on Irish feminism in

Britain, remarks,

There is a growing debate between Irish feminists here and in the two parts of Ireland, and also vast areas of unresolved debate amongst Irish feminists in Britain, which need to be aired in print. We do not have the resources to develop a whole separate feminist media and, even if we did, most Irish feminists have no desire to retreat into total exclusivity.[71]

It is however essential that Irish women in Britain, North America, Australia, New Zealand and elsewhere 'come in from the cold' and ensure that their experiences, unlike those of their sisters in past generations, are committed to history.

Notes

1 E. J. Hobsbawm, *Industry and Empire, The Pelican History of Britain*, vol. 3 (Harmondsworth, 1968).
2 Bronwen Walter, *Gender and Irish Migration to Britain*, Geography Working Paper, 4, School of Geography, Anglia Higher Education College (Cambridge, 1989).
3 Robert Kennedy, *The Irish: Emigration, Marriage and Fertility* (Berkeley, 1983).
4 R. Swift and S. Gilley, eds, *The Irish in the Victorian City* (London, 1985).
5 R. Swift and S. Gilley, eds, *The Irish in Britain, 1815–1939* (London, 1989).
6 Anna Davin, 'Women and history', in *The Body Politic, Writings for the Women's Movement in Britain, 1969–1972*, compiled by Michelene Wandor (London, 1972) p. 215.
7 M. Lennon, M. McAdam and J. O'Brien, *Across the Water: Irish Women's Lives in Britain* (London, 1988).
8 Ide O'Carroll, *Models for Movers: Irish Women's Emigration to America* (Dublin, 1990).
9 Maude Casey, *Over the Water* (London, 1987).
10 Moy McCrory, *The Water's Edge and Other Stories* (London, 1985).
11 London Irish Women's Centre, *Our Experience of Emigration, Report of the London Irish Women's Conference, 1984; Living in England, Report of the Second London Irish Women's Conference, 1985; Irish Women, Our Lives – Our Identity, Report of the 1987 Irish Women's Conference, 1987; Irish Women Today, Conference Report, 1988; The Fifth London Irish Women's Conference Report, 1989*.
12 Bronwen Walter, *Irish Women in London, the Ealing Dimension* (London, 1989).
13 Hasia R. Diner, *Erin's Daughters in America: Immigrant Women in the Nineteenth Century* (Baltimore, 1983).
14 Janet A. Nolan, *Ourselves Alone: Women's Emigration from Ireland, 1885–1920* (Lexington, 1989).

15 Lynn Hollen Lees, *Exiles of Erin, Irish Migrants in Victorian London* (New York, 1979).

16 Kerby A. Miller, *Emigrants and Exiles, Ireland and the Irish Exodus to North America* (Oxford, 1985) p. 193.

17 Gearóid ó Tuathaigh, 'The Irish in nineteenth-century Britain: Problems of integration', in Swift and Gilley, eds, *The Irish in the Victorian City*, p. 14.

18 Kennedy, op. cit., p. 27.

19 David Fitzpatrick, 'A curious middle place: the Irish in Britain, 1871–1921', in Swift and Gilley, eds, *The Irish in Britain, 1915–1939*, pp. 16–19.

20 Nolan, op. cit., p. 100.

21 Maxine Seller, 'Beyond the stereotype: a new look at the immigrant woman, 1880–1924', *Journal of Ethnic Studies* 3 (Spring, 1975) p. 64.

22 Kristian Hvidt, 'Flight to America: the social background of 300,000 Danish emigrants', in *Studies in Social Discontinuity* (New York, 1975).

23 Kennedy, op. cit., p. 22.

24 Lynn Hollen Lees, 'Mid-Victorian migration and the Irish family economy', *Victorian Studies* (Autumn, 1976) p. 26.

25 ibid., p. 26.

26 ibid., p. 27.

27 ibid.

28 Gearóid ó Tuathaigh, 'The role of women in Ireland under the new English order', in M. Mac Curtain and D. O'Corrain, eds, *Women in Irish Society, the Historical Dimension* (Dublin, 1978) pp. 28–9.

29 Mary E. Daly, 'Women in the Irish workforce from pre-industrial to modern times', *Saothar* 7 (1981) pp. 74–82.

30 Joseph Lee, 'Women and the Church since the Famine', in Mac Curtain and O'Corrain, eds, op.cit., p. 37.

31 Frederick Engels, 'The origin of the family, private property and the state', in *Karl Marx and Frederick Engels, Selected Works* (London, 1970).

32 Hugh Brody, *Inishkillane, Change and Decline in the West of Ireland* (London, 1973) pp. 111–12.

33 *Report of the Commission on Emigration and Other Population Problems* (Dublin, 1954) p. 72, Table 57.

34 Eugene Hynes, 'The great hunger and Irish Catholicism', *Societas* 8, 2 (Spring, 1978) pp. 147–8.

35 Pauline Jackson, 'Women in 19th century emigration', *International Migration Review* 18, 4 (1984) pp. 1011–12.

36 David Fitzpatrick, '"A share of the honeycomb": education, emigration and Irishwomen', *Continuity and Change* 1, 2 (1986) pp. 217–18.

37 Diner, op. cit., p. 52.

38 ibid., p. 52.

39 Rita M. Rhodes, *Women and the Family in Post-Famine Ireland: Status and Opportunity in a Patriarchal Society*, unpublished Ph.D. thesis, University of Illinois, Chicago (1986).

40 Letter, Julia Lough (December, 1888) National Library of Ireland, MS 8347.

41 Anna Kelly, 'I went to America', *The Bell* (February, 1942) p. 356.

42 Hollen Lees, 'Mid-Victorian migration', p. 38.
43 Hollen Lees, *Exiles of Erin*, p. 95.
44 ibid., pp. 111–16.
45 Jill Liddington and Jill Norris, *One Hand Tied Behind Us: The Rise of the Women's Suffrage Movement* (London, 1978).
46 Fitzpatrick, '"A share of the honeycomb"', pp. 218–20.
47 *Report of the Commission on Emigration*, p. 119, Table 89; p. 116, Table 87.
48 Mary E. Daly, *Social and Economic History of Ireland Since 1800* (Dublin, 1981) p. 163.
49 ibid., p. 77.
50 John Archer Jackson, *The Irish in Britain* (London, 1963) pp. 102, 103.
51 ibid., p. 104.
52 ibid., p. 106.
53 E. J. B. Rose, *Colour and Citizenship, A Report on British Race Relations, London* (Oxford, 1969).
54 Kate Kelly and Triona Nic Giolla Choille, eds, *Emigration Matters for Women* (Dublin, 1990) p. 15.
55 Kelly and Nic Giolla Choille, eds, op. cit., p. 17.
56 *Guardian* (2 September 1987).
57 Sheridan Gilley, 'Irish Catholicism in Britain, 1880–1939', in *Catholics and their Church in Britain c. 1880–1939*, Warwick Working Papers in Social History (Warwick, 1988).
58 Nira Yuval Davis and Floya Anthias, eds, *Woman–Nation–State* (London, 1989) pp. 7–9.
59 M. Lennon, M. McAdam and J. O'Brien, op. cit.
60 ibid., pp. 99–100.
61 Liam Ryan, 'Irish emigration to Britain since World War II', in *Migrations, the Irish at Home and Abroad*, ed. Richard Kearney (Dublin, 1990) pp. 59–60.
62 Walter, *Irish Women in London*, p. 28.
63 Quoted in Muirin O'Briain, *Irish Immigrants in London*, unpublished M. Phil. thesis, The City University, London (1981) p. 122.
64 Quoted in Kelly and Nic Giolla Choille, eds, op. cit., p. 13.
65 'Across the water, Irish Women's Abortion support group', *Feminist Review* 29 (Spring, 1988) pp. 68–9.
66 Ann Rossiter, 'Granting civil rights to the foetus in Ireland, a victory to Christian fundamentalists worldwide', *Women Against Fundamentalism Newsletter* 1 (1990) pp. 8–10.
67 Margaret Ward, *Unmanageable Revolutionaries, Women in Irish Nationalism* (London, 1983).
68 Dave Russell, 'Some early Irish movements in South London' in *South London Record*, South London History Workshop, 2 (1987) pp. 17–21.
69 *Women Behind the Wire: Bulletin of the Armagh Co-Ordinating Group*, 1 (1981).
70 *Women Behind the Wire, 2 (1984)* and *Working Together to end Strip Searching: Report of a Conference, 5th December, 1987* (London, 1988).
71 Marian Larragy, 'Looking back, looking forward', in *Spare Rib* 215, (August, 1990) p. 43.

14 Missing the boat
The Labour party and the Irish question

Jonathan Moore

In the summer of 1981 a member of the British House of Commons, Bobby Sands, starved himself to death in a prison hospital a few miles outside Belfast. The cause of this extraordinary protest was Sands's demand that Irish Republican Army (IRA) prisoners be accorded political status. The government refused to budge from their criminalization policy and so, after sixty-six days of painful protest, Sands died.

The refusal of the Thatcher government to give in to Sands's demands was met with widespread international condemnation. There were anti-British protests in many countries and Lech Wałesa called Sands 'a great man who sacrificed his life for his struggle'.[1] The story was very different in Westminster, where the British Labour party rallied in support of the Conservative government's action. Critical voices were virtually absent. Days before Sands's death, the Labour spokesman on Northern Irish affairs, Don Concannon, visited Sands in the Maze prison in order to tell the ailing prisoner that he could expect no support from Labour.[2]

The behaviour of the Labour party in 1981 was illustrative of the position that Labour has taken towards the Irish question since the re-emergence of political violence there in the late 1960s. A general failure to differentiate the Labour party's Irish policy from that of the Conservatives has been the norm, and Conservative governments have normally been able to depend on the support of the Labour party when dealing with Irish questions.

Such unanimity is very unusual in the British political system, which is based on adversarial politics. That it has been practised in the recent context of the Irish issue is very illuminating. Its roots lie in the Labour party's troublesome relationship with the Irish issue: Ireland has rarely appeared to be an issue with which Labour has felt comfortable. This chapter will examine why this has been the case, and will look also at some individuals and groups who have attempted to articulate a clear and separate Irish policy within the party.

THE ORIGINS OF LABOUR PARTY POLICY

Concern about the Irish question was prevalent amongst many socialists in the late nineteenth century. For example, Henry Hyndman of the Marxist Social Democratic Federation (SDF) argued in 1881 that the principal reason for the existence of the SDF was the 'action of the government in relation to Ireland'.[3] However, despite this interest in the issue from those on the left they usually failed to differentiate their Irish policy from that of the Gladstonian Liberals. There was no discernable separate Labour policy. Speaking in 1892, Kier Hardie spoke of his support for Home Rule 'provided the supremacy of the Imperial parliament be maintained unimpaired'.[4]

In his study of the Labour party and Ireland during this period, Barry Stubbs observes that the party leadership were thoroughly frustrated with the Irish issue by the time of the First World War. Ireland was perceived as an issue which was consuming a vast quantity of parliamentary time. 'Many necessary social reforms'[5] were therefore blocked. In the Parliamentary Labour Party (PLP) report to the 1913 conference, the party's attitude towards Home Rule is summed up: the priority was 'to get the measure carried and put out of the way'.[6]

The enthusiasm of people such as Hyndman for the Irish issue was not represented within the PLP. A crucial reason for this appeared to be that Home Rule was a major concern of the old, pre-Labour, political system. It was not part of the new reformist agenda that Labour had brought into parliament. Ramsay Macdonald reflected this mode of thinking in 1914 when he stated that with respect to Ireland the Labour party would 'take the position of a detached party listening to what is said'.[7]

The dramatic results of the 1918 General Election, which resulted in the virtual obliteration of the old Home Rule party and its replacement by Sinn Féin did not lead to any dramatic change in Labour's perspective on Ireland. As late as 1920, by which time a separatist Irish Dáil (parliament) existed in Dublin, J. R. Clynes, the chairman of the PLP, argued that the level of self-determination available to Ireland could only be maximized in line with 'the unity and the safety of the United Kingdom in time of war'.[8] The language of national self-determination, so much in vogue in the conference halls of Versailles in the previous year, was not to be applied to Ireland.

There simply was no concept of a separate and identifiable Labour policy, despite the fact that the policy of the Liberals and Conservatives had been demonstrably rejected by the Irish electorate. The rejection was explained by the Labour party paper the *Daily Herald* in the following, patronizing terms

We believe that if Ireland were free to decide whether she would remain within the Empire or become completely separate from it, the Irish themselves, upon mature consideration would decide that the link should not be completely severed.[9]

There were voices in opposition to this approach but they were few and far between.[10] It was not to be political reflection, but electoral need which was to lead to a reappraisal of policy. In April 1920 there was a by-election in Stockport. The sizeable Irish community there put up a leading Irish trade unionist and 'political prisoner' as candidate, and he polled over 2,000 votes. Labour would have lost the election anyway,[11] but the warning was clear.

The fear that continued support for the government and its Irish policy carried with it probable electoral costs would appear to have been a major contributory factor in Labour taking the unusual step of abstaining during the crucial stages of the 1920 Government of Ireland Act debate. The PLP would not only not be voting on the bill but, according to Clynes, taking 'no part whatever in the progress of the bill'.[12] One Labour MP, Neil Maclean, had no doubt why Labour ought to distance itself from the legislation. He explained

In this country those who are identified with the working-class movements in districts where Irish men form a considerable portion of the Industrial population are absolutely opposed to this bill.[13]

Under mounting pressure from sections of the party's rank and file, a Commission of Inquiry was set up by Labour to investigate the disturbances in Ireland. The commission's report was highly critical of government actions in Ireland. At a special conference held in December 1920 to discuss the commission's report, there was a call for 'the withdrawal of all armed forces'.[14] Labour did not combine this call with an endorsement of Sinn Féin's demands for an Irish Republic. Any future Irish constitution, the conference agreed, 'should prevent Ireland from becoming a military or naval menace to Great Britain'.[15] Labour was caught between two stools. Clynes noted that partition would never 'secure the approval of the majority of the Irish people',[16] but commented on the Anglo-Irish

Treaty which confirmed partition, that it was 'a triumph of national spirit'.[17] Confusion was rife, but the Labour party was delighted to see the back of this 'troublesome business'.[18]

FROM PARTITION TO CIVIL RIGHTS

Partition in Ireland carried with it major political problems. The fact that half a million Catholic nationalists were left as a minority within the new Northern Irish state created a situation which was fraught with problems. How was this group to be treated by the Unionist dominated parliament, which was now to be in charge of domestic policy in Ulster?

From 1921 onwards a policy was adopted by both the Labour and Conservative parties not to intervene in Northern Irish affairs. Following partition, the Unionist majority were to be left a free hand to consolidate the new situation. Such freedom allowed the Unionist government to use whatever means it saw as necessary to nullify the political, economic and social power of the half-million-strong Catholic nationalist minority.[19] The Cameron Report, published in 1969, documented the full extent of discrimination used by the various Unionist authorities.[20]

The response of both British political parties was to try, as far as possible, to ensure that discussion of these serious and embarrassing problems did not cross the Irish Sea, and in particular did not reach the floor of Westminster. Following Speaker's rulings in 1922 and 1923,[21] matters devolved to the Northern Irish parliament could not be raised in either House at Westminster. Since devolution was virtually complete in the field of domestic policy, there was little left to talk about. This was only a convention, but few at Westminster had any desire to question it.

Between the two wars, the lack of interest in Irish affairs within the Labour party appears to have been absolute. Sam Kyle of the Northern Ireland Labour party visited the 1926 Labour conference and concluded that the delegates who 'attended the conference did . . . [not take] any particular interest in this problem'.[22]

The election of the first majority Labour government in 1945 led some nationalists in Ireland to believe intervention was close at hand. James McSparran, Chairman of the Anti-Partition League (APL), asked whether the new government might 'consider it an opportune moment to weigh up the expediency of maintaining a government in Northern Ireland which detests the very name of Labour'.[23] McSparran and his fellow nationalists were to be sorely disappointed by the actions of Attlee's government in its Irish policy. Rumpf and Hepburn succintly summed up the attitude of the government

It became clear at a very early stage that no one in the Attlee Cabinet was inclined to upset the Unionist applecart in Northern Ireland.[24]

A new concern over Ireland had now gripped the attention of both Conservative and Labour parties. Following Ireland's neutrality during the Second World War, there was real concern about Ireland's strategic importance. When in 1949 Ireland ceded from the Commonwealth and became a Republic, Herbert Morrison noted that

it will never be to Great Britain's advantage that Northern Ireland will form part of a territory outside Her Majesty's jurisdiction. Indeed it seems unlikely that Great Britain would ever be able to agree to this even if the people of Northern Ireland desired it.[25]

If the Labour leaders were to disappoint the nationalists with their every move, there were people within the PLP who were keen to see government intervention in Northern Irish affairs. In November 1945 an organization called 'The Friends of Ireland' was formed from members of the PLP. The group was led by Dr H. B. Morgan, but its most vocal members were Geoffrey Bing and Hugh Delargy. In theory the group rose to about a hundred in number by 1948, but much of this was a nominal membership. In terms of active membership 'The Friends' was a minute group.[26]

As well as being very small, the group never really married together socialism and nationalism. As Purdie has demonstrated, some of the 'Friends' wanted links with the non-nationalist NILP, others were simply interested in self-determination for the whole of Ireland. Purdie notes that 'there was rich potential for conflict'[27] among the small membership. The problem of the two approaches can be seen in the cases of Bing and Delargy. Bing, in his best selling *Tribune* pamphlet *John Bull's Other Ireland*[28] analysed the problems of Northern Ireland in class, rather than national terms. On the other hand, a far more traditional nationalist approach was taken by the Falls Road-born Delargy, who scorned the idea that any problems could be solved until 'the nationality problem was settled'.[29]

The high point in the short life of 'The Friends' occurred in the drama which followed the announcement by John A. Costello, the Taoiseach, in September 1948, that Ireland was to become a Republic. The response of Labour was to introduce the Ireland Bill, in which the position of Northern Ireland in the United Kingdom was strengthened. The salient feature of the change had already been announced by the British Prime Minister in the Commons in October 1948

> The view of His Majesty's Government . . . has always been that no change should be made in the constitutional status of Northern Ireland without Northern Ireland's free agreement.[30]

Despite the tone of this comment, it did signify an important change in Northern Ireland's position. For the first time, the six counties were being explicitly offered self-determination. It would be the Ulster Unionists and not the British government who would now decide the future constitutional status of Northern Ireland. In the government, there was criticism from Lord Packenham, the Minister of Aviation, who argued that such an 'explicit guarantee of the territorial integrity of Northern Ireland would be wrong'.[31]

The constitutional guarantee was condemned by both Delargy and Bing in their different ways. Their criticisms were rejected by the government, who had the wholehearted support of the Conservative opposition. However, nearly fifty Labour MPs joined with Delargy and Bing in supporting various amendments to the bill. It was to be the only time in this period that Labour MPs were, in any numbers, to reject the prevailing orthodoxy of two-party unanimity.

Quite simply, the Labour leaders had overplayed their hand on this occasion. It was one thing to ignore Northern Irish problems, it was quite another publicly to endorse partition in this fashion. 'The Friends' never reached this level of influence again. Bing and Delargy continued to speak, but the issue of Ireland was not to raise itself again until the 1960s. Purdie, in analysing their failure as a group, points out that for the traditional Labour left Ireland was simply not an issue on the political agenda.[32] It was not until the Irish question presented itself in language with which Labour could sympathize that action was taken. Until that time Herbert Morrison spoke for most Labour MPs when he commented in 1949, 'I hope that none of us will encourage . . . this Irish issue . . . to become an embarrassing issue in British politics again.'[33]

THE IMPACT OF THE CIVIL RIGHTS MOVEMENT AND THE RISE OF THE CDU

The return of a Labour government to Westminster in 1964, after thirteen years in opposition, was greeted with some enthusiasm in the nationalist community of Northern Ireland. Particular faith was placed in the new Prime Minister, Harold Wilson, who was seen as sympathetic to the plight of nationalists in the north. Shortly before the 1964 election, Wilson had written to a new civil rights group 'The Campaign for Social Justice', in the following terms

> I agree with you as to the importance of the issues with which your campaign is concerned and can assure you that a Labour government would do everything in its power to see that infringements of justice to which you are so rightly drawing attention are effectively dealt with.[34]

Interest in Wilson's views on the situation in Northern Ireland was further fuelled by various off-the-cuff announcements in favour of a united Ireland and by gestures such as the return of the remains of Sir Roger Casement to Ireland. Wilson's 'surrogate Irish nationalism'[35] was now going to be tested.

The election of the Labour government coincided with important changes in Northern Irish politics. Among increasingly large sections of the Catholic community, there was a realization that the political obsession with partition had achieved nothing. As a result of this, civil rights organizations were formed which focused on the widespread discrimination against the Catholic minority. Interest in the 'chimera of Irish unity'[36] was played down.

Labour MPs, particularly those newly elected in 1964, responded to these changes in Northern Ireland. Typical of these was Paul Rose, who prior to 1962 did not 'have the remotest idea about the situation'.[37] However, through contact with the left-wing Republican group, the Connolly Association, Rose became aware of the level of discrimination in Ulster. From the start, his interest in Irish politics was not to do with the border, but 'with the rights of Northern Irish Catholics as United Kingdom citizens'.[38] The stress of Rose and other Labour MPs on the fact that 'the border is not an issue'[39] was to be the catalyst allowing mainstream Labour MPs to feel comfortable with Northern Ireland. Labour MPs did not see this as the re-emergence of the old 'Irish issue'.

On 2 June 1965, the Campaign for Democracy in Ulster (CDU) was formed. It quickly gained the support of nearly fifty MPs. Rose was elected chairman and Lord Fenner Brockway, the veteran peace campaigner, president. The aims of this new pressure group were threefold. First, it wanted to secure a full and impartial inquiry into the administration of government in Northern Ireland and into allegations of discrimination against Catholics. Second, it wanted to examine the electoral law, and in particular the vexed question of electoral boundaries. Third, it demanded that the Race Relations Act be applied in Northern Ireland, and that it be amended to include religious discrimination and incitement. What was not mentioned here was any question of the border. This was clear evidence of the striking difference between the CDU and groups which had traditionally campaigned on Irish issues. The very use of the word 'Ulster' in the name of the organization was a deliberate attempt to prevent it being seen as a nationalist group. The CDU stated in 1967

> the people of Ulster (particularly the Catholic minority) should have the same rights as the rest of the United Kingdom. The border is considered irrelevant to the issue, and the CDU relates its campaign to those parts of the United Kingdom over which the British Government has control.[40]

The call was for 'British standards' for British people. There was talk of gerrymandering but not of partition. Unionism amd Republicanism alike were seen as ancient political philosophies of no relevance to the Ulster of the 1960s. The CDU wanted their cause to be akin to the civil rights movements flourishing around the world at this time

> Under the able secretaryship of Paddy Byrne, Catholic, Protestant, Jew and Humanist worked together and poignantly illustrated our concern for the totality of human rights by inviting Dr Pitt, a West Indian, to chair a delegate conference of the Labour movement in London. 'We shall overcome' was now heard in Derry and Deptford with an Irish lilt that was never expected in Alabama.[41]

THE SUPREMACY OF ORTHODOXY: THE FAILURE OF THE CDU

In April 1967 representatives of the CDU visited Northern Ireland, and produced a scathing report on the state of democracy in the six counties. Underlying the tactics of the CDU was a belief that the justice of their cause was so undeniable that once the Labour government heard the facts, they would be forced to act. However, the Home Secretary, Roy Jenkins was very reticent about probing into the situation. He seemed to fear that any serious investigation of the allegations could have grave constitutional ramifications.

> We cannot simply put aside the constitution of Northern Ireland. Successive governments have refused to take any steps which would

inevitably cut away not only the authority of the Northern Ireland government but also the constitution of the province.[42]

Prime Minister Wilson's attitude is perhaps best summed up by a comment made in 1964, 'Any politician who wants to become involved in Ulster ought to have his head examined.'[43]

Wilson sustained this non-interventionist attitude apparently because of his belief that the Northern Irish Premier Terence O'Neill was a genuine reformer. His view of O'Neill in 1966 was that 'he had already made much progress in a matter of two or three years in attacking problems of discrimination and human rights'.[44] In fact there was precious little evidence of O'Neill's reforming instincts. As the NILP stated in 1967

No attempt has been made by the . . . government to knit the community together; there has been no electoral reform, no review of electoral boundaries . . . there is no ombudsman . . . not merely has Captain O'Neill dashed the hopes he himself raised, he has added a new bitterness and disappointment to the grievances of the minority.[45]

Wilson must have been aware of such arguments but he would not act. When pressed by the London Federation of Trades Councils, which had passed a motion calling for an inquiry into the workings of government in Northern Ireland, Wilson replied

While the UK Government are wholly opposed to all forms of discrimination, the questions about which allegations of discrimination are made in Northern Ireland fall within the competence of the Northern Ireland authorities.[46]

The fact that senior government ministers refused to move on this issue rendered the CDU's strategy futile. They later complained that 'letters . . . to Home Secretaries have been treated with contempt'.[47] The inaction of the government leaders was assisted by the fact that the CDU never developed into anything approximating a mass-movement within the party. Only three constituencies ever affiliated to the organization. The CDU concluded that Northern Ireland was simply not an attractive proposition to the average British socialist.[48]

The rational arguments of the CDU achieved nothing. Their failure was due to the fact that they did not understand that the Labour party leaders were genuinely terrified by the prospect of reopening the Irish question. The fact that the evidence of discrimination was so clear-cut counted for little in comparison with this. It took the Royal Ulster

Constabulary riot in Derry on 5 October 1968, so graphically shown on television throughout the world, to force Wilson and his colleagues to move. As Paul Rose later recalled

> It was not until millions of television viewers saw a British MP, Gerry Fitt, with his head streaming with blood from a police baton charge that the nation woke up to what some of us in the Commons have been campaigning about month after month in the last five years . . . it is the tragedy of the situation that it was not until heads were broken in Londonderry that the attention of the British press, public and Parliament were focused on Northern Ireland.[49]

LABOUR AND THE FAILURE OF REFORM

Following the Derry violence of October 1968, the Labour government moved very fast to force the Unionists to implement a wide-ranging reform programme. In essence, the Wilson government adopted the programme of the CDU. The fundamental demands of the CDU (and therefore, by implication, of the civil-rights movement) had been enacted by the Unionist government by 1970. But this did not bring about the peace that Labour MPs and others had hoped for.

Underlying the dashed hopes of the reformers as Northern Ireland went headlong into two decades of violence, were fundamental problems of analysis. For men such as Paul Rose, the discrimination that pervaded the Northern Irish scene was based on simple bigotry and sectarianism. The material and constitutional roots of the oppression of Catholics were never considered.[50] The fact that the main aim of discrimination against the minority was to nullify their political power, and that any attempt to attack discrimination would therefore be perceived as a threat to the constitutional position of Protestants within the United Kingdom was not understood by anyone in the Labour party. In essence, reform produced a far more hardline form of Unionism in the shape of Paisleyism, and this wrecked any real chance of accommodation between the two communities. As Rose later admitted 'we never realized the extent that Protestants would oppose simple reform'.[51] And the reason for this was that reform was intrinsically tied up with the national question.

Labour policy (and there were few disagreements within the party) was directed towards reforming the north but leaving its running to the Unionist administration. In pursuit of this objective, there was a concerted attempt by the government to carry the opposition with them. Wilson was later to recall how important this bi-party unanimity was to his strategy: '[we] . . . maintained a constructive bi-partisan approach . . . one can see in retrospect what dangers might have followed if that had not been so.'[52]

The danger was that Ireland would divide the British political system in the way that it had during the Home Rule period. For both Wilson and James Callaghan avoidance of this division became a central plank of their policy. As Callaghan observed

> Anyone who studies the history of Ireland from the mid-19th century onwards must conclude – in marked contrast to the present nature of the parties – Irish problems were made much worse by the absence of any agreement between the . . . parties.[53]

After the defeat of the Wilson government in 1970, the significance of these words became more relevant. Despite the fact that the Conservatives had supported Wilson's handling of the crisis, policy underwent important changes with the arrival of Edward Heath's government. Most significantly, the army was given far more freedom to act as it saw fit.[54] The Catholic population, who had welcomed the troops in 1969, rapidly came into violent conflict with them. By early 1971 the Provisional IRA were on the streets with wide support in the Catholic ghettos.

The response of the government: to increase the military pressure on the nationalist population, furthered the violence. In August 1971 internment was introduced, with disastrous results. Violence reached unprecedented levels. Labour leaders tried to combine criticism of the 'drift in policy' with continuing bi-party unanimity.[55] Kevin McNamara, a leading member of the CDU, believed that

> Wilson was so concerned that Labour ought not to be seen criticizing British soldiers, that he lost sight of the rapidly deteriorating situation which had been brought about, in no small way, by the actions of the army.[56]

The demands of the CDU were that the parliament in Northern Ireland be suspended 'as a matter of the utmost urgency'.[57] After the 'Bloody Sunday' killings, this became inevitable and Stormont was dissolved in March 1972.

In the aftermath of the end of the Stormont regime, the Conservative government accepted nearly all the arguments of the Labour leaders and the CDU. There was to be a new power-sharing government in Northern Ireland and new constitutional ties with the Republic of Ireland. The new Secretary of State for Northern Ireland, William

Whitelaw, could depend on far greater support from the Labour benches than from his own. He later commented: 'Labour were very supportive. On our own side, there were far greater misgivings. My job would have been very difficult if Labour had not been so supportive.'[58]

Labour's policy was based on the idea that Northern Ireland could be reformed. There were few in the PLP that disagreed with this. Support for the radical Anti-Internment League (AIL)[59] was almost non-existent within the PLP.

The problem of Labour's approach was that they failed to understand, once again, the problems of the reforming role. The object of the bi-partisan strategy was to get agreement between constitutional parties in Northern Ireland. If a moderate consensus could be achieved, then the extreme wings on both sides would be left isolated. The problem was that the nature of the Northern Irish situation meant that nearly all the reforms granted were gains for the nationalist community and losses for the Unionists. From the position where Unionists had a virtual monopoly of power, power was now being taken away and given to nationalists. By the end of 1973, a power-sharing government was in place and the Sunningdale Agreement was signed, whereby Dublin was given a say in the running of Northern Irish affairs.

The inevitable result of this was a Unionist backlash and the rejection of any accommodation with nationalism. The Ulster Workers' strike of May 1974 paralysed Northern Ireland. It was supported by large sections of the Protestant working class, and crippled the fragile power-sharing executive in Belfast.

CONCLUSION

Underlying the problems of the Labour party with respect to the Irish question has been a basic failure of analysis. Ireland has rarely been regarded as a Labour question. The response of the party has therefore been to ignore the question, or to refuse to treat it in its proper context. In the period prior to partition, there was a constant desire to get the issue out of the way. There was never any attempt to apply a specific socialist approach to Ireland. Home Rule was an issue for the other parties, it was not a Labour issue. Following the settlement of 1921, the party consensus was to ignore the issue, despite all the evidence that there were serious breaches of human rights occurring within Northern Ireland. The issue only reappeared in the 1960s and then the CDU denied that the question facing them was the Irish question. This later mistake was to fail to understand the real underlying causes of the civil rights conflict.

Since the failure of Sunningdale in 1974, little has really changed within the ranks of the party. The unease with the issue is clearly still present. The best way to understand this phenomenon is to look at the roots of Labour party ideology. These roots were labourist and reformist. The question of Ireland has never fitted easily within these two frameworks. The application of the concept of self-determination to Ireland has rarely been on the Labour agenda. The reason for this is, in all probability, due to the proximity of Ireland to Britain. Internationalist perspectives are difficult to apply so close to home. This failure of analysis has cost the Labour party, and more importantly the Irish people, very dearly.

Notes

1 Padraig O'Malley, *Biting at the Grave: The Irish Hunger Strikes and the Politics of Despair* (Belfast, 1990) p. 4.
2 'There were loud cheers from all parts of the Commons yesterday as Mr Michael Foot, leader of the Labour Party, placed himself squarely behind Mrs Margaret Thatcher in her firm rejection of the demands of the IRA hunger strikes', *The Times* (6 May 1981).
3 Geoffrey Bell, *Troublesome Business: The Labour Party and the Irish Question* (London, 1982) p. 3.
4 ibid., p. 9.
5 Barry Stubbs, *The Labour Party and the Irish Question* (unpublished University of London M. Phil, 1970) p. 23.
6 ibid., p. 38.
7 *House of Commons Debates*, vol. 134, cols 1416–17.
8 ibid., vol. 127, cols 940–52.
9 *Labour Party Conference Report 1920* (London, 1921) p. 6.
10 The most notable critic was Neil Maclean, the Labour MP for Glasgow Govan.
11 The prominent Irish trade unionist William O'Brien received 2,336 votes and Labour lost by over 6,000 votes. Bell, op. cit., pp. 49–50.
12 *House of Commons Debates*, vol. 129, col. 1328.
13 ibid., col. 1350.
14 *Labour Party Conference Report 1921* (London, 1922) p. 23.
15 ibid., p. 161.
16 *House of Commons Debates*, vol. 147, cols 1407–8.
17 ibid., vol. 149, cols 18–22.
18 Bell, op. cit., p. 42.
19 The best account of this is contained in Michael Farrell, *Northern Ireland: The Orange State* (London, 1982) pp. 39–80.
20 *Cameron Report: Disturbances in Northern Ireland: Report of the Commission appointed by the Governor of Northern Ireland*, Cm 532 (Belfast:

HMSO, 1969).

21 The best discussion is contained in Derek Birrell and Alan Murie, *Policy and Government in Northern Ireland: Lessons of Devolution* (Dublin, 1980) pp. 11–15.

22 *Labour Party Conference Report 1926* (London, 1927) p. 245.

23 Bob Purdie, 'The Friends of Ireland', in Tom Gallagher and James O' Connell, eds, *Contemporary Irish Studies* (Manchester, 1983) p. 82.

24 E. Rumpf and A. Hepburn, *Nationalism and Socialism in 20th Century Ireland* (Liverpool, 1977) p. 107.

25 Bell, op. cit., p. 81.

26 According to Purdie, 'Only some eight MPs were positively identified . . . as belonging to the group'. Purdie, op. cit., p. 83.

27 ibid., pp. 81–2.

28 Geoffrey Bing, *John Bull's Other Ireland* (London, 1950).

29 Purdie, op. cit., p. 90.

30 *House of Commons Debates*, vol. 457, col. 239.

31 Bell, op. cit., p. 87.

32 Purdie makes the important point that leading pro-Soviet MPs such as Zilliacus saw Ireland as 'not my cup of tea'. This attitude was not unusual. Purdie, op. cit., pp. 83–4.

33 Bell, op. cit., p. 88.

34 CDU papers, Northern Ireland Public Record Office (NIPRO) 3026/1 10559.

35 Paul Bew, Peter Gibbon and Henry Patterson, *The State in Northern Ireland 1921–1972* (Manchester, 1979) p. 190.

36 ibid., p. 169.

37 Paul Rose, interview with author.

38 ibid.

39 CDU papers, NIPRO 3026/2 10559.

40 ibid.

41 *Irish Times* (4 February 1970).

42 *House of Commons Debates*, vol. 713, col. 1686.

43 Sunday Times Insight Team, *Ulster* (London, 1972) p. 80.

44 Harold Wilson, *The Labour Government 1964–70* (London, 1971) pp. 348–9.

45 CDU papers, NIPRO 3026/2 10559.

46 ibid.

47 ibid.

48 For example, there were only three resolutions on Northern Ireland submitted for the 1968 conference and only five for the 1969 conference.

49 *Labour Party Conference Report* (1969) p. 177.

50 Paul Rose and Kevin McNamara, interviews.

51 Paul Rose, interview with author.

52 *House of Commons Debates*, vol. 813, col. 260.

53 James Callaghan, *A House Divided* (London, 1973) p. 12.

54 The best account of this is in the Sunday Times Insight Team, op. cit.

55 Merlyn Rees, interview with author.

56 Kevin McNamara, interview with author.

57 Paul Rose, interview with author.

58 William Whitelaw, interview with author.

59 Formed in 1971, the AIL became the focal point for left activity outside the Labour party. It had the support of around fifty branches in Britain. The MP closest to them was Jock Stallard. The AIL called for an end to internment and to this end organized two large marches in early 1972. To some extent the suspension of Stormont in March 1972 ended the unity of the AIL. Following this, they tended to split between those who wanted democratic reform and those who called for 'victory to the IRA'. The former drifted away after the IRA offensive of the summer of 1972. Source interview with John Gray, organizer of the AIL, 1971–2.

Index